The Southern Railway

BURKE DAVIS

The Southern Railway
Road of the Innovators

The University of North Carolina Press
Chapel Hill and London

© 1985 Southern Railway Company

All rights reserved

Manufactured in the United States of America

Library of Congress Cataloging in Publication Data

Davis, Burke, 1913–
The Southern Railway.

Includes index.
1. Southern Railway (U.S.) I. Title.
TF25.S7D38   1985   385'.09755   84-15343
ISBN 0-8078-1636-1

Contents

Preface / vii

ONE
Putting Out the Fire / 3

TWO
"The Strongest Management" / 10

THREE
The Birth of the Southern Railway / 19

FOUR
Sam Spencer's Grand Design / 33

FIVE
In the Steps of the Founder / 45

SIX
"How Many Blisters Do You Have?" / 53

SEVEN
"We Have an Abiding Faith" / 71

EIGHT
"What a Bold Conception!" / 94

NINE
FFVs and Tar Heels Take to the Rails / 107

TEN
Westward the Rails / 118

ELEVEN
Casualties of War / 166

Contents

TWELVE
Out of the Ashes / 180

THIRTEEN
"We Were Happy, and It Showed" / 199

FOURTEEN
"The Best Executive I Ever Saw" / 212

FIFTEEN
Bill Brosnan: "It Can't Be Done" / 226

SIXTEEN
Graham Claytor and His Team / 250

SEVENTEEN
Stanley Crane: "If We Are Smart Enough" / 267

EIGHTEEN
Harold Hall: "One of the Very Best" / 278

Index / 295

Preface

Ours was a young country in the early years of the nineteenth century—largely rural, largely agricultural. The South, especially, was a paradox by modern standards. Here was an agricultural society on the threshold of maturity that still lacked an adequate transportation system.

Great plantations had grown up in the Tidewater regions by the ocean shores, and along the rivers that laced this fertile land. But in the developing Piedmont areas beyond the fall line of the streams, only a few crude roads penetrated to the frontier landholdings. Much of the South was still a wilderness, barely scratched by such wagon ruts as Boone's trail across the Alleghenies and the dangerous Natchez Trace.

Events were taking shape that would change all this, and a varied assortment of pioneer railroaders had much to contribute to the change that was coming. Some of them gave up promising careers in other businesses and professions to pursue the new idea of transportation on twin rails. All of them were builders.

They built with iron and dreams and determination, with hard cash and difficult credit. When war left their dreams charred wreckage, they stooped and built again. Somehow they seemed to understand that they were creating a South-wide transportation system and leaving a legacy of growth to generations they would never see. Part of that legacy is the 10,500-mile network of rails with which Southern Railway System serves the South and a wide area beyond it.

Although Southern has existed as a company only since 1894, its story reaches back to the little railroads that were only scattered threads of pine and iron in the vast earth-colored tapestry of early America. In South Carolina, Virginia, Tennessee, Alabama, indeed, across the South, enthusiasts sought to build the first local rail lines, which they saw as the key to prosperity for communities and, eventually, for entire regions. In time, these came to be the framework for today's Southern.

Bringing into print the story of Southern Railway has not proved much easier than the task of uniting all the small lines—125 or

Preface

more—that combined and recombined over more than a century to form Southern Railway System. This book has been twenty-five years in the making, and it represents the efforts of three writers.

The colorful and complex story of Southern Railway has now been cast in highly readable form by the biographer and popular historian Burke Davis, author of more than forty published works. His account of the men and forces that shaped the modern Southern Railway paints a vivid picture of a rail system as old as the first beginnings of railroads in America and as new as their latest advances. Davis was fortunate to have interviewed five of the Southern's nine presidents and numerous staff members, and his narrative thus has a remarkably human flavor that is unique among railroad histories.

Basic research on which most of this volume is based was begun a generation ago by the late Carlton J. Corliss, railroad historian and former public relations officer of the Association of American Railroads. His work took him to original sources throughout Southern's territory and provided a sound basis for the final manuscript.

Keith Bryant, Jr., an experienced historian who is now head of the Department of History at Texas A&M, added to the quality of this research by updating and completing the Corliss manuscript.

Southern Railway's combination with Norfolk and Western Railway on 1 June 1982, under the banner of Norfolk Southern Corporation—when Davis was nearing completion of his work—created a particularly appropriate closing for the published history of Southern Railway System.

With warm thanks to the three historians who have served as guides, and with the hope that the reader will find this journey out of the past toward the future both interesting and informative, here is the story of Southern Railway. We have subtitled it *Road of the Innovators* because, since its beginnings, that is what Southern Railway has been.

Harold H. Hall
President and Chief Operating Officer
Norfolk Southern Corporation
(Last president of the independent
Southern Railway Company)
October 1984

The Southern Railway

ONE

Putting Out the Fire

On the sunny afternoon of 17 June 1953 a venerable steam engine—the heavy Mikado Number 6330—chuffed into the yards of the Southern Railway System in Chattanooga. Engineer C. F. Case, a thirty-five-year veteran, eased the old Mike and its string of freight cars into the congested area and brought his train to a ceremonial halt.

At one side of 6330 was a gleaming red-and-black replica of the tiny Best Friend of Charleston, the progenitor of American steam railroading, and at the other was one of Southern's four-unit diesel-electric locomotives of the latest design.

A few dignitaries gathered in the heat beside Case's engine while photographers recorded the scene, and soon the old locomotive was pulled to the ashpit, where its fires were drawn for the last time. A sentimental railroad man who watched wrote of its last moments: "The whine of the headlight generator faded to a whimper, the feather of steam faded from her pops, the sobbing choke of her cylinder cocks stopped. There was nothing more for the 6330 to do."

Walter Gay, an ashpit man, hosed down the coals of its last fire on the tracks and the old locomotive was ready for the scrap heap. Only two of its parts had been found useful enough to be saved—the bell was destined for a church, and the steam whistle for a factory.

The Southern's days of steam had come to an end. The System was the first major American railroad to become completely dieselized, almost a century and a quarter after the nation's steam era had opened in the heart of its territory.

When Southern's President Harry A. DeButts declared from Washington, "It took us 123 years to put out that fire," Southern was saluting a predecessor line and its Best Friend of Charleston, which had made its first run on Christmas Day 1830—the first steam locomotive in regular scheduled passenger service on the American continent. DeButts was paying a personal tribute when he added later, "A lot of the romance went out of railroading when the steam engine disappeared."

4
Putting Out the Fire

The brief ceremony in the Chattanooga yards marked the completion of a technological revolution on one of the nation's most innovative railroads. The great regional carrier had already been revitalized by the change from steam to diesel power. In return for an investment of $120 million in diesel locomotives, Southern had doubled its motive power and cut its fuel costs in half. The new era of progress that lay ahead for Southern promised to be its brightest.

The System was already setting new mileage records that railroad veterans found fantastic. Passenger diesels were averaging about fourteen thousand miles of service each month, 300 percent more than the steam locomotives they had replaced. Two divisions—Charleston and Columbia, South Carolina—had recently reported that forty-one diesels were doing the work of one hundred and fifty steam locomotives. Throughout the System, road freight diesels were averaging nine thousand miles per month, and road switchers six thousand miles. Even yard diesels were now kept busy about nineteen hours daily, or seven thousand hours per year, an increase of 136 percent over the performance of steam switchers of a decade earlier.

The new power had made Southern a system in more than name. In contrast to the former practice of operating locomotives over only one or two districts within an operating division, diesels were now dispatched on a regional basis, and overall planning was on a systemwide basis. Many diesel assignments covered all three of Southern's operating regions.

The process of dieselization of the System was already fourteen years old when Engineer Case took 6330 on its farewell run. In 1939, under the aggressive leadership of President Ernest E. Norris, who preceded DeButts, Southern had entered the diesel era. On the recommendation of these two leaders, the Board of Directors had approved the experimental use of diesel-electric locomotives on branch-line passenger trains in hope of improving economy and efficiency to help meet competition from automobiles and buses. Though Southern management began its pioneering effort on a limited scale, this decision required courage and foresight, for diesel power on railroads was still in its early stages.

Norris first ordered six small 750-horsepower locomotives for local passenger trains, and on 24 September 1939 Southern celebrated a historic event when the Goldenrod entered daily service between Columbus, Mississippi, and Mobile, Alabama. A week

5
Putting Out the Fire

later a second diesel-powered train, the Joe Wheeler, named after a celebrated Confederate cavalry general, made the first of its runs between Chattanooga, Tennessee, and Tuscumbia, Alabama. These were soon followed by a third train, the Cracker, operating between Atlanta and Brunswick, Georgia.

Norris and his staff were so impressed by the efficiency of the new passenger units that they ordered six larger diesel locomotives of two thousand horsepower, as well as six stainless-steel trains for long-distance passenger service. Norris also ordered eight diesel switching engines in 1940, and in May 1941 placed his order for Southern's first F-type freight diesel locomotive, the four-unit 6100.

Southern thus made more history on 26 May 1941, when it accepted delivery of the 6100—the first road-freight diesel-electric engine ever built. This powerful unit had been completed late in 1939 but had been demonstrated on other roads before Norris made his purchase.

The Santa Fe and the Great Northern railroads had bought diesel-electrics of later manufacture in the interim and had put those into service. But it was the pioneer 6100 that captured the imagination of railroaders.

After the tractive power of the huge unit had been questioned, the 6100 became the lead unit of a four-unit road diesel that developed fifty-four hundred horsepower. In tests on other roads, which lasted for over a year, the units had been operated for more than eighty-three thousand miles, on twenty different railroads, through thirty-five states, and had performed magnificently. After reconditioning, the 6100 quickly convinced Norris and DeButts that the future of railroading lay with the diesel locomotive.

A typical steam engine of 1941 was a heavy USRA 2-8-2 Mikado, whose performance on such runs as the "Rat Hole" division between Cincinnati and Chattanooga left something to be desired. These steam locomotives could pull no more than 3,100 tons on the run from Cincinnati, Ohio, to Danville, Kentucky, and their rating dropped to a mere 1,750 tons when they were used on the backbone of the run, over rugged terrain between Danville and Oakdale, Tennessee. The touring 6100, by contrast, made light work of the taxing grades, hauling 4,000 tons over the entire route while slicing an hour from the normal run of six hours from Danville to Oakdale.

Southern's management now pressed toward full dieselization. There was an enormous fleet of aging steam engines to be retired

Putting Out the Fire

and scrapped. Southern had used an assortment of types during the three decades prior to dieselization, a total of some twenty-four hundred—most of these Consolidations, Mikados, Pacifics, Santa Fes, six-wheel switch engines, and ten-wheel passengers.

The future president William ("Bill") Brosnan remembered, "We had a good fleet of steam engines, but they stood too long for servicing and repair. Also they were hard on track due to reciprocating parts. Norris made a wise decision to go diesel. They were more efficient, could pull more tonnage, and had a very high availability for service, about like that of an automobile."

By 1947 one of Southern's veteran diesel locomotives, the 4100, had already logged 400,000 miles and had only begun its useful life. By the following year Southern had put into service its first F-7s, which were to become the workhorses of the era.

The first all-diesel division of Southern had been the New Orleans & Northeastern, whose last steam engine made its final run in December 1948, thus placing this separate member company of the System among the first Class 1 railroads to make the vital change.

By March 1949, when 10 percent of Southern's locomotives were diesels, the newcomers handled 60 percent of the System's gross freight ton-miles; passenger diesels, then only 19 percent of the Southern fleet, accounted for 56 percent of passenger train-miles. The vision of Southern executives initiated the new era, but it was the hard work of the System's union laborers—members of the railway brotherhoods—that made possible the new accomplishments. Some of the brotherhoods were suspicious and resentful of the diesel revolution for a time, but their members adapted quickly to the new ways.

In the end, the coming of the diesel completely changed the face of the railroad and revamped its operations. Many coal and water stations and roundhouses disappeared in the first phase, and the machinery and equipment of the old shops was eventually replaced.

Crews were instructed in the new techniques in touring classroom cars whose instructors were provided by the mechanical and operating departments. In three years these cars offered class sessions for ten thousand students, the demonstrations made effective by the use of cutaway models and samples of the new equipment. The transition also necessitated a systemwide on-the-job training program.

Southern practiced a dual system during the transition years to

7
Putting Out the Fire

maintain its steam equipment while moving more fully into diesel operations. Older facilities were phased out gradually. The reduction of shop forces brought a reduction of locomotive crewmen, a circumstance that led to a protracted and occasionally violent confrontation between the railway brotherhoods and the resolute Brosnan, who had become vice-president, Operations, by the time Southern's crisis arose.

"We had trouble enough in the changeover," Brosnan recalled later, "and then there was a national effort by the firemen's organization to disrupt this and require a fireman on every unit. A strike resulted, there was some shooting at locomotives and other rough-housing, but the work went on."

Brosnan's assault upon featherbedding in his locomotive cabs became legendary in the industry. His view of the challenge was simple: the diesel had rendered firemen obsolete, and their retention as unproductive employees would endanger profitability and perhaps the existence of Southern. He was resolved to resist with every legal means the effort of the brotherhoods to keep firemen on the job. Thanks to Brosnan, Southern was able to reduce the high cost of maintaining all of its firemen before it was too late; other roads would be unable to follow Brosnan's example in later years.

Brosnan began by allowing attrition to reduce the ranks, until there were too few firemen to man all runs. With his candid approach, he managed to hold the loyalty of most of his people, including firemen. He pointed out that the arrival of the automobile, milking machines, and mechanical refrigeration had displaced many thousands of workers. Railroads, he insisted, fell into the same pattern with the diesel locomotive. To the dismay of the firemen's union, he won his point.

"When the fireless diesel took the place of the coal-burning steam locomotive whose fire the fireman was hired to tend, there was no longer any need for a fireman," Brosnan said. "The employment of *new*, unneeded firemen would ... worsen the job security of all employees who get their livelihood from Southern."

About this time a presidential commission named by Harry Truman found that firemen were not needed on diesels and recommended that firemen with fewer than ten years' seniority be laid off permanently. Brosnan declined to lay off any of his men. "All our firemen and their families ... deserve fair treatment. Each man now holding seniority as a fireman will work out his time until retired or he becomes disabled, unless dismissed for cause.

8
Putting Out the Fire

There is no threat to the jobs of any of Southern's firemen as is posed to firemen of other railroads by the recommendation of the Presidential Commission."

Brosnan refused to go beyond that: "Certainly we are not obligated to hire new men, including men not yet born, for whom there is no need. We will not do so. No business could do such a thing and survive." As he pointed out, the Southern's agreement with the Brotherhood did not require the hiring of new firemen.

Brosnan ran trains with reduced crews when the lists of firemen had been exhausted—an engineer and a brakeman handled the locomotives. Brosnan said this crew was more than adequate. "The firemen had nothing to do anyway—no fire to tend, no boiler to watch." For several years Southern's trains ran safely and efficiently under this system, and Southern soon established an extensive record of safe operation with the smaller crews.

The brotherhood filed a complaint and a federal court in Washington, D.C., ordered Southern to resume its hiring of firemen. Brosnan laid his plans and waited. He recalled these tense days years afterward: "Our lawyers badgered me to hire firemen but I wouldn't budge. We needed time to study the matter. Finally, late one night, the lawyers told me that we must hire firemen or be in contempt of court. I told them to go to bed and forget it."

That same night, however, he called security officers at division points and gave them orders: "Go out and hire the firemen we need for all trains. But not just anybody. They must be at least seventy years old, and preferably black. Education doesn't matter. They won't have to be able to read or write. There'll be no physical exam, and no work exam. Just hire 'em and we'll put 'em on."

Brosnan stayed by his telephone until 4 A.M., when the last of his officers had reported the job done. The aged black men—and a number of women—rode the trains, performing no duties whatsoever. "All they had to do," Brosnan said, "was climb into the locomotive, sit still and do nothing, beyond going to the bathroom."

Southern's lawyers continued to call, but Brosnan reassured them, "There's no problem. These people are firemen, and we've complied with the court order. Since the new firemen have no duties to perform, it's obvious that anyone, regardless of age, race, sex, education, or state of health, could do the job—just sitting in a comfortable seat."

The Brotherhood, as Brosnan remarked, "did not seem to appreciate Southern's effort," and later demanded that Brosnan be cited for contempt. Brosnan was firm with his anxious lawyers: "I

Putting Out the Fire

have every right to decide who is to be designated as a fireman and what his duties are." He also pointed out that the union was in a vulnerable position, since its contracts provided that new men to be hired must be white, in violation of the Constitution.

The court agreed with Brosnan, ruling that he had complied with its orders and that he was within his rights to select Southern's firemen and set forth their duties.

Brosnan later disclaimed any Machiavellian purpose in his hiring strategy. "Since the money was to be largely wasted, it seemed to me to be sensible to give it to older people, and to catch up on our hiring of blacks. I thought it was the best way to help needy people. So we did it that way. We still—in the 1980s—have to hire firemen we don't need, but we're much better off than we would have been if I'd rolled over and played dead."

The issue was to be fought out over more than twenty years, for it was 1972 before Southern reached a final agreement with the brotherhood, providing that firemen would be required only on passenger and hostling services and as a source of supply for promotion to engineer. Though the union resisted to the bitter end, it was overcome by Brosnan's relentless pressure.

In 1954 Brosnan was elected to the Board of Directors, on the suggestion of DeButts. Six years later he was named to the new post of executive vice president in charge of both operations and traffic. It was now virtually certain that he was to become president when DeButts retired, and become the third in a Southern triumvirate which directed the System's affairs over a crucial period of three decades: Norris, DeButts, and Brosnan.

TWO

"The Strongest Management"

In the late 1970s and early 1980s, almost a generation after becoming an all-diesel road, the Southern consistently ranked among the top two or three railroads in profitability despite its ninth-place position in size. A leader in the application of new technology and innovative management, it continued to break its own records in earnings and revenues and in 1974 had been named by *Dun's Review* as one of the five best-managed corporations in America, along with American Telephone & Telegraph, Kerr-McGee, Merck & Company, and Reynolds Industries.

Its 10,250-mile network of gleaming rails threaded a thirteen-state region—from Washington, D.C., to Jacksonville, Florida, and from East St. Louis, Illinois, to New Orleans, Louisiana. Though the heart of its territory was the old Confederacy—the rapidly growing Southeast—it also served parts of the Midwest. Generally regarded as a road of the open country, with its main stem traversing the southern Piedmont, it was in truth a mountain line, with the great "X" of its lines crossing the Alleghenies through some of the most forbidding terrain on the eastern half of the continent. Its Saluda grade in the North Carolina hill country was, at 4.7 percent, the steepest mainline on a major American railroad.

The System's western reaches also included the Cincinnati, New Orleans & Texas Pacific, celebrated as the "Rat Hole" division, whose sharp curves, plunging grades, and long, narrow tunnels had once tested crews in their passage of the Cumberland Mountains between Cincinnati and Chattanooga. There was also the Asheville division in western North Carolina, whose builders had fought their way over sharp ridges by dragging locomotives with mule- and oxen-power. On the western flank of the Old South, the System's enormous bridges carried rails over the Ohio, Cumberland, Tennessee, Black Warrior, and Tombigbee rivers. The network touched the Mississippi at three points: New Orleans, Memphis, and East St. Louis.

Along the eastern seaboard, trending south, the system served

"The Strongest Management"

the growing ports of Norfolk, Morehead City, Charleston, Brunswick, Savannah, Jacksonville, Mobile, and New Orleans.

In the decade following the mid-1960s more than $1 billion had been invested in Southern's plant and equipment. As one of the most carefully maintained of the world's railroads, Southern had led the fourteen major American rail systems in expenditures for maintenance of way during the period. In 1981 Southern owned more than 75,000 freight cars and had 1,459 diesel locomotive units, all well maintained and replaced on regular schedules.

The System carried a highly diversified billion-dollar traffic mix with major traffic volume in coal, chemicals, pulp and paper products, agricultural and food products, automobiles, lumber and wood products, stone, clay, glass, and concrete products. In an industry that had traditionally struggled to earn a fair return, Southern had repeatedly operated at remarkably high levels with such traffic. For six years its revenues had topped $1 billion, and in 1981 its revenues were $1,790,669,000, and its net income $212,080,000.

As *Dun's Review* pointed out in 1974, Southern's earnings had "grown faster than those of any other railroad in the past decade. And of the three major roads engaged exclusively in the rail business, it is the only one whose earnings have grown consistently over the past five years." The System's "solid, long-term growth" was cited as Southern's chief accomplishment, one made possible by farsighted management: "It is a succession of prescient decisions by chief executives over the past two decades that has allowed Southern to remain one of the very few railroads in the country that could successfully stick to its last."

Some of the System's leaders gave credit for that management strength to their third president, Fairfax Harrison, who had established a unique management-training program before World War I—training that involved an introduction to the pick and shovel and the hard facts of maintenance of way. Though it went unsaid in this instance, an equally vital factor in Southern's growth was the dedication of its laboring force.

Among the less tangible assets of the Southern was the corporate spirit that had made possible its rise—a high level of morale that had persisted for decades. Many observers noted the brisk, commonsense style of Southern's management, the close bond of communication that seemed to be companywide, and the maintenance of discipline remarkable in the permissive atmosphere of

"The Strongest Management"

the 1970s and 1980s. As one president pointed out, this morale owed much to the policy of hiring men and women from its own region to a large extent, and to a long-established policy of promotion from the ranks. The System's morale was thus continually reinforced by its officer corps.

In an industry noted for its positive leadership by chief executive officers cast in a rugged mold, Southern's nine presidents had been outstanding. Samuel Spencer, the founder, had risen from the status of a boy cavalryman of the Confederacy to a position of influence with the banking firm of J. P. Morgan. Harold Hall, the last president of the independent Southern, began as a boy telegrapher in a mountain village. Of the nine presidents, five were still living in 1982, as the Southern prepared to surrender its corporate identity in a merger with the Norfolk & Western.

The Southern's presidents and their terms are:

Samuel Spencer of Georgia	1894–1903
William W. Finley of Mississippi	1903–1913
Fairfax Harrison of Virginia	1913–1937
Ernest E. Norris of Illinois	1937–1952
Harry A. DeButts of Virginia	1952–1962
D. William Brosnan of Georgia	1962–1967
W. Graham Claytor, Jr., of Virginia	1967–1976
L. Stanley Crane of the District of Columbia	1976–1979
Harold H. Hall of North Carolina	1979–1982

Though Southern's progress had been fairly consistent from the start, the leadership of Harry DeButts and Bill Brosnan in the 1950s gave it the impetus to become one of the premier railroads in the United States. In Southern's infancy, around 1900, security analysts hailed the Pennsylvania Railroad as the "Standard Railroad of the World." By the 1930s and 1940s the Atchison, Topeka & Santa Fe Railroad was generally acclaimed as the foremost. But by the 1960s, when the Brosnan revolution had begun to bear fruit, the respected observer David P. Morgan, editor of *Trains*, declared Southern to be the leader of the American railroad industry. The System continued to exhibit this leadership during the 1970s in a time in which several railroads collapsed, and into the uncertain business climate of the 1980s—still achieving record levels of profitability and improved service.

Southern's highly motivated work force of some twenty-one thousand ranked among the most productive in the industry, as well as the most safety-minded. Twice in the late 1970s and again

"The Strongest Management"

in 1981 the System won the E. H. Harriman Memorial Gold Medal, the top honor for employee safety. The annual Harriman awards were initiated in 1913 in honor of an American railroad pioneer; the program today is carried on by his son, Governor W. Averell Harriman.

The Southern's position of leadership, achieved by DeButts and Brosnan, rested largely on its program of early mechanization. As *Railway Age* reported late in 1979, "Southern had men like Bill Brosnan, who, earlier than anyone else, recognized the threat that the escalating cost of labor would pose to a well-maintained right of way; as a result, Southern, earlier than anyone else, began to mechanize: when the machines were not available, Southern invented them; and Southern, more than most railroads, has been able to produce the earnings that could be plowed back into the roadway." At that time Southern was investing only sixty-four cents in labor for each dollar of track material installed—as compared with a figure of ninety cents for the industry as a whole.

One veteran student of the industry was quoted by a national business magazine: "Anybody who tries to play catch-up now has to do it at 1970s prices. Southern is so well up on its maintenance that it has the option of cutting back on routine maintenance if it should run into difficult times, and still keep its earnings up."

Innovation and technological advancement on the Southern, rather than slowing with the coming of diesel power, began to accelerate. Once the faster and more dependable locomotives had focused attention upon the bottlenecks that the System's classification yards had become, Southern began a modernization program that moved with all possible speed. The opening of major new facilities in Knoxville and Birmingham in 1951 and 1952 was only the beginning. By 1979, the seventh of these strategically located and highly efficient new yards had opened at Linwood, North Carolina. These yards were geared to speeding traffic on its way through the use of closed circuit television, radio communications, and radar speed meters, and despite the heavy investments for such equipment, it soon paid for itself.

Welded ribbon rail, laid in quarter-mile sections, replaced the old short jointed sections on Southern; this change promised much in improved speed, safety, and maintenance. By 1981, Southern had more than 7,000 miles of welded rail in place and was adding more at the rate of about 350 miles annually.

The first microwave system developed for the railroad industry covered more than 4,720 route miles, and was the largest private

"The Strongest Management"

communications network of its kind in the eastern United States. As an early convert to the computer age, Southern had become the first industrial user of IBM's Model 705. In 1980 its Atlanta computer center could locate any car on the System almost instantly and reveal its cargo and destination. The center also linked the microwave and hotbox-detection system to computers, dispatched trains, received signals of train movements, and ordered priorities in passing of trains, cutting delays in transit by 25 percent on the division where it was first tried experimentally. By monitoring with test cars, the computers also recorded a profile of track conditions.

Modern marketing had also been a key to Southern's growth since World War II. With the introduction of the unit train system in coal fields in 1960, Southern pioneered a marketing system that utilized special cars whose design and use originated with the System. The unit trains were used in fast turnaround service between coal mines and electric power plants. Following their introduction, Southern brought out other special cars, enabling the System to share in the growth of furniture, lumber, textile, paper, chemical, and other regional markets. The first of these cars, a giant aluminum hopper car called Big John, had revolutionized the grain-carrying trade and created a healthy livestock industry in the Southeast.

While other railroads imposed broad across-the-board rate increases during this period, Southern was making selective reductions and increases, with special attention to the most profitable traffic. With its greater efficiency Southern managed to hold this traffic in face of ever-fiercer competition and, in fact, was able to retain its profit levels at relatively lower rates. Michael R. Armellino, a securities analyst with Goldman, Sachs and Company, commented, "The difference between Southern and the old-line companies is that the old-line companies start with operations; they have the line and they let the customers come to them. But the Southern starts with marketing, and it has been very clever about soliciting the best business."

In a companion effort, as an aid to marketing, Southern had been a leader in industrial development since its earliest days, when its first efforts promoted immigration of farm families into the South, and helped to develop a diversified agricultural production. Much later, with the identical goal of building traffic, Southern had introduced the concept of the industrial park, which became an important factor in encouraging diversified industrial

"The Strongest Management"

growth in its territory. The success of the industrial program was reflected in annual reports of an ever-increasing tide of industrial immigration to the South. In 1981, new and expanded plants and warehouses involved investments of $1.1 billion in the Southern's territory—developments expected to add some sixty-one hundred jobs and an increase of about $42.5 million annually in freight revenues.

Southern began as a substantial carrier of the freight in its region, but was best known to the public for its passenger service, whose crack trains first became famous in the days of the Washington & Southwestern Vestibuled Limited and the New York & Florida Limited, hailed around the turn of the century as "the most luxurious train in the world." This was a tradition that continued with the Florida Express, and the Crescent Limited which, as the Southern Crescent, was in its turn hailed as the world's finest passenger train. During the 1920s and 1930s the green-and-gold Pacifics and their matching cars made Southern trains favorites among the nation's travelers.

The end of Southern's passenger era—marked by the final run of the Southern Crescent in February 1979—had followed an especially significant phase of the System's history. Under the leadership of W. Graham Claytor, Jr., the first nonrailroader to become Southern's president, the Company's management practices were restructured and broadened, long-range planning and budgeting were introduced, and a new balance was struck between operating and commercial divisions.

The Southern's own history in many ways closely paralleled that of the South it served, leading some observers to contend that the System's progress was due to the burgeoning of the southern economy. But, as the Harvard economist Daryl Wycoff pointed out, the railroad itself "contributed significantly" to this general regional growth—and in addition the road outperformed its rivals by a wide margin. Graham Claytor observed that the Southern, with its lean system, was the beneficiary of a unique regional legacy: since capital had been limited in the Southeast during the early era of railroading, there were no burdensome appendages of marginal or duplicating lines such as plagued railroads in other regions.

Whatever Southern's natural advantages, and the acclaim it had won for innovative methods in technology and management, its leaders single-mindedly pursued a goal of satisfying their customers. As President Harold Hall put it, "We are not in business to fix tracks, or repair locomotives, or to run a management committee *per se*. We are in the transportation business purely and simply to be of service to the shipper."

That concept guided Southern into the uncertain economic climate of the 1980s. In the wake of the merger of the Chessie System and Seaboard Coast Line Industries into the nation's largest rail system, Southern, with its highly diversified traffic mix, planned a merger with Norfolk & Western, a perennially profitable road whose great strength was in hauling coal. This combination, under a holding company known as Norfolk Southern Corporation, seemed to augur success for the two industry leaders, in a time when economists hesitated to forecast the future of American railroads.

Energy was expected to exert a critical influence on rail performance, and in case petroleum shortages dictated greater coal usage, the Southern–Norfolk & Western system stood to become a major beneficiary. In the event of petroleum scarcity, railroads in general would have a great advantage over other forms of mass transportation. A National Science Foundation study of 1973 found that railroads were four times more efficient than trucks in use of petroleum, and sixty-five times more efficient than air cargo carriers. There remained the threat of coal pipelines, but this was a challenge Southern had overcome in the past. Deregulation of railroads, generally welcomed by Southern and other railroads, though with reservations, opened the prospect of a new competitive environment that had not existed in the United States in modern times.

Perhaps the chief factor that would shape Southern's future was the prospect of continued growth in the South itself. Economists agreed that the outlook for the region was positive, with industry and population continuing to migrate into the Southeast. Much of the anticipated development would be within Southern's territory.

If the Southern, still a youngster at the age of eighty-eight, could look forward to a future as promising as that of any other American railroad, it could also look back upon a history remarkable in an industry whose story was so strongly linked with the nation's history. History and heritage have always been major concerns of the Southern—the history of the emerging South as well as that of the railway system, as the two had been linked since the distant beginnings of the railroad movement in America.

Southern's history, in any case, which began properly with the

"The Strongest Management"

men who put the Best Friend of Charleston on the rails, had been written by remarkable people, some of whom were familiar figures in American annals: John C. Calhoun, Joel Poinsett, Jefferson Davis, John C. Breckinridge, Abraham Lincoln, and the Confederate generals John B. Gordon and Nathan Bedford Forrest. The major currents of regional history had shaped the modern railroad system and its growth: the rise of King Cotton, the era of internal improvements in the second quarter of the nineteenth century, the manifold contributions of black labor, the Civil War and Reconstruction, the New South. But though the Southern Railway System bore the unmistakable stamp of its region in personnel and outlook, its vigorous management style was its own, and it was that which had made it a model for its industry.

Of numerous dates prominent in the System's past, two are of signal importance: 25 December 1830, when Southern's oldest predecessor line, the South Carolina Canal & Rail Road Company, began the first regularly scheduled steam passenger service in America—and 1 July 1894, when the Southern Railway Company was organized from the wreckage of the bankrupt Richmond & Danville Railroad. In the years between these milestones some 125 smaller railroads had been combined, recombined, and reorganized to form the nucleus of the Southern Railway System.

They were a mixed lot of enterprises, their lines ranging from a remote village on Florida's St. Johns River to Alexandria, Virginia, and from Norfolk on the Atlantic to the river towns of the Mississippi.

Despite failures that had been so numerous and the war ravages that had been their common fate, these roads were regarded with pride, or with bemused good humor by Southerners.

Inevitably, jocular nicknames had been concocted to correspond to the initials displayed on freight cars of the lines:

The Georgia & Florida—G&F: God-Forgotten.
The New Orleans & Northeastern—NO&NE: No Omelettes, No Eggs.
The Georgia, Florida & Alabama—GF&A: Gophers, Frogs & Alligators.
The Georgia Southern & Florida—GS&F: Go Slow & Flag.
The East Tennessee, Virginia & Georgia—ETV&G: Eat Turnips, Vinegar & Greens.
The Live Oak, Perry & Gulf—LOP&G: Lean Over, Push & Grunt.

18
"The Strongest Management"

The new company into which so many of these battered little railroads were to be merged was a creation of the banking house of Drexel, Morgan and Company, but the moving spirit of the enterprise was as much a southerner, a Confederate—and a railroader—as any among the colorful personalities of the Southern railroad scene to this time. His name was Samuel Spencer, and though he had come to the leadership of the Southern Railway by a divergent route, he was one of their own.

THREE

The Birth of the Southern Railway

Samuel Spencer was one of a numerous band of Confederate veterans who rose to prominence in national affairs during the tumultuous period following the Civil War. The son of a Columbus, Georgia, cotton merchant and planter, he was born in 1847, an only child. His mother was the daughter of Isaac Mitchell, a pioneer settler of Columbus.

The Spencer family had lived on Maryland's Eastern Shore near St. Michael's since the mid-eighteenth century, but Samuel's father, Lambert Spencer, had migrated to the sparsely settled Georgia-Alabama border at the age of eighteen and had made his fortune there. Young Samuel lived a life of ease traditional in wealthy southern families of the day, tended by servants, visiting frequently on the plantations of relatives, and introduced to an outdoor life at an early age. His mother died when Samuel was ten and the boy was brought up by black servants and cousins who were scarcely his senior.

The coming of the Civil War ended this idyllic life. In the midst of the war Samuel entered the Georgia Military Institute at Marietta, when he was about fifteen years old, and in 1864, at the age of seventeen, he enlisted in Nelson's Rangers, a cavalry troop that included several boys from Columbus. Private Spencer and his troop campaigned in Mississippi and Alabama, served for a time under the celebrated cavalry chief Nathan Bedford Forrest, and finally joined the army of Gen. John B. Hood. The impetuous Hood, driven from Atlanta, now marched into Tennessee, hopeful of luring Gen. W. T. Sherman out of Georgia. This army's move resulted in the bloody battle of Franklin, Tennessee, a disaster for the Confederate cause.

When the war ended in the spring of 1865, young Spencer returned to his father's plantation near Columbus, where he spent several months recuperating. In January 1866, when the University of Georgia reopened, Samuel Spencer enrolled as a member of the junior class, along with a number of his army companions. An excellent student, Samuel became the valedictorian of his graduating class the following year. Spencer wrote his father that

The Birth of Southern Railway

he realized he was expected to enter the family cotton business, but he longed for the more active life of a civil engineer. Lambert Spencer replied that though the engineering profession seemed to be overcrowded, with ex-army officers seeking employment, he would not oppose his son's plans. He then enrolled his son at the University of Virginia.

Spencer also led his class at Virginia, where he applied himself with single-minded zeal. He did not return home for Christmas vacation because of the expense of the trip. In 1869 Samuel returned home and worked briefly for the Columbus city waterworks. A few months later he landed his first railroad job, as a rodman with the Savannah & Western (now part of the Central of Georgia), which was building a line from Opelika to Birmingham, Alabama. Spencer was launched on the career that was to end with his founding and directing the Southern Railway System.

Samuel was soon promoted to assistant engineer and in 1871 became principal assistant engineer of the road, assigned to survey and stake a new line. A few months later, promoted to chief engineer, he was deeply involved in the railroad's most vital affairs, learning the cost of construction, locomotives and cars, and other equipment. He became so involved in his work that when he married Louisa Benning, of a leading Columbus family, in February 1872, the honeymoon had to be postponed.

Spencer's advance toward the upper levels of railroad management began in earnest with the arrival of Thomas R. Sharp on the Savannah & Memphis as general superintendent—the Colonel Sharp who had won fame with Stonewall Jackson during the war, capturing Baltimore & Ohio (B&O) locomotives in West Virginia and hauling them over dirt roads into Confederate territory. Sharp quickly recognized Spencer's superior abilities and named him resident engineer in charge of all construction on the railroad.

When Sharp resigned about six months later to become superintendent of the New Jersey Southern Railroad, Spencer became acting superintendent of the Savannah & Memphis, but he soon became dissatisfied and followed Colonel Sharp to New Jersey in the summer of 1872. Within a few days both Sharp and Spencer had been hired by the B&O Railroad, Sharp as assistant master of transportation and Spencer as supervisor of trains on the Hagerstown and Strasburg branch of the B&O. Spencer recognized his opportunity. He had written his wife to say that he preferred the B&O over any other American road, and wrote his father that his new job was a stepping stone to a superintendency: "My duties

The Birth of Southern Railway

will be to attend to the proper running of all trains on the branch, the looking after the enginemen, conductors and agents ... and while I have no control over the machinery and auditing departments, I will necessarily have to see that all duties pertaining to them are faithfully and efficiently performed." Here, too, he worked so conscientiously that he was unable to leave for a Christmas holiday with his wife and newborn son, Henry—a pattern of work that was to endure for years.

Spencer soon came to the attention of his superiors and was promoted to supervisor of trains on the Harrisburg, Pennsylvania, branch. He had now won the approval of one of the nation's leading railroad executives, John W. Garrett, the dynamic president of the B&O, who saw in Spencer an exceptionally able, forthright, and energetic young man.

Samuel Spencer in his late twenties had already acquired the arresting presence that was to mark him in later years—erect and manly, with an air of quiet but forceful competence. Though he was a reserved man of few words, he was always noted for his consideration of blue-collar workmen on the railroads, whose hard labor produced small incomes. When a friend praised him for this trait, Spencer only said tersely, "I was a poor man once myself."

Through his increasingly close association with Garrett, Spencer met influential politicians and business leaders in Washington and Baltimore. His duties became more varied. In the period 1875–77 he dealt with such matters as lobbying bills favorable to railroads through the Virginia legislature, relocation of a local depot amidst a noisy controversy, establishing freight rates for shipment of peaches, and bringing to book an agent who had lost $260 of company funds. From such experiences he learned to deal with many types of men and began to develop a shrewd judgment of his fellows.

Spencer continued to devote himself to work. He once wrote his wife to explain his refusal of an invitation for Christmas dinner, "My position here is not strong enough to admit of so many absences, and while it would have been very pleasant I don't think it would have done me any good. The B&O does not look with favor upon social enjoyment." He spent that Christmas Day of 1876, like so many others, at work.

In the following year Spencer left the B&O, with Garrett's approval, to become superintendent of transportation on the Virginia Midland Railroad (now part of the Southern), a line that

The Birth of Southern Railway

Garrett hoped to influence and perhaps absorb. Spencer felt the new experience would further his career, though the salary of $2,500 did not impress him.

But Spencer had hardly joined this road when Thomas Sharp beckoned him once more. After a costly strike that had been ended by federal intervention, Sharp had left the B&O to become president and receiver of the Long Island Railroad—and he immediately offered Spencer the position of superintendent, at a salary of $5,000. Sharp urged Spencer to accept: "If you have any hesitancy in assuming so much responsibility, I will shoulder all you do not want.... I do not know of any one that I am willing to make Gen'l Supt. but yourself."

Another of Spencer's friends in New York—a former director of the Savannah & Western—also advised him to make the move: "These railroad men here lack the varied experience and railroad knowledge you have acquired.... I think you had better take Col. Sharp's offer."

Spencer did so and once more won the attention and respect of an influential sponsor who was to play a leading role in his career—this time J. Pierpont Morgan, whose banking firm was heavily involved in the troubled Long Island Railroad. The management of Sharp and Spencer was so effective as to delight Drexel, Morgan and Company, and Morgan in particular came to trust Spencer's knowledge, tact, and ability. Spencer served on the Long Island Railroad for about eighteen months, but was recalled to the B&O by John Garrett and his son Robert, who had come to realize the value of the young Georgian's services. In October 1879 Spencer became assistant to President Garrett, a position from which he directed daily operations of the B&O—and was especially charged with "the judicious and economical use of our cars."

Within a few months Spencer reported that car movements were faster and more efficient than ever on the road. When John Garrett was on vacation in 1881, Spencer operated the road; the president was pleased enough with his work to give him one of his prize cows as a mark of his approval.

An enduring anecdote reveals the closeness of the relationship between Garrett and Spencer at this time. The two met at a New York steamship pier, where Spencer had gone to bid farewell to his chief, who was sailing to Europe. Garrett insisted that Spencer accompany him: "You must get on this steamer, Spencer, and go to Europe with me. You know Baltimore & Ohio and I have to have

The Birth of Southern Railway

money for the property. You are the very man to talk to those bankers over there."

Spencer went along and apparently made an effective plea, for the B&O secured a loan, and Spencer returned home as third vice-president. He was soon promoted to second vice-president, and two years later, after the death of John W. Garrett and the elevation of Robert Garrett to the presidency, Spencer became the B&O's vice-president, and had charge of operations. The death of the elder Garrett, however, marked the beginning of a long decline for the railroad. Spencer himself was as competent as ever and continued to win praise for his work in the face of increased responsibilities. He was soon involved in negotiations with connecting railroads on tariff and other matters; he also carried through a number of business deals for oil and coke properties in West Virginia and Pennsylvania in which B&O directors had interests. In these dealings he was praised as "adroit, resourceful, and sound."

But the B&O now began to experience serious financial instability, largely as a result of building a costly branch line into Philadelphia to compete with the Pennsylvania Railroad. In the absence of Robert Garrett, who was in England, Spencer sought to cope with unreliable subcontractors who undertook the work at low prices and absconded without paying laborers when they found their contracts unprofitable. Irate workmen retaliated by seizing Spencer's superintendent of construction and a clerk, holding them until their wages were paid.

It was also Spencer's duty to report to directors that 1885 had been the least profitable of the past eight years. The B&O was forced to seek new loans, and Robert Garrett returned to Europe to enlist the aid of bankers on the Continent. In Garrett's absence, Spencer and the road's general counsel, John K. Cowen, also approached Drexel, Morgan and Company for emergency financing, a move that set in motion a complex series of events which made Spencer president of the B&O. Morgan formed a syndicate of New York, Boston, and London investors to advance fresh capital to the B&O.

Morgan had agreed to finance the railroad with the understanding that he choose the executive officers. When it was rumored that Spencer was his candidate for president of the B&O, Robert Garrett, who heard the rumors in London, became quite upset at the prospect of being forced out of the company. Spencer asked Morgan to cable Garrett and to publish a full and accurate account of the transaction in London newspapers, but when Morgan declined, leaving the task to his London office, Spencer himself published a statement in the New York *Herald*, an explanation that gratified Garrett—but did not mollify his bitter feelings toward Morgan.

Spencer was elected president of the B&O in December 1887 at a salary of $25,000, a princely income for the day—but the road was not prospering and there were signs of growing troubles. The B&O's Board of Directors was composed of seven members named by the city of Baltimore, four by the state of Maryland, and twelve elected by private stockholders—an arrangement dating from the chartering of the railroad. Several members of the Board and others began to oppose Spencer, and opposition grew as the new president launched a vigorous attack upon the road's basic problems, which were largely political in nature.

When Spencer took office, the B&O's floating indebtedness amounted to almost $9 million, an excessive burden for the time. Spencer insisted upon a restatement of the book values of the company assets, which were set unrealistically high. He found that aging locomotives, obsolete for many years, were carried at their original cost—at least 30 percent too high. Obsolescence and deterioration had not been taken into account in any of the company's bookkeeping.

With the backing of Drexel, Morgan and Company, Spencer insisted upon a reappraisal of all equipment and the conservative valuation of the company's holdings of stocks, bonds, and accounts receivable—alterations that reduced the profit-and-loss-statement totals by about $22 million.

Spencer went further. He sold the express, sleeping-car, and telegraph businesses that had been established by John W. Garrett, eliminating heavy expenses. With funds from the sales, he reduced the road's debts—but drew criticism from those who favored continued B&O ownership of these services.

The report by Spencer and his committee on the true state of the B&O's financial condition, published in the annual report of November 1888, provoked an outcry from a shocked public. A new system of bookkeeping was inaugurated and dividends were suspended for the year. Most railroad men and financiers were impressed by the clarity and honesty of Spencer's report, but some Maryland and Baltimore politicians were outraged, and bent upon revenge. According to a Spencer family tradition, at least, the searching report had revealed numerous rebate arrangements

The Birth of Southern Railway

from which political figures profited at the expense of the railroad's stockholders. These payments were halted.

The anti-Spencer element soon had its way. Representatives of private investors on the Board decided to end the association with Drexel, Morgan and Company, and, to accomplish this, had to remove Spencer from office. In December 1888 the Board ousted Spencer in favor of a Baltimore merchant, Charles F. Mayer, by a vote of 13 to 8. Mayer went immediately to the president's office and began issuing orders. Spencer, who was at lunch when the move took place, never returned. (Mayer's leadership was to plunge the B&O into receivership within a short time.)

As the historian of the B&O wrote, "Samuel Spencer always spoke with great simplicity—and great honesty. For his sincerity and honesty at Baltimore, he paid—with his high position.... He became, in certain high quarters, *persona non grata*.... He had occupied the highest executive post of the B&O just one year and nine days."

Spencer was offered several other positions, but he declined to consider those outside the railroad field. In March 1889 he joined Drexel, Morgan and Company as its railroad adviser, a position that he was to hold until his death. This connection with the celebrated banking firm led to the climactic work of his career, the creation of the Southern Railway System.

Spencer's good fortune, as one observer said, was that he entered railroading during the period of expansion after the Civil War, when professional railroad men had begun to replace entrepreneurs as managers of large lines. Most professionals who rose to leadership in the industry followed paths similar to that of Spencer—through engineering and construction to operations, a training that gave them broad knowledge in the field and made of them "a new kind of informed executive." In Spencer's case, an equally vital asset was his dedication and honesty of character. Linked to his outstanding ability, it made him the leading candidate when J. P. Morgan began his search for a man to create the Southern from the wreckage of the Richmond & Danville line and the holding company that controlled it—the Richmond Terminal System.

This rich, varied, and sometimes frustrating background brought Spencer the unique opportunity to found a great new regional railroad system in the South. And because of his character and background, the Southern was to begin life with assets that most competitors lacked.

The Birth of Southern Railway

Spencer's first assignment with Drexel, Morgan and Company was further preparation for the work to come. He was put in charge of organizing the Elgin, Joliet & Eastern Railroad in Illinois and Indiana, and served as its president for nine years. In 1894, while he was still involved with this western road, the collapse of the Richmond & West Point Terminal Railway & Warehouse Company provided Spencer with the opportunity to found a successor system and direct it through its crucial formative years.

Richmond & Danville's decline began in 1891 with the onset of a depression that found the holding company dangerously overextended. There were no fewer than seventy mortgages, many bearing high interest rates and in need of refunding. The Terminal was just then at its peak in size and prestige, controlling almost eight thousand miles of rail lines, about one-sixth of all the roads in the South. It was at that point the second-largest American rail system, exceeded in length only by the Atchison, Topeka & Santa Fe. The rail and water lines (in the Chesapeake Bay) controlled by the company represented assets of $92 million, the greatest concentration of capital in the region. Terminal was doing an annual business of $42 million.

Once the depression's added pressure made it difficult for Terminal's management to obtain new financing, the end came swiftly. President John Hamilton Inman invited six leading railway financial experts to devise a plan to save Terminal, but when their report recommended creation of a new corporation with a capitalization of $350 million, it was rejected—largely because Terminal's stock- and bondholders were to be favored over investors who held the underlying securities. The crisis actually arrived in March 1892, when Georgia courts annulled the lease of the Central of Georgia, one of Terminal's largest components. Disintegration of the regional network followed rapidly. President Inman resigned rather than accept receivership. By July 1893 Samuel Spencer, F. W. Huidekoper, and Reuben Foster were appointed receivers of the Richmond & Danville and East Tennessee, Virginia & Georgia components of the Terminal system. By the end of the year nearly every property in the system was under receivership. The Terminal was not alone, for seventy-four American railroads, with more than twenty-seven thousand miles of line, entered receivership in 1893, more than in any other year in the nation's history.

Drexel, Morgan and Company was asked to revive the ruined Terminal system. A new committee composed of Charles H.

The Birth of Southern Railway

Coster of the Morgan firm, George Sherman, and Anthony J. Thomas was formed to draw up a plan for refinancing the enterprise. Samuel Spencer was named as consultant to the committee. The new plan appeared in February 1894, calling for the formation of a new corporation, the Southern Railway Company, capitalized at $305 million (with $120 million in 5 percent first consolidated mortgage and collateral trust bonds secured by mortgage of all company property; $60 million in 5 percent noncumulative preferred stock; and $125 million in common stock).

Security holders of the old Terminal Company accepted the proposal, but there were to be years of court actions before the legal maze was untangled. The Virginia legislature granted a charter to the Southern Railway Company on 20 February 1894, Samuel Spencer was elected president of the new road in June, and Southern began operating on 1 July—starting life with more than two thousand miles of line that had been the nucleus of the old system. For several months many former affiliates of the Terminal emerged from receivership and joined the Southern, so that the System embraced 4,392 miles by the end of the year. The new company forged into a single system more than thirty railroad companies, many of which had led a precarious existence for most of their corporate lives.

The Southern brought to an end the series of failures and bankruptcies that had marked the early period of Southeastern railroading and brought a new stability to rail transport of the region. The thirty corporations whose interlocked affairs and securities had caused such confusion were united and thirty sets of directors and accounts disappeared, with most of the seventy mortgages involved. About forty of these mortgages were eliminated in the reorganization, and the complex system of majority stock control which had infuriated minority holders was a thing of the past. Security holders of the older rail lines were by no means unanimously happy, but the majority accepted the new peace and the promise of greater regional prosperity.

Of equal importance, the bitter infighting between the East Tennessee, Virginia & Georgia, and the Richmond & Danville lines was ended. Though they were under common ownership in the Terminal days, jealousy between the two was so marked that they often turned over business to outside connections rather than give it to each other. Under Spencer's Southern these conflicts gave way to unity and cooperation.

The Reorganization Committee bought the Richmond & Dan-

The Birth of Southern Railway

ville properties at a foreclosure sale on 15 June and three days later met in Richmond to complete the new organization. A document, called the Articles of Agreement, was signed between Charles Coster and Anthony J. Thomas, purchasers of the Richmond & Danville, and Spencer, Col. Alexander B. Andrews, Francis L. Stetson, and W. A. C. Ewen, their associates. It was at this meeting that Spencer was named president. Vice-presidents were Colonel Andrews and W. H. Baldwin, Jr.; general counsel was Francis L. Stetson; secretary was W. A. C. Ewen; and auditor was George S. Hobbs. Control was firmly in the hands of the house of Morgan.

Spencer, who had been chosen by J. P. Morgan, selected his own associates carefully. Colonel Andrews, a former North Carolina farm boy who had worked on the North Carolina (NC) Railroad's construction at age seventeen, was an able operating and construction executive who was to aid Southern's first two presidents. The builder of the Western North Carolina Railroad, Andrews held the presidency of a dozen Southern railroads at various times, and was a director of numerous other lines. He was to serve with the Southern until his death in 1915.

William H. Baldwin, Jr., a Harvard man, was a New Englander who had begun his career with the Union Pacific and advanced to assistant vice-president before becoming vice-president of the Pere Marquette Railroad. Young Baldwin, who was to head Southern's operations and traffic departments, was praised by *Railroad Gazette* as "a man of clear and powerful mind, of quick comprehension, of extraordinary rapidity of decision, and absolutely without fear. He would have been a great soldier." Baldwin served under Spencer for two years before leaving to become president of the Long Island Railroad.

Francis Lynde Stetson, general counsel, was a leading lawyer of his day, representing no fewer than nine other railway companies during his career. He was noted for his courtesy and social graces, and had served as legal adviser to the Reorganization Committee. If Spencer chose his chief officers, Drexel, Morgan and Company selected the Southern's early directors: President Spencer, Charles H. Coster, and Anthony J. Thomas, from New York; Aubin L. Boulware of Richmond; Harris C. Fahnestock and Samuel Thomas of New York; Skipwith Wilmer of Baltimore; and the romantic figure Thomas Fortune Ryan, the Virginia orphan who became one of the financial barons of Wall Street. In 1895 Ryan and Samuel Thomas were succeeded by Samuel M. Inman of Atlanta

The Birth of Southern Railway

and George W. Maslin of New York. Thereafter, the Board's membership was to remain unchanged for several years.

Spencer opened operations with a main stem reaching from Alexandria, Virginia, southward through Charlottesville, Lynchburg, and Danville, Virginia; Greensboro, Salisbury, and Charlotte, North Carolina; Spartanburg and Greenville, South Carolina; and Gainesville, Georgia, to Atlanta. There were key branch lines to Strasburg, Richmond, and West Point, Virginia; Durham, Raleigh, Goldsboro, Winston-Salem, Asheville, and Murphy, North Carolina; and to Athens, Georgia.

Two months after operations began, Southern's mileage more than doubled from the acquisition of the East Tennessee, Virginia & Georgia, with its 1,791 miles; the Charlotte, Columbia & Augusta, with 191 miles; the Columbia & Greenville, 165 miles; the Georgia Pacific, 660 miles; and the Louisville Southern, 123 miles. In the same period, two independent lines came under Southern control: the Danville & Western, 83 miles; and the Blue Ridge, 34 miles. At the opening of 1895, Southern owned or operated more than 4,500 miles of line in seven states. With the exception of 491 miles from Goldsboro to Atlanta, which were leased, the Southern owned its entire system outright. (It also owned about 150 miles of water lines in the Chesapeake area.) Critics complained that northern capitalists were ruthlessly gobbling up southern interests, but there was no hope for the bankrupt small lines, and consolidation continued here, as elsewhere.

The System as it began represented an investment of $269 million, with authorized stocks at a par value of $170 million and a funded debt (as of 30 June 1895) of $74 million. In its first year Southern grossed $17.1 million, with net railway operating revenues of $5.1 million—and profits after interest and taxes of $896,000.

Spencer began with a fleet of 629 steam locomotives, 487 passenger cars, 18,305 freight cars, and 329 units of road-service equipment.

Among the new president's first moves was the reorganization of the traffic department under Vice-President Baldwin, with the veteran John W. Culp, formerly of the Richmond & Danville, as traffic manager for the system. The officers set out to increase traffic and revenues in order to pay the system's interest-bearing obligations, and this attempt continued a program of acquisitions.

In 1895 Spencer scored a coup by purchasing control of the Alabama Great Southern Railway, which brought Southern con-

The Birth of Southern Railway

trol of the Cincinnati, New Orleans & Texas Pacific (CNO&TP) Railway, which was in turn the lessee of the Cincinnati Southern. The CNO&TP became part of the Southern four years later, giving the System access to both New Orleans and Cincinnati through the rich territory of the Queen & Crescent Route.

Southern strengthened its base in Georgia by purchase of the 102-mile Atlanta & Florida in June 1895, entering an important lumbering and agricultural region on the route from Atlanta to Fort Valley. This dilapidated line was restored and made profitable only after heavy expenditures for track, structures, and rolling stock. In a kindred move, in July 1895 Spencer bought control of the Georgia, Southern & Florida Railway, which ran for 285 miles from Macon to Valdosta and thence to Palatka on the St. Johns River, crossing one of the South's important lumbering regions, one also rich in naval stores, cotton, fruits, and vegetables. Spencer's interest in lines to Florida, however, looked to the future, for winter travel to that state was already increasing, and new rail lines were pushing down both the east and west coasts, under the leadership of Henry M. Flagler and Henry B. Plant, both former directors of the Terminal Company.

But Spencer's chief concern in this period was for reaching a deep-water port on the Atlantic, the traditional keystone for successful railroads in the South. He accomplished this by pushing to Pinner's Point, near Norfolk, Virginia, by obtaining trackage rights over the Wilmington & Weldon and the Norfolk & Carolina lines between Selma, North Carolina, and Pinner's Point. Though this was not an ideal solution to his problem, he acquired acreage in the Norfolk area and built yards, wharves, and docks on both sides of the Elizabeth River, preparing for a growth in foreign trade. By 1 January 1896 Southern was operating from its Norfolk base.

The Southern's growth was closely paralleled by that of its regional rivals. The Atlantic Coast Line, organized in 1889 under leadership of H. G. Walters of Baltimore, had grown to 1,337 miles by 1894, having merged fifteen railroads in the process. The Louisville & Nashville (L&N) had grown as rapidly, adding 1,300 miles to its system between 1885 and 1894. By the time Southern began operations, the L&N operated 4,800 miles of line in the seven southern states, Indiana, and Illinois. There was also the Seaboard Air Line Railway System, founded in 1889 by the Baltimoreans John M. Robinson and R. C. Hoffman. By 1894 this line included six rail lines with a network of 1,000 miles. Spencer and the

The Birth of Southern Railway

Southern, however, rapidly outstripped their rivals in mileage, traffic, and investment.

Spencer also took a pioneering step by negotiating with Collis P. Huntington of the Southern Pacific (SP) to exchange traffic and open an all-rail route from Washington to San Francisco. Though results were not spectacular, traffic exchange with the SP did increase at Southern's New Orleans terminal.

The first of Spencer's serious problems arose in North Carolina when Governor Daniel L. Russell surprised Southern with an attack on its lease of the NC Railroad, the heart of the Southern's System. Loss of this lease would almost certainly have been fatal to the new enterprise, and the issue was a close one for some months. Russell's attack had been inspired in part by rival interests who proposed to lease the NC Railroad at higher rentals—but it was also a patriotic Tar Heel protest against Southern's linking its lines to a Virginia port, rather than to one in North Carolina. The conflict over this lease kept the state legislature in turmoil for an entire session before the members rejected the governor's recommendations and refused to annul the Southern's lease. Despite this action, the Southern applied for an injunction restraining state and NC Railroad officials from dissolving the lease. This injunction was granted, and later court rulings held that the lease had been made in good faith and was not fraudulent. Thereafter, Southern was assured of the continuance of the lease, which covered the lines between Goldsboro and Charlotte, North Carolina.

Spencer had only begun to expand. In 1898, the Spanish-American War broke out and put heavy demands on Southern facilities. Southern purchased the 332-mile Memphis & Charleston Railroad, giving the System a second line to the Mississippi. This acquisition, made for more than $9.5 million, pushed Southern's lines above 5,000 miles. Spencer was to acquire 1,200 more miles during the next two years.

Southern gained control of the South Carolina & Georgia (SC&G) Railroad (the former South Carolina Railroad), extending from Charleston to Augusta, Columbia, and Chester, with an extension from Augusta to Tenille, Georgia, under lease. These key acquisitions carried the Southern into Charleston itself, the chief city and seaport of South Carolina—and also brought into the Southern family the South's oldest railroad and the heritage of the first steam-powered railroad operated in the New World. The SC&G road operated 323 miles of track, represented an investment of some $11 million, and had an annual gross of about $1.25 million. This road, too, having recently emerged from receivership, demanded heavy investments to bring its track and equipment up to Southern's standards.

Four other acquisitions were made during this phase of Spencer's ambitious program. In Alabama, he acquired the Mobile & Birmingham, 148 miles long, from Marion Junction to Mobile, the state's chief port; and the Northern Alabama, 96 miles long, from Parrish on the Birmingham-Greenville line, northwestward to Sheffield on Southern's Chattanooga-Memphis route. The Northern Alabama thus gave Southern a direct connection between Birmingham and Memphis. In North Carolina, Spencer bought control of the Atlantic & Yadkin, running from Sanford through Greensboro to Mount Airy, a total of 131 miles, including branches. In Georgia, Spencer added the Northeastern Railroad of Georgia, 39 miles long, connecting with Southern's Piedmont Air-Line at Lula, operating to Athens. This line was bought at a bankruptcy sale for $307,000. All of these lines added significantly to future traffic volume, and helped to round out a network covering virtually all important points in the region.

FOUR

Sam Spencer's Grand Design

Spencer knew the importance of his role as founding father of the Southern, and he began with the broad concept that, since the railway system was part of the South, it was his mission to promote the two simultaneously, a pattern which would endure. He was quick to realize that the Southeast was rich in natural resources as well as in labor and potential business leaders, and he began a program to acquaint the public with economic opportunities along Southern's rails. The region's lacks, as Spencer knew so well, were capital and leadership for development. He assigned all his traffic representatives to encourage new industry in the region. In 1896 he established a Land and Industrial Department.

The incipient migration of the New England textile industry to the South was an early fruit of Spencer's aggressive program. Northern manufacturers were bombarded with booklets outlining the advantages of operating in the South, adjacent to the cotton fields—and with the added bonus of dramatically lower freight rates if they shipped manufactured cotton goods out of the region (these rates were much lower than those for shipping raw cotton). There was also a drumfire of other appeals: plentiful labor anxious for work, a milder climate, economical sources of power, materials available close at hand. The magic began to work. By 1900, forty-eight textile plants were already located along Southern lines, and more were added each year, a trend so powerful that half of American cotton spindles would be located in the South by the mid-1930s, and 91 percent of them by 1950. From Spencer's day to the present, the Southern became a major beneficiary of this movement.

Spencer's men also wooed furniture manufacturers, lumber mills, iron and steel manufacturers, and users of the vast deposits of marble, granite, limestone, and high-quality clays in the region. A diversified industrial base, though in its infancy, was already discernible before Spencer's career ended.

The founder also saw great potential in development—and diversification—of southern agriculture. One of his first moves as president was to appoint M. V. Richards, a resourceful promoter,

Sam Spencer's Grand Design

as land and immigration agent. Richards surveyed farmlands available in the railroad's territory and launched an imaginative campaign to attract farmers from Europe, Canada, and other parts of the United States. *The Southern Field*, a monthly bulletin on southern farming, appeared in 1895 and was circulated in English, German, and French editions, listing farms for sale and offering homestead excursions carrying prospective settlers to see farm properties along Southern's lines.

Richards also distributed booklets on a variety of topics: *The Black Soil of Alabama, The Southern States and What They Offer, A Land for Settlers*. There was also a market bulletin, listing farms and farm products for sale, information for livestock breeders, dairymen, and crop farmers. There were fervent testimonials from northern farmers who had made the move, praising the southern climate and its long growing season. The bulletin also told the stories of European bands now living in the South—Germans in Virginia; Waldensians in North Carolina; Swedes, Bohemians, and Hungarians in Alabama.

As if he represented a head of state, Richards took his exhibits and literature to fairs and expositions all over the United States and to Europe in an effort to lure newcomers. At one time he had twenty-five full-time agents in the field, many of them scattered through large cities in the North and Midwest; he maintained an immigration agent in London for several years. The program resulted in a substantial influx, including colonies of some size. Their arrival, and their farm practices, inspired natives to diversify crops.

As an adjunct to these programs Spencer sought to promote trade with Latin America, and his exhibit at the Cotton States and International Exposition in Atlanta in 1895 stressed the expansion of this trade—a process that was accelerated by the outbreak of the Spanish-American War in 1898, when Southern was called upon to transport troops and materiel for operations in Cuba.

In 1895, only a few months after the founding of the new System, Spencer hired a young man who was already a veteran railroader, and who was to become important in the continuity of Southern's management—William W. Finley, a native Mississippian whose varied experience with other roads had made him an accomplished traffic manager. Finley began as third vice-president, and soon made himself indispensable to Spencer.

The two faced immediate and pressing needs for new equip-

Sam Spencer's Grand Design

ment. Spencer had begun operations with a collection of inherited locomotives—a menagerie, it was called. Many of these, though still in service, were antiques fit for exhibition. Locomotive records were so scanty as to provide no information on repair costs and efficiency of operation. Most of these old engines were small Americans (4-4-0) or Moguls (2-6-0), incapable of hauling long, heavy trains over some parts of the System. Southern was never to buy a new American, and Spencer soon scrapped most of the 200-odd with which he had begun. The remaining Americans and Moguls were shifted to branch lines as quickly as possible. The road did have 225 tenwheelers and bought a few more of this type.

By 1900 Southern was fitting most of its passenger trains with new steel-frame cars, and 4-4-2s of the Atlantic type took over the main-line runs, since their seventy-nine inch drivers enabled them to pull longer trains at high speed. With the advent of all-steel cars, however, these locomotives were also sent to branch lines.

The most powerful locomotives available to Spencer in his first years were the Consolidations (2-8-0), which were to remain in service for decades. The Southern purchased 750 additional 2-8-0s from several builders in the years between 1897 and 1912. These workaday, "no-frills" engines produced about forty-four thousand pounds of tractive power with drivers of fifty-six or fifty-seven inches, and hauled trains over the rugged Murphy branch in the North Carolina mountain region, as well as in the less demanding Piedmont, where runs were longer. The useful lives of these engines were extended by the later installation of superheaters and mechanical stokers.

In 1903 Spencer placed an order with Baldwin Locomotive Works for five light Pacific 4-6-2s, the first of a breed that was to become legendary on the Southern. Over the years until 1914 more Pacifics arrived on the system, some with superheaters and seventy-two-inch drivers, and Spencer's initial purchase flowered into a gradual improvement in motive power.

Spencer's untiring search for new sources of revenue for Southern led him to hasten the day when relentless competition from trucks, buses, and private automobiles would endanger the stability of railroads. In 1901, when no one could foresee the development of a vast network of highways threading the American continent, Spencer joined the "good roads" movement with a vengeance. The Southern's prosperity then depended upon improving roads so that traffic, largely animal-drawn, could reach its depots; the competitive aspect of highway development would not be understood for at least a generation.

Thus, in 1901, Spencer sent a special "Good Roads Train" over the system to exhibit the latest methods of road building. His engineers rode the train on a five-month tour through the Southeast, covering four thousand miles, talking with thousands of people who came to see exhibits of pavement samples—asphalt, cement, brick, crushed stone, and tar. Photographs and diagrams depicted the latest developments in highway construction. Press coverage was extensive, and Southern was praised for its progressive outlook. Eighteen separate stretches of improved roads were actually built by Southern's experts during the tour, prompting local interest in building all-weather roads.

Spencer's personal life at this time reflected the interests of his youth, for he spent vacations and other spare time hunting quail in the South or fishing, usually for salmon in Canada's Petit Saguenay River. His status as a leading fisherman of his day resulted in the display of his tackle in the American Museum of Fly Fishing. By now Spencer's son Henry was working with Southern, and he was to become a vice-president by the time of World War I, when he departed with the onset of the federal takeover and became founder of the Fruit Growers Express.

The opening of the twentieth century found the Southern the largest railroad in the region. In January 1900 the six-year-old system boasted almost seventy-two hundred miles of track, nearly eight hundred locomotives, and more than twenty-eight thousand freight cars. Since 1895 its freight volume had doubled; in the first year of the new century it exceeded one million carloads for the first time, giving the System a commanding lead over rival lines. Passenger service had also burgeoned, by 85 percent, and produced about a quarter of revenues.

Spencer and his vice-president, William W. Finley, lavished attention upon their passenger trains. The Washington & Southwestern Vestibuled Limited, which had begun its runs three years before Southern's incorporation, now carried passengers from New York to New Orleans in forty hours. This luxury train offered the finest and most modern sleeping, dining, library, and drawing-room cars. But the pride of Southern's fleet was the New York & Florida Limited, cited by the *Official Guide of the Railways* as "the most luxurious train in the world." This train left New York near noon daily, passing through Washington, Charlotte, Columbia,

Sam Spencer's Grand Design

and Savannah, to reach Jacksonville after a run of twenty-five hours and fifty-five minutes. Southern also offered the Florida Express and the United States Fast Mail, both with through Pullman cars to Pinehurst, Aiken, and points in Florida.

In January 1901 Southern opened direct passenger service from Chicago to St. Augustine, launching a Florida-Midwest service that was to be offered for more than sixty years. The Royal Palm, as many thousands of midwesterners discovered, was a welcome escape route from their snow-covered home country to Florida's sun-drenched beaches. James Whitcomb Riley, the homespun Indiana poet, reported that the Royal Palm "glided me in palatial comfort to the all too sweet and amiable sunshine of Florida."

The year 1900 also ushered in the heyday of the excursion train, with trips to holiday celebrations, baseball and football games, prize fights, horse races, camp meetings, and state and county fairs. Vice-President Finley reported 484 excursions operated in 1900, an increase of about 40 percent over the previous year. Spencer and Finley realized that such promotions could add little to profits—but felt that they helped create public goodwill for the young system.

In his six years at the helm, Samuel Spencer had merged sixty-eight railway properties operating under 109 charters, and now had the satisfaction of seeing them function within a harmonious system with far greater efficiency than had been achieved by any predecessors in the region. This consolidation had also been accompanied by heavy capital spending to improve the physical plant to Spencer's exacting standards.

The founder continued his expansion. In January 1901 he established another Southern outlet to the Mississippi by purchase of the bankrupt Louisville, Evansville & St. Louis Consolidated, whose 265-mile main line offered the shortest route between Louisville and St. Louis. This road's checkered history traced back to 1836, when the young legislator Abraham Lincoln helped to give it life. With its acquisition, Spencer outflanked his rival, the L&N. He quickly built a profitable volume of through freight and passenger traffic to the major gateway city of St. Louis, where he now connected with a dozen rail systems.

He was not content. Southern still lacked a connection with Chicago, one of the nation's key terminals. In July 1902 he joined with the L&N to buy control of the Chicago, Indianapolis & Louisville, commonly known as the Monon—a move that gave both partners access to Chicago and important Indiana cities. The arrangement

Sam Spencer's Grand Design

was to endure for forty-four years, before bankruptcy of the road wiped out Southern's investment. Spencer made a larger purchase in that year which was also to end in loss—but only after thirty years. He bought the Mobile & Ohio, which ran from Mobile to Columbus, Kentucky.

Southern made more permanently profitable moves by buying the New Albany Belt & Terminal Railroad across the river from Louisville—and joined with thirteen other roads in buying the Terminal Railroad Association of St. Louis. Southern now had substantial connections on both sides of the river.

Spencer did not neglect his other fronts, north or south. In July 1901 he joined the Pennsylvania, B&O, Atlantic Coast Line (ACL), Seaboard, and Chesapeake & Ohio (C&O) in acquiring control of the Richmond, Fredericksburg & Potomac, a vital link between Washington and Richmond.

Looking southward, Spencer built a line from Valdosta, Georgia, to Jacksonville, Florida, and joined the ACL, Seaboard, and Florida East Coast in acquiring Jacksonville Terminal Company. Southern now had the connection with Florida East Coast, which it had long coveted, and other agreements gained it trackage rights over ACL tracks from Savannah to Jacksonville and an exchange of traffic with ACL's lines into southern Florida.

Attracted by prospects of increased traffic via the Panama Canal, then under construction, Spencer moved into the New Orleans market. He bought the New Orleans Belt & Terminal Company, which owned the extensive Port Chalmette terminal just below New Orleans, flanking both the Mississippi and the celebrated battlefield where Andrew Jackson had defeated a British army in 1815. Spencer's purchase also brought the Southern a belt line connecting with several railroads entering the city from the north and east.

Within a few months in the first two years of the new century, Spencer had extended the Southern System to give it the structure of a truly regional railroad, providing it with access to two important ports destined for spectacular growth. The extensions established new positions on the Mississippi, reached into the Chicago market, and ensured an outlet for the Southern through northern Virginia to the Mid-Atlantic corridor.

Fortunately for Southern, Spencer had been supplied with capital to make these strategic moves in a time when his competitors were at a disadvantage. The expansions of this period generated such an immediate increase of traffic as to overburden Southern

Sam Spencer's Grand Design

lines, particularly the main stem between Washington and Atlanta. Crews began laying a second track on the main line early in 1903, and extensive grade and curvature changes were made here, and on the mountain lines, as cash flow permitted. Spencer also launched a program to expand yards and shops and build new ones, in order to cope with growing volume. During this time Southern pioneered the use of the block signal system on a large scale. Officials of other railroads made frequent visits to observe the new system, which contributed so much to improved safety and efficiency. But by an ironic twist of fate, Southern at this time suffered its most celebrated fatal accident.

On the morning of 27 September 1903, Mail Train Number 97 pulled out of Washington, D.C., fifty-two minutes behind schedule. Manned by elite crews on the demand of the Post Office Department, the all-mail train was on its 1,530-mile run from Jersey City to New Orleans on the fastest long-distance express schedule Southern had attempted—forty-four hours and forty minutes. After the delay in Washington, where slow loading of cargo exasperated the crew, Old 97 picked up speed until it reached the way point of Monroe, Virginia, where engine and crews were changed.

Joseph ("Steve") Broady, who had been a Southern engineer only one month, boarded with his crew, which included two firemen to keep steam pressure high. Old 97 was now more than an hour behind schedule. It was Broady's first run on this train, but he was a veteran from Norfolk & Western, and was somewhat familiar with this line.

While clerks sorted the mail in cars behind him, Broady eased his Tenwheeler locomotive, Number 1102, out of Monroe and was soon speeding southward. As the four-car mail train neared Danville, hurtling down the track, Broady entered a three-mile downgrade on White Oak Mountain, leading to Stillhouse Trestle. Signs on either side of the track read: "Slow up, Trestle!" Broady held his speed.

"He'll never make it!" a witness screamed from the trackside, unheard, as 97 roared down upon the trestle.

Broady then set his brakes—too late. The engine stack blew sparks and black smoke, mail clerks fell to the floor as speed dropped abruptly. Old 97 flew from the tracks, smashed the corner of a factory building, and plunged some one hundred feet into the ravine of Cherrystone Creek, carrying part of the trestle as it fell. The engine buried its nose in the stream bank.

Rescuers hastened to the jumbled wreckage, where they found

Sam Spencer's Grand Design

ten men already dead and six injured, some fatally. Only one man had escaped unharmed. Engineer Broady and thirteen other train crewmen, most of them postal clerks, died in the crash.

Suddenly, the air above the train was filled with a golden swarm and eerie song, as thousands of canaries, freed from their shipping cages, circled over the wreckage. Many survivors of the five thousand songbirds were captured by spectators while the rescue work went on below.

Police, firemen, and ambulances were soon on the scene, joined a few hours later by road-wreck crews from Spencer and Lynchburg. Investigation failed to pinpoint the cause of the tragedy: the track was in excellent condition, there was no failure of the air brakes, and no evidence of excessive speed. Broady had no orders to disregard the posted speed limit, and would have ignored them if he had. In a time when train wrecks were almost as common as automobile accidents of a later date, the disaster at Stillhouse Trestle attracted little attention, and after a few days of excitement, the fate of Broady and the thirteen other victims was apparently forgotten.

It was not until twenty-one years later that "The Wreck of Old 97" appeared as a copyrighted song, a ballad that was to become one of the most familiar of all American railroad songs. The publisher was Triangle Publishing of New York, and the accredited author was Henry Whitter of Fries, Virginia. The simple lyrics had been set to the tune of a traditional ballad, "The Ship that Never Returned."

America took the song to heart, even before it was recorded. Victor reproduced "The Wreck" on records and grossed more than $400,000 on it during the 1920s, a bonanza for the day. The song immediately became a classic, a "standard" that entered the repertoire of all folk and country ballad singers.

In 1927 the song created bitter controversy, when a new claimant to authorship made himself known, David G. George, a sometime railroad brakeman, farmer, mule skinner, boxer, revenue agent, and amateur musician from Beaver Dam, Virginia. George heard the recording of "his" song and brought suit that led to twelve years of litigation before the U.S. Supreme Court upheld George's authorship, but declined to rule on his compensation. The Victor Company, which said it had already paid three claimants, would pay no more. The song's popularity never waned. Of its numerous versions, that of 1924 has remained the most familiar:

Sam Spencer's Grand Design

On a cold, frosty morning in the month of September
When the clouds were hanging low,
Ninety-seven pulled out of the Washington station
Like an arrow shot from a bow.

Oh, they handed him his orders at Monroe, Virginia,
Sayin': 'Steve, you're away behind time,
This is not Thirty-eight, but it's old Ninety-seven;
You must get 'er in Spencer on time!'

Oh, he looked around his cab at his black greasy fireman,
Sayin': 'Shovel in a little more coal,
An' when we cross that White Oak Mountain
You can watch old Ninety-seven roll!'

It's a mighty rough road from Lynchburg to Danville
And the line's on a three-mile grade.
It was on that grade that he lost his air brake,
And you see what a jump he made.

He was goin' down hill at ninety miles an hour
When the whistle broke into a scream.
He was found in the wreck with his hand on the throttle
And a-scalded to death with the steam!

Now, ladies, you must take warnin',
From this time ever more,
Never speak harsh words to your true lovin' husbands;
They may leave you never to return!

The ballad, an unpretentious blend of fact and fiction, long outlived the chief actors in the tragedy, as well as the equipment, and the wreck scene itself. Wrecking crews retrieved Locomotive 1102 from the creek, and after repairs it survived as a working locomotive until 1935. Train 97 was operated until 1907. Ten years later, Southern relocated its line into Danville and eliminated the White Oak Mountain grade and the trestle. Today, motorists cross the tracks at the point where Old 97 plunged off into space. The lone reminder of the wreck is a state historical marker. The song itself is still sung frequently in all parts of the country, occasionally lifted to new heights of popularity by a well-known performer—as it has been in recent years by Johnny Cash.

Samuel Spencer and William Finley continued to work to make the Southern safer and more efficient, and Spencer, in particular,

Sam Spencer's Grand Design

began to focus on public relations. It was he, in fact, who first used the term "public relations" as it applied to railroads. In an era when a few press agents handled the sparse news reported by railroads, Spencer took the lead in creating a public relations program for the industry at large. He did so in the face of a serious challenge.

In 1904 the Esch-Townsend bill was introduced in Congress, and passed by the House, a bill that would empower the Interstate Commerce Commission (ICC) to set all American freight rates, subject only to judicial review. Eighteen ranking railroad officials met in New York to lay plans to meet the threat. Spencer was chosen to lead a counteroffensive. He organized a national campaign to defeat the proposal, and in the process created the Railroad Literary Bureau, based in Chicago, where a small staff distributed pamphlets, articles, and copies of speeches to businessmen, legislators, and editors. Out of this beginning was to grow the Bureau of Railway Economics, an extensive transportation library that was finally merged into the Association of American Railroads.

Spencer himself crossed the country, making speeches against the bill whose effects he feared would cripple the railroad industry. He conceded that some railroads had abused their trust, but insisted that the great majority of railroad men were honest and efficient. In one address he urged stronger laws banning rebates and secret agreements and said that any railroads found guilty of such acts should be fully exposed. "But," he said, "it is un-American and unfair... that every manager, every president and director, shall be subject to indiscriminate public condemnation, and that innocent investors shall have their property jeopardized, and their rights infringed, because [law-enforcement officers]... fail to find the offender, and to punish him."

As to rates, he pointed out that those in the South were already low and that, as a result, investors were timid and private capital was difficult to raise. Though these southern roads were improving rapidly, they could not prosper if their rates were lowered still further. Largely as a result of Spencer's work, the Senate defeated the threatening bill and railroads were spared, for a time, the burden of "overregulation" of which Spencer warned.

This campaign was one of Spencer's final contributions to Southern and the industry. By a tragic irony, he died in a train wreck on the railroad he had created and guided through its formative years. Spencer had taken some guests on a Thanksgiving

Sam Spencer's Grand Design

quail hunt near Greensboro, North Carolina, in the autumn of 1906. The four men were sleeping in his office car near Lawyer's Station, Virginia, on the night of 26 November when a fast train from the south, following faulty signals, crashed into the car at full speed. The charred bodies of Spencer and three of his guests were found in the wreckage.

The Southern bade its founder farewell ceremonially, on the day of his funeral in Washington. All trains and locomotives stood still for five minutes, and several thousand employees bowed in silence as the System's telegraphs reported that the funeral rites had begun in St. John's Episcopal Church. Many national dignitaries attended the funeral, including Vice President Charles W. Fairbanks, Associate Justice Edward D. White of the Supreme Court, cabinet members, senators, and congressmen. Among Spencer's railroad friends were Edward H. Harriman and J. Pierpont Morgan, and hundreds of Southern's officers and employees.

Thirty thousand Southern employees made contributions toward erecting a monument in Spencer's memory, and in 1910 a bronze statue of heroic size, by sculptor Daniel Chester French, was unveiled at Atlanta's Terminal Station. Both the statue and the station were to remain for generations as a tribute to "The Father of the Southern Railway System." When the old terminal was razed to make way for a federal courthouse and office building, the statue was moved to the suburban Brookwood Station.

Spencer left behind him a giant of regional transportation. In twelve years he had created from the chaos of earlier days an efficient, highly integrated Southern System, whose practices were already the envy of the industry—and whose success was envied by woe-begone investors in earlier roads now assimilated. Astute expansion had made Spencer's system the leading factor in southeastern transportation, and his network between the Mississippi and the Atlantic, and Washington and the Gulf of Mexico, laid the foundation for a great railroad of the future. With a commanding lead over its competition, it appeared that the Southern would remain dominant for many years to come.

During his dozen years as president, Southern's mileage had increased from about 4,400 to more than 7,500. Revenues had climbed from $17 million to more than $53 million. Freight volume was up from some 6.5 million tons to 27 million tons; passengers had increased from fewer than 3.5 million to over 11.5 million. The most favorable portent for the future was that Spencer's management had provided revenues to invest in new locomotives

Sam Spencer's Grand Design

and cars, double tracks, yards and stations, block signals and line acquisitions.

Not the least of his acomplishments had been the training of William W. Finley, whom he had schooled in railroad management for seven years. Finley, already a veteran of a lifetime on other railroads when he joined Southern, said of his mentor, "I learned more from Samuel Spencer in those seven years than I had learned in all my life on railroads." With the loss of its founder, Southern turned to Finley for leadership.

FIVE

In the Steps of the Founder

Southern found in William Finley a man ideally suited to carry on and build upon the policies established by his predecessor. Finley, who was now fifty-three, had been railroading since the age of twenty, when he became a stenographer in the office of the president of the New Orleans, Jackson & Great Northern (now a part of the Illinois Central Gulf System).

Finley was serving as assistant general freight agent ten years later when he left to join the Texas & Pacific Railroad in a similar position. He soon became the general freight agent for this road and for the next twelve years worked for various southwestern railroads and for several traffic associations. He had arrived in Atlanta in the latter capacity, where he attracted Spencer's attention.

For seven years, as director of Southern's traffic department, Finley had built it into one of the most effective American railway sales organizations. As Spencer's most trusted lieutenant, he had also been grounded in the management principles of the founder and acted as Spencer's alter ego in the last years of the first president's life.

A southerner who had been "gently born and gently bred" in Pass Christian, Mississippi, Finley was eight when the Civil War began, and he bore vivid memories of its devastating effects upon his family and neighbors. Denied a college education, he was forced to go to work on his own, like so many boys of his region who grew up amidst the chaotic conditions of the Reconstruction era.

Now, as Spencer's chosen successor, Finley was determined to carry out the founder's operational, financial, and public relations policies. He surpassed his mentor in the latter field—for the new president covered twenty-one thousand miles on tour during his first five months in office, making innumerable speeches and public appearances and seeking contacts with shippers and government officials.

Finley's vision went beyond Southern's own needs. In one of the most intensive public relations campaigns ever undertaken personally by a railroad president, Finley sought to allay public distrust of American railroads at large, and did much to improve the industry's image. His goal was to convince the public that an efficient national rail transportation system was essential. He spoke before groups of bankers, newspapermen, and railroad men, as well as chambers of commerce, farm organizations, and boards of trade. His speeches indicated the scope of his interests: "Industrial Development in the South," "Conservation of Southern Forests," "Banking and the Railroads," "Southern Export Trade," "Transportation—A Basic Need." Invariably, he stressed the community of interest shared by the public and the railroads.

In his conduct of the System, Finley resolved to build on Spencer's accomplishments, rather than expand the Southern as his predecessor had done. The Southern's map had been made, and it was to remain virtually unchanged for many years to come. Finley's aim was to preserve Spencer's work and to consolidate the Southern's rather spectacular early gains.

The need for Finley's public relations offensive soon became apparent. It was an era when railroads were favorite whipping boys for political demagogues, and the public had come to regard the industry as an insatiable monopolistic giant. This animosity toward the railroads, an outgrowth of the Granger movement in the 1870s, intensified during the railroad failures of 1873 and 1893; there was a public outcry over poor service and high rates. State laws in Southern's territory reflected these attitudes and soon posed a crisis for Finley. Alabama took the lead in regulation of railroad rates, largely through the agitation of its railroad commissioner, Braxton B. Comer. After Comer became Governor in January 1907, his fight for lower rail rates and passenger fares spread throughout the Southeast. Average revenues per passenger mile dropped almost 12 percent from 1907 to 1909, and freight revenues fell by 2.6 percent. Reduced revenues added to the already painful financial difficulties experienced by the Southern during the recession of 1907–10, for revenues in 1909 fell by $2,725,000.

In North Carolina, Finley and the Southern directly confronted the antirailroad movement. The North Carolina legislature of 1907 had set a maximum fare of 2.25 cents per mile for intrastate passenger service, with penalties of 500 dollars for each violation—and fines and imprisonment prescribed for railroad agents who violated the act. Soon after passage of this law, a Southern ticket agent in Asheville was arrested for having overcharged for a

In the Steps of the Founder

railroad ticket and was sentenced to thirty days in jail. Other prosecutions followed.

While negotiations between the governor and the railroads were under way to effect a compromise, state officials in Raleigh, unaware of these discussions, issued an order for the arrest of President Finley, who was then in Asheville. Newspapers that announced Finley's arrest also revealed that the Southern had yielded to the authority of the state of North Carolina. Finley appeared in court and was released on bond after explaining that only a few hours earlier he had sent a representative to Raleigh to accept the governor's terms. Meanwhile, the state had seized the railroad within its borders, an act that set off litigation which ended only when Finley's officers convinced the courts that they had no intention of violating the law.

Finley realized that this episode revealed the need for greater public understanding of railroad problems, a need made all the more pressing as the nation entered the severe recession of 1907. The prosperity of the previous year had led Finley to make large capital expenditures for double track and larger yards, and the boom continued rising to a peak in October 1907, when Southern established new record revenues of almost $5.5 million. In late October a financial crisis abruptly struck the nation, paralyzing business activity. The Southern's earnings dropped precipitously. Average daily earnings of $199,000 in late October fell to $161,000 in late November, and to $131,000 by January 1908—a drop of 35 percent in less than three months.

Finley faced a precarious situation, and a problem new to management. The ratio of operating expenses to revenues, the accepted standard for measuring the financial health of the railroad, was 89.14 percent, the highest in Southern's history before, or after, excepting only the period of federal control during World War I. Finley's problem, as he saw it, was "one of retrenchment of expense of operation in greater proportion than in the decline of revenues." Cost reductions that merely matched the shrinkage of gross revenues would doom Southern to bankruptcy because of unavoidable fixed costs—interest on the funded debt, rental of leased lines, and taxes.

Finley acted promptly—even ruthlessly—to guide Southern through the emergency. He reduced train service and laid off employees and consolidated operating divisions. He revised train schedules, car distribution, coal consumption, and handling of packaged freight. He sought to standardize equipment and estab-

In the Steps of the Founder

lish uniform practices to save money. Operating costs dropped rapidly, but Southern's cash flow continued to ebb and Finley prepared for the worst. The System was on the verge of bankruptcy. In the early months of 1908 it appeared that the Southern Railway might come to an end after only fourteen years of service.

Finley turned for help to Fairfax Harrison, his financial vice-president, who had joined Southern in 1896 at the age of twenty-seven. Harrison was a descendant of Lord Fairfax, a legendary land baron of colonial Virginia, and was related to several prominent Virginia families. He was the son of Burton Harrison, who had served as secretary to the Confederate president, Jefferson Davis, during the Civil War, and of Constance Cary Harrison, a popular novelist and southern belle of the wartime era.

Young Harrison had been educated at Yale and Columbia, where he studied law, economics, and languages. His abilities in law and finance had been noted by Samuel Spencer, who made him his assistant. With Finley's ascension to the presidency, Harrison had become vice-president, finance and accounting.

The young Virginian proved himself on his first foray into the New York financial markets, where Finley sent him early in 1908, under instructions to obtain loans to tide the Southern through its crisis—even if only for a few weeks. The need was desperate. The railroad's credit was poor, and Harrison walked the city's streets from one banking house and insurance firm to another, meeting with refusal at every turn.

But the persistent, optimistic Harrison was successful at last. He borrowed a total of $2 million from J. P. Morgan and Company, First National Bank, and the Hanover Bank at the then-exorbitant rate of 10 percent interest. The Southern was saved for the moment, but only for the moment. Harrison was soon back in New York seeking a permanent loan of $10 million, when funds were now even more difficult to obtain. The Southern's mounting problems continued to challenge Finley and Harrison—maturing obligations, lack of a public market, and bankers caught in the general despair generated by the panic.

By the most stringent economies, the railroad weathered the depression. New construction was suspended and purchase of locomotives and cars was reduced to the minimum. Dividends on preferred stock were suspended from October 1907 until April 1911, when, in the spring of that year, improved conditions enabled the Southern to resume payments on its preferred—1 percent in 1911, $4 a share in 1912, and $5 in 1913.

In the Steps of the Founder

Once the worst of the recession was over, Fairfax Harrison was moved to a new assignment, as president of the Monon Railroad (the Chicago, Indianapolis & Louisville, owned jointly by Southern and the L&N Railroad).

Business in 1911 improved so dramatically that traffic soon taxed Southern's capacity. Finley then began investing heavily in improvements to a total of $49 million during his presidency. He built several hundred miles of second main track, installed heavier rail, built Citico Yard at Chattanooga and Inman Yard at Atlanta, expanded terminals and built new passenger stations at New Orleans, Mobile, Chattanooga, and Birmingham. He also built new bridges over the Ohio River at Louisville and the Kentucky River at High Bridge. Joining with the Mobile & Ohio, the Southern expanded wharf, harbor, and warehouse facilities at Mobile, Alabama, to handle growing traffic with Latin America.

Southern also pioneered in improved technology during this period. Oil-burning steam locomotives and a few gasoline-electric locomotives were introduced. The block signal system was expanded and trains were now dispatched by telephone.

In 1911 Finley purchased Southern's first 2-8-2 (Mikado type) from Baldwin Locomotive, and it performed so well that the System eventually bought 430 "Mikes." These clean-lined, traditional locomotives were assigned to the mountain divisions, especially between Cincinnati and Asheville, and were to serve Southern for many years, some of them with the addition of modern equipment such as feedwater heaters and Baker valve gear. New Mikados were to come into the System over the years until 1929, when Baldwin delivered the last order.

Finley foresaw that the opening of the Panama Canal would have a major impact upon the Southern and its territory. He believed that the Southeast would become a manufacturing region in response to the needs of South and Central America, Asia, and the Pacific Islands. He opened freight and passenger agencies in the Midwest and on the Pacific Coast and in Canada, creating an extensive network to develop freight and passenger traffic, as well as to encourage immigration of new industries and rural settlers.

Finley's interest in diversifying southern agriculture intensified in 1910 with the appearance of the devastating boll weevil in cotton fields of the region. He supported the efforts of the industrious M. V. Richards, who launched a program to help farmers combat the new pest, while pressing for introduction of new crops. The railroad's Cotton Culture Department, with thirteen field agents, became an influential force in the field. Southern also hired livestock and dairy experts to educate farmers. A Southern Dairy Car moved from town to town offering lectures to farmers—about thirteen thousand of whom attended. Richards and his agents also encouraged development of fruit, vegetable, sweet potato, and corn production. Southern's horticulturist, George E. Murrell, introduced the tung tree to southern Mississippi, where thousands of acres were soon producing tung nuts for their valuable oil, providing a new cash crop for the region. Murrell also introduced Satsuma oranges and pimientos in the region, and originated the profitable peach-growing industry in South Carolina. The sweet potato was one of his enthusiasms, and he promoted it vigorously, distributing printed leaflets on its culture and featuring potato dishes in dining cars.

Finley also advanced Spencer's work in the industrial field, with such success that more than eight thousand new industries located along Southern's tracks between 1900 and 1913, and twenty-five hundred existing plants were expanded. Finley also continued the "Good Roads" movement as a spur to highway development, one of whose fruits would be expanded rail traffic.

Finley's management of the Southern and his public relations campaigns in particular, had attracted national attention. In June 1913, when the New York *American* polled leading bankers to name the dozen outstanding railroad men in the country, Finley was named third. The *American* hailed him:

> W. W. Finley was called upon to fill a big position when he succeeded Samuel Spencer as President of the Southern Railway in 1906.... Spencer was an ardent expansionist... but Finley adopted a safer, if less spectacular, course. He is a traffic getter, worthy to be rated with J. C. Stubbs [of the Union Pacific]; operating 450 miles fewer than when he took command, he has increased gross earnings $10 million since 1908 ... he has devoted much attention to acquainting the public with the place the railroads fill in the life of the nation, and in his own territory he has been brilliantly successful in encouraging more scientific methods among farmers.... He is a good writer and a clever orator.

But Finley's unremitting efforts to improve the Southern had taken their toll. In September 1913 ill health forced him to curtail his activities. Responding to rumors of his resignation, Southern

In the Steps of the Founder

issued a denial. Finley was responding to medical treatment, but died of a stroke on 23 November. He was mourned by thousands of Southern employees who had come to realize how effectively he had managed the System in the face of severe handicaps.

Despite the recession of 1907 and its aftermath, Finley's seven-year presidency had seen a growth in capital investment from $357 million to $373 million. Revenues had risen by 21 percent, and, more important, income available for dividends (though largely invested in the plant) had risen by almost 210 percent. These accomplishments were made possible by high morale throughout the company, fostered by Finley's policy of promotions from within and frequent rewards for meritorious service. Finley's foresight was to result in a vital corporate asset over many years.

Though the System had shrunk by almost 500 miles during his time, Finley had seen gross earnings per mile of road rise by 40 percent. Double track had increased from 136 to 385 miles, and the ratio of side-track mileage to main-line had risen from 26 percent to 35 percent.

By the end of his term Finley had replaced virtually all the old iron rail with heavier steel, and wooden bridges with steel structures of much higher load capacity. Many key freight and passenger terminals had been enlarged and the most modern freight classification yards had been built. Hundreds of larger and more powerful locomotives and thousands of improved cars had come into service. Signal and communications systems had been improved. In addition, Finley had inaugurated a merit system for advancement. Of special interest to stockholders and the officers he left behind, Finley's administration had seen the cost of Southern's funded debt rise by only 3 percent—though the debt itself had grown by 40 percent. Samuel Spencer's successor had been worthy of his challenge.

The Southern had now established an enviable record of progress. Ton-miles of revenue freight had risen 145 percent over 1895, the first full year of operation. Passenger miles had grown by 179 percent, gross income by 143 percent—and net revenue by 361 percent.

This progress had a parallel in the South at large, where a long trend of growth had begun. In the twenty-year period ending in 1910, farmland values in the Southeast had risen by 128 percent; value of farm products was up by 102 percent; capital invested in manufacturing by 279 percent; value of manufactured products by

In the Steps of the Founder

182 percent; and bank deposits by 180 percent. Finley's death found both the Southern and its region in a flourishing condition, looking forward to a new era of growth.

The Southern News-Bulletin said of Finley, "He was essentially a gentleman ... fair and just in all his dealings, courteous to all men, slow to anger, but fierce in his resentment of injustice in others. Partisan in his love for and belief in the South and its future and in the Southern Railway as an important factor in that community, he convinced his associates that he never allowed his partisan feeling to color his judgment to such an extent that he could not always see the other side; but a policy once determined, he set about its accomplishment with a characteristic belief in the potency of persistence and an unhesitating use of all the power at his command."

Finley's successor, Fairfax Harrison, was elected president of the Southern on 1 December 1913. He was to serve for a quarter of a century, far longer than any other president in Southern's corporate history. Within a few months he was to face the formidable problems rising from global warfare and, ultimately, to lead the System through grave hours of financial crisis.

SIX

"How Many Blisters Do You Have?"

Fairfax Harrison was a singular figure in the story of American railroading. A Virginia patrician in manner and appearance, courtly but aloof, he was scholarly and brilliant. He read Greek and Latin and had translated Cato's *Farm Management* for circulation among his friends. He was to write books on the distinguished Harrison family of Virginia, on the thoroughbred horses of his native state—and on Traveler, the war-horse of Gen. Robert E. Lee.

Harrison was equally at home with the intricate financial affairs of the railroad and with esoteric fields of study. He sometimes baffled Southern's engineers with discussions of Santayana's sonnets or by asking their opinions of Ming dynasty ceramics.

Harrison was physically imposing and was gray-haired from his middle age onward. Harry DeButts, a protégé who was to become a president of Southern, remembered of him, "Harrison was very technical in all his work, and rather difficult for people to know—a little cold when you first met him, but underneath he was a very warm, admirable, capable and wise man. He did many things for the railroad that we've seen bear fruit in modern times."

The forty-four-year-old Harrison was hailed as a symbol of a "new breed" of railroader, a spokesman and champion of the New South who foresaw great prosperity for the region. Trained under both Spencer and Finley and seasoned by his three-year term as president of the Monon, Harrison was well equipped to conduct the legal and financial affairs of the Southern System, and despite his aristocratic air, his approach to management was highly practical in most aspects.

One of the early innovations during his presidency was to be long remembered as a major contribution to Southern's success—a "training for management" program for promising southern college graduates in engineering, designed to give them intimate working knowledge of the daily tasks of the railroad, including maintenance of track and equipment. Civil engineers were put to work with pick and shovel, and mechanical engineers began as shop helpers at the most menial chores. Harrison's foresight was

"How Many Blisters Do You Have?"

to produce hundreds of seasoned executives for the System in future years, men who knew railroading from the bottom up. Among the graduates of this program were to be at least five presidents of other railroads and numerous officers of high rank who led distinguished careers in the industry—not to mention two of Southern's best-known presidents.

These trainees were selected after study of academic records, character references, and interviews by Southern officers. Harrison himself frequently served as counselor to the trainees and made a point of visiting them on his rounds. He would summon the youngsters, in their grimy work clothes, to his office car and press them for reports on their work: "How many blisters do you have? ... How do things on the railroad look to you?"

After a talk of half an hour or so, the apprentices returned to work, unaware of Harrison's purpose in his inquisition. A veteran of the program recalled, "He was checking right then on who among us would go on up the ladder—by the time we got to be section foremen he had already started the weeding-out process. The ones who stayed did go on up—and it's surprising how many stayed."

Harrison also established an apprentice program to teach basic mathematics and other high school courses and shop classes, to provide a cadre of skilled younger workmen who might rise to supervisory levels. To improve morale, he assigned locomotives to specific engine crews and had the names of veteran engineers stenciled on their cabs.

Harrison took office amidst an era of unprecedented prosperity for the nation, for the South, and for Southern. The year 1913 brought the railroad new operating and tonnage records; income and employment were at new highs across the nation and foreign trade was flourishing. The world was at peace and there were no hints that a great European war was to erupt within a few months and draw the United States and Southern itself into the conflict.

When business declined in 1914 and wages were reduced, Harrison cut his own salary by 20 percent and ordered proportional reductions throughout the System—salaries of $2,500 were cut by only 2 percent. He initiated safety programs to discover and prevent the causes of accidents. He made awards for fuel efficiency, for gardens around depots, and for successful athletic teams within the company.

Harrison felt he had to face four areas of responsibility as chief of Southern: to the government, to the public, to shareholders,

"How Many Blisters Do You Have?"

and to employees. Years later *Railway Age* wrote of him, "He looked upon his obligation to the stockholders of the Southern in the light of a solemn trusteeship." The magazine praised Harrison's "feeling for the individuality of the property" and noted that he instilled that attitude in his staff.

The new president made no sweeping changes in management techniques or personnel. He retained the staff developed under Spencer and Finley and expressed confidence in the railroad's entire personnel in his first report to stockholders. Harrison did change the makeup of the Board of Directors, increasing its involvement in the affairs of the company. He abolished the five-man Executive Committee, which had previously made important decisions and brought all matters requiring action to the full Board. Southern's directors began the new regime with renewed interest in Southern's progress.

The System passed a corporate milestone in June 1914 when the Voting Trustees, who had been appointed as part of the agreement of 1894, withdrew and passed full authority to stockholders and the Board. For twenty years the Trustees had represented major investors in the nomination of directors and in matters of capital spending by the railroad. The final report of these Trustees paid tribute to Southern's "financial strength, conservative management and excellent physical condition," and reported that the System's growth had been accompanied by a surge in regional population, wealth, and industrial development—a trend "largely due to the activities of Southern Railway Company in promoting the commercial and industrial enterprises along its lines."

At this time Harrison completed his revamping of the Board of Directors, making its membership almost entirely southern. Previously dominated by northern men representing investors in New York, Boston, and Philadelphia, the Board now became regional, and from 1915 onward, southerners comprised a majority of the membership, most of them men who lived within the System's territory.

Five new directors, all southerners, were elected in 1914, two of them of such unconventional background as to spark controversy: Edwin A. Alderman, president of the University of Virginia, and the Rev. John Carlisle Kilgo, bishop of the Methodist Episcopal Church, South. In defense of these nominations at a Board meeting in Richmond, Harrison explained them as public relations moves, based upon "the policy of recognizing the public interest in railroads, of securing so far as possible public approval of the

"How Many Blisters Do You Have?"

company by the people living along the line of the railroad." These proposed directors, as men of wide influence, would win public respect for Southern, Harrison said, and their election would indicate that "the policies of the Board are consistent with the best interests of the Southern people."

Approval was not unanimous. T. P. Mayo of Richmond queried Harrison: "I would like to know what a college professor and a bishop know about running a railroad."

"They represent the public opinion of the communities served by the company," Harrison said. "Public opinion has become one of the most important factors in running a railroad. And in that way they do know how to run a railroad."

Three years later Harrison was able to report to the Board that Alderman and Kilgo had been "of substantial service to the Company" and had increased public confidence in Southern. The president added that directors chosen exclusively from among major investors would be unknown to the public, but that outside business and professional men from southern cities would enable communities to "measure the policies and purposes of the Company by their private affairs."

This innovation, which attracted widespread attention at the time, became an enduring company policy, under which many distinguished southerners from many fields served the System. Harrison was not content to man the Board with southerners. He also established a policy of hiring officers and employees from towns along the railroad, seeking men with intimate knowledge of the region and its heritage. He insisted that his officers have an understanding of, and respect for, the thousands of blacks on the company payrolls. This policy of regional unity contributed to improved morale that was to mark Southern's operations for generations to come.

Morale and resources were soon tested by the outbreak of war in Europe. Harrison had been in office only seven months when, in June 1914, the assassination of an Austrian archduke set off the violent four-year storm of World War I. The shock to the American economy was immediate. Transatlantic trade and travel were cut off, business in the United States declined sharply, and railway traffic was especially hard hit. With the disappearance of the European market for cotton and other products, the Southeast was virtually paralyzed for a time. As the nation's busiest cotton carrier, Southern felt the impact at once, and suffered a 12 percent loss in revenue during the year ending in June 1915.

"How Many Blisters Do You Have?"

It was now, almost unnoticed amid the wartime excitement, that Fairfax Harrison warned of the automobile as a threat to rail prosperity. In Southern's annual report of October 1915, Harrison noted that passenger revenues had declined by 34 percent during the past year, and added, "The increased use of automobiles, especially for short-distance travel, is the only prominent cause contributing to a reduction of railway passenger travel.... While it costs more to travel by automobile than it does by train, the automobile affords a convenience of time to which no railway schedule can be adjusted." It was a forecast of disaster ahead for the nation's passenger trains, then in their heyday.

After six months of stagnation, the economy and the railroad gradually began to recover from the effects of the war's first shock. By the fall of 1915 demand for cotton was nearing normal levels. American railroad traffic recovered and soon reached record volume. By April 1917, freight volume was almost 45 percent above that of 1915, and most lines and equipment were strained to the limit. Harrison and his staff had prepared Southern to meet the emergency more readily than had other railroads. Some $67 million had been invested in plant and equipment in the decade ending in 1916, and through the purchase of 476 more powerful locomotives and 27,000 steel cars to replace predecessors, the System's capacity was expanded.

Southern was now experimenting with locomotives by placing the cylinders, frame, and running gear of retired locomotives under the tenders of 2-8-2s as auxiliary power. Engineer W. S. Brown of the Knoxville division aided the process by inventing a lighter and simplified valve gear, which was applied to several classes of locomotives.

In 1917 Southern's first truly modern power appeared—thirty Mountain-type 4-8-2s for passenger service,* built by Baldwin. The Mountain weighed 315,000 pounds and its 69-inch drivers delivered 50,000 pounds of tractive power for the runs out of Asheville, North Carolina, and from Memphis to Spencer, North Carolina. Baldwin also delivered thirty-eight new 2-10-2s of the Santa Fe type the same year, and these freight engines were destined to make a major contribution to the war effort. The Santa

---

*Under the Whyte system, steam locomotives are classified by the number and arrangement of their wheels. Thus, in the three-number designation 4-8-2, there are four pairs of wheels under the front truck, eight pairs of driving wheels, and two pairs of wheels under the trailering truck. Four sets of numbers—e.g., 2-8-8-0, etc.—indicate that the tender's truck wheels are also included.

"How Many Blisters Do You Have?"

Fes weighed 538,000 pounds and required the construction of new turntables in roundhouses. They went to work hauling long trains on mountain runs, but could not be used on the "Rat Hole" between Cincinnati and Chattanooga because their smoke filled the tunnels and blinded crews. This was not the first of Southern's efforts to use increased power on its mountain runs; it had sought to use Mallet or Articulated locomotives in the hills, and as early as 1909 had bought Big Liz, an enormous 2-6-8-0, from Baldwin. Two more of the type followed before the road went to 2-8-8-0s, with 80,000 pounds of tractive power.

Harrison also began a renewed program of double-tracking of the main line between Washington and Atlanta, a distance of 638 miles. This key project, begun in 1913, would continue through the war until its completion in 1919. In addition, Harrison directed the building of Forrest Yard in Memphis, a bridge over the Tennessee River, several freight warehouses, new signal systems, and a grade separation program. The Southern staff sought to utilize these new resources to the fullest, but found itself overwhelmed by the demands of war. Camps and training centers sprang up across the South and passenger traffic soared. Much of the building material for the sprawling new camps was carried by Southern, at the expense of civilian shippers and their needs. The railroad adopted the slogan, "Make one car do the work of two"; shippers were urged to load cars more efficiently and promptly—but the inflow of traffic proved to be more than the system could handle.

The coming of the war had found Southern in a new phase of expanding foreign trade. In 1914 Harrison had created a foreign freight traffic department with R. L. McKeller at its head and agents at Mobile and New Orleans. The war postponed plans to capitalize on Southern's strategic location between the Mississippi and Atlantic and Gulf ports, but the campaign was to be pressed with renewed vigor after the Armistice. In 1916 Harrison acquired the line from Meridian, Mississippi, to New Orleans, to augment the System's services to the busy port. With this move, Southern attained the eight-thousand-mile, thirteen-state network that was to mark the limit of its territorial expansion for nearly half a century.

American involvement in the war increased steadily, under pressure of hostile acts by the German navy, until, in April 1917, the United States declared war and prepared to go to the aid of the Allies. Within a week after the declaration of war, Harrison met

"How Many Blisters Do You Have?"

with about fifty other railroad presidents in Washington in response to a call from the Council of Defense, and presented a resolution that the nation's railroads coordinate their services to provide the utmost efficiency. The proposal was accepted and Harrison was named chairman of a five-man railroads' War Board, charged with the creation of a national rail system. With little warning or preparation, hundreds of American railroads were to surrender their competitive roles and join a vast system with more than 250,000 miles of line, more than 1.75 million workers, 66,000 locomotives, almost 2.5 million freight cars, and 56,000 passenger cars. This unprecedented step was expected to provide an efficient national rail system to speed the war effort. These optimistic hopes were soon dashed.

Atlantic harbor and port facilities were soon choked with traffic and long lines of boxcars crowded rails and sidings, all loaded for overseas shipment. Meanwhile, elsewhere in the country, shippers waited desperately for freight cars. By November 1917 there was a shortage of more than 150,000 cars. The railroads, which were unable to coordinate their services completely for fear of antitrust action, and were unwilling to surrender competitive advantages, could not meet the challenge. In December 1917 President Woodrow Wilson proclaimed federal control over the nation's railroads, on the theory that government operation would improve efficiency. The United States Railroad Administration (USRA) was formed under William Gibbs McAdoo. He became the virtual czar of the transportation system in the nation.

Eugene H. Coapman, Southern's vice-president and general manager, was named a federal manager with jurisdiction over the Southern System, and since railroads under federal control were required to maintain separate corporate organizations, both Coapman and Harrison were forced to resign from Southern.

Railroad competition ended once McAdoo assumed control of the USRA. Offline traffic offices were abolished at once and many other traffic solicitation jobs were eliminated. The Southern absorbed some of these employees in other departments, but most of them were dismissed. Thousands of others, including highly skilled workmen, left Southern for military service, or to work in munition plants and shipyards. The effect upon Southern's operations was profound. More and more women appeared in shops, yards, and storehouses, taking over jobs once held by men.

Despite the changes, the Southern worked harder than ever, and more efficiently. By 1918 the average Southern locomotive

"How Many Blisters Do You Have?"

was performing 83 percent more service (based on ton-miles and passenger miles) than in 1913. Traffic increased to levels undreamed of in prewar years. Passenger traffic for 1918 was 89 percent greater than for 1913, the last year of peace, and freight traffic was up 58 percent. For three years following 1915 the railroad provided more freight and passenger service per locomotive, car, train, and employee than ever before. But costs were also soaring. Coal prices more than doubled. The average wage of train service employees rose from $1.29 per day to $2.00.

In the final year of the war Southern established still more records. Gross operating revenues exceeded $100 million for the first time, and the System handled more passengers and freight—and spent more money in operations—than ever before.

The war's end on 11 November 1918 was marked by Southern with a two-minute work stoppage and silent prayer, "that our nation will never again be drawn into armed conflict." A pandemonium of ringing bells and wailing whistles followed as the men and women of the railroad celebrated the Armistice. Federal control, which had been exercised for a little over two years, ended on 29 February 1920, when shareholders and management resumed direction of the Southern.

The USRA experiment had cost taxpayers dearly, for its managers had run up operating deficits of $2 million per day—a total of $1.8 billion for the duration. Southern stockholders also suffered. The road faced huge rehabilitation and adjustment costs, but was denied adequate compensation as provided by USRA's own formula. The agency offered railroads compensation equal to their average annual operating income for three years ending in June 1917, a formula that would have awarded Southern more than $1.5 million per month. The USRA penalized the System for its high profitability, ruling that this amount was excessive, and finally paying Southern only $28,000 per month of federal operation.

Upon reassuming control in March 1920, Southern had the option of remaining under the federal guaranty for six months, or operating independently without a guaranty of any kind. The directors chose independence—and ended the six-month period with a profit of $7.5 million they would have lost under government control.

These initial earnings were doubly welcome, since Southern's treasury had been empty at the end of federal control—but even this newly earned surplus vanished overnight when the govern-

"How Many Blisters Do You Have?"

ment ordered the railroad to pay employees several million dollars in back wages. Thus, by September 1920 the Southern's treasury was empty once more.

Fortunately, traffic and earnings growth over the next two years restored the surplus, which Harrison held in reserve as working capital—a tactic that prompted a clamor of protest from some stockholders, who demanded that dividends be paid. Southern had paid no dividends on its common during its history, and only a modest return on its preferred. Harrison defended this policy before the stockholders' meeting in October 1923, and managed to convince a majority of the prudence of his plan.

One investor, wryly conceding defeat, paid tribute to Harrison's glib and extended defense: "Mr. Chairman, you can go down deeper, stay longer, and come up drier, than any man I ever saw."

Holders of Southern common were soon to be rewarded, however. When the Board of Directors met in New York in March 1924, the financier Jeremiah Milbank demanded that a dividend be declared, adding that since he owned $20 million worth of stock, he had virtual control of the company. The directors obliged him by ordering a dividend of $5 per share. Payments were to increase to $7 in 1926 and $8 in 1928 as business continued to flourish.

The unexpected news of the initial dividend on Southern common set off brisk trading in the stock, which rose from 50¼ to 55 in a single day, reaching the highest recorded price. The price of the common had been rising for two years, however, from a low of 17⅛, in anticipation of a dividend payment. The year 1924 marked the first time in Southern's thirty-year history that returns were paid on all classes of its $455 million in securities. The structure included $275 million in bonds, $60 million in preferred, and $120 million in common stock.

Wartime inflation had altered every phase of Southern's operations. Despite record wartime traffic volume, increased revenues had lagged behind rising costs of materials and equipment, and the operating ratio (expenses to revenues) had risen from almost 70 percent in 1917 to 75 percent in 1918—and to more than 90 percent in 1919, the latter the highest in company history. The ratio would have meant disaster for a privately operated railroad, since the remaining 9.19 percent would have been insufficient to meet rental and interest charges.

Private postwar operations opened amid signs of a spectacular boom period, with Southern's operating revenues for 1920 reach-

"How Many Blisters Do You Have?"

ing a record of nearly $153 million, an increase of 68 percent over 1917—but even this notable growth could not be translated to net income because of the much more rapid growth of expenses and taxes.

In three years prior to June 1920, total expenses had more than doubled: wages were up 86 percent, fuel by 94 percent, and new rail by 47 percent. Meanwhile, average revenue per passenger mile was up only 38 percent and ton-miles of freight only 36 percent. Harrison and his staff approached the task of controlling costs with such vigor that the operating ratio fell at a gratifying rate, from over 90 percent in 1919 to 86 percent in 1921, 80 percent in 1922—and 70 percent in 1925.

This encouraging trend was set in motion despite unprecedented managerial difficulties caused by the sea change in the American economy. The power of labor had increased significantly, and the railroad's employees were now able to enforce some of their demands. Southern's officers found that they must now spend eighty-five cents to produce each dollar of revenue—as against sixty-eight cents per dollar in 1911. Taxes had increased from $2.8 million annually to $6.9 million in nine years, while operating income was up only $4 million. In response to this new economic environment the Interstate Commerce Commission allowed railroads to raise rates, but Southern did not choose to follow the rest of the industry. Nationally, average rail rates rose by 55 percent from 1913 to 1923, but they rose only 32 percent on the Southern. Finley and Harrison had set a precedent that would assume greater significance a generation later.

In the postwar boom that swept the South, Harrison saw his traffic pattern undergoing rapid change, as new industries began pouring out manufactured products, providing Southern with a sharp increase in this category. Harrison now devoted much of his time to southern industry, in pursuit of increased revenues. He became a familiar figure throughout the System, traveling in his twin cars, Carolina and Virginia, the only railroad president who used two cars. The Carolina was used for sleeping; the Virginia, which was used largely by Southern directors, boasted a dining room and kitchen, crew quarters and an observation section.

Harrison was also continuing his quest for greater motive power, and under his leadership the steam era reached its zenith on Southern. His maintenance supervisors made careful analyses of the System's veteran Pacifics and created specifications for the class of 1923—the P-4s, which were to become celebrated. South-

"How Many Blisters Do You Have?"

ern's experts judged the performance of drivers of various sizes, valve gear, and cylinders, and then sent a complete set of specifications to Baldwin's Schenectady Works, which built Numbers 1375 to 1386 of the new class in 1923—with 73-inch drivers, feedwater heaters, Baker valve gear, and 47,500 pounds of tractive power.

These Pacifics were assigned to the Atlanta-Washington run, where they quickly established records for speed and dependability. More Pacifics of the same design arrived over the next three years, changed only by the addition of larger tenders. Passengers and railfans admired the Pacifics, but it was Fairfax Harrison who made them so appealing that the nation took them to its heart.

Touring England in 1925, Harrison took a fancy to the colorful locomotives, particularly the green engines of the London & North Eastern Line. He returned and ordered the Pacifics painted "Virginia" (forest) green, trimmed with gold lettering and stripes, with silver running boards, cylinder heads, and wheel rims. Cab roofs were painted brick red. These handsome locomotives became symbols of Southern steam power, especially when they roared along with the Crescent Limited, whose cars were painted to match. Harrison's color scheme did much to popularize the Pacifics and Southern's passenger service as well. His trains were the most dazzling sights on American rails, and were almost certainly the inspiration for the poetic outbursts of the author Thomas Wolfe, who wrote so ecstatically of trains rushing through the night.

Southern had made careful, expensive preparation for passenger trains of the 1920s. All-steel cars had been bought before the war, replacing wooden cars with steel frames; short-haul and branch lines had new equipment, including some gas-electric motor cars. Stimulated by the Florida land boom, Harrison had created his new luxury fleet. In 1921 the Suwannee River Special began runs between Chicago, Detroit, and Cleveland to Tampa and St. Petersburg. Two years later, in vain hope of meeting the heavy demand, Harrison acquired fifty new Pullman cars. Numerous coaches were added each year; the Pullmans were longer and heavier than their predecessors, and they rode on six-wheel trucks to give a smoother ride. They were fitted with green plush seats, electric fans, and a new ventilating system.

By 1924 the Southern was operating forty-eight dining cars and nine cafe-parlor cars on forty-five trains, carrying on a tradition that had begun in the South in 1891 on the Richmond & Danville's

"How Many Blisters Do You Have?"

Washington-Atlanta run. By the mid-twenties a staff of almost 450 stewards, cooks, and waiters was serving 1.25 million customers on Southern's dining cars, featuring regional cuisine. This dining fleet expanded in 1925 with the arrival of eight new seventy-eight-foot-long cars that seated thirty-six passengers in ornate and luxurious style, with Oriental carpets, walnut chairs upholstered in Spanish leather, and large electric fans.

A new train of 1925, the Crescent Limited, became the pride of the fleet, with its runs from New Orleans to New York in thirty-seven hours and fifty minutes. Its five sets of equipment cost $2 million and were staffed by a crew of 130. The Crescent carried a valet in the club car, a maid in the ladies' lounge, and a telephone in the observation car, itself a sensation of the day. The train offered fifty-four sections, eight drawing rooms, and eight compartments—all available for an extra fare of only $5. Within a few months this train was being drawn by new Pacifics between Atlanta and Washington, sporting gold crescents on their cylinders and "Crescent Limited" emblazoned on the tenders. New cars were decorated in green and gold with green curtains and leather or plush chairs. There was a porcelain tub in the men's bath. Salons were furnished with reed chairs and tables. These amenities made the train one of the most popular in the United States. In its first five years the southbound Crescent was late only 33 times in 1,793 trips; northbound, only 75 times in 1,751 trips. In its day the steam-powered Crescent ran nearly 7.5 million miles.

The stock market crash of October 1929 found Harrison re-equipping his crack train in even grander fashion, with the exterior paint of the thirty-five cars matching the green and gold Pacifics that pulled them. In the boom year of 1928 Harrison bought the last new steam engines ever purchased by Southern—Pacifics and giant 2-8-8-2s, which hauled freight on the demanding mountain runs, including coal hauling from Appalachian mines. The new engines were single-expansion articulated locomotives developing ninety thousand pounds of tractive power, equipped with modern superheaters, stokers, power reverse, air brakes, and cross-compound pumps.

Throughout these prosperous years, Harrison expanded the public relations program established by Spencer and advanced by Finley. He made numerous speeches annually throughout the region and in 1924 launched an institutional advertising campaign designed to make the railway and its service familiar to the southern people. Advertisements in all newspapers within the system

"How Many Blisters Do You Have?"

soon made the slogan, "The Southern Serves the South," a household phrase. This was an appeal to the public as well as to shippers, for the System, like other roads, still had its critics. This slogan had been conceived in 1915 by L. E. Jeffries, vice-president and general counsel, who designed Southern's logo. It had been a rather casual birth. Jeffries was riding the line one day when he idly took a half dollar from his pocket, placed it on a sheet of paper, and drew a circle about it with a pencil. He then placed a quarter inside this and drew a second circle.

In the inner space, Jeffries roughed out the initials *SR*, and in the outer space, after a few false starts, printed the slogan: *The Southern Serves the South*. This simple, direct, and expressive motto was to endure for many decades, after making its first appearance in timetables of September 1915.

Harrison's monthly newspaper ads about the System's affairs attracted attention in the North as well as the South. He included reports on Southern's improvements in its plant, made possible by a policy of plowing back millions of dollars of earnings into the property, rather than creating a massive debt through bond issues, as many railroads were doing. In 1922 Harrison reported that Southern had invested some $77 million in improvements in the past ten years. Major investments of the time included grade reductions, double tracking of several lines, use of heavier rail, a new double-track bridge over the Ohio River at Cincinnati, installation of electric block signals and automatic train control devices, hundreds of miles of added passing tracks, and extensive application of ballast. Finley Shops in Birmingham and the John Sevier Yard in Knoxville were built at this time.

Though there were few signs of imminent economic collapse, the mid-1920s found the Southern, like many other railroads, caught in the familiar pattern of vulnerability caused by the rising labor demands. Southern now spent 45.5 cents of each dollar of income on wages. By 1922 the System had nearly fifty-one thousand people on its payroll. Labor contracts provided for bonuses for "efficiency and cooperation" as well as higher wages and mileage rates. The Southern Railway System Employees' Pension Association provided health and accident insurance and in the late 1920s employees voted for the establishment of a retirement system.

In these years Harrison brought to completion what some of his successors considered his most valuable service to the Southern—the financial stabilization of the line by eliminating overlapping

"How Many Blisters Do You Have?"

indebtedness and acquisition of minority interests in subsidiary and component lines. Through extended negotiation Harrison removed many of Southern's smaller lines from threat of loss by the parent, consolidated interests, and in favorable situations acquired all issued stock for Southern. The task required years of effort and a thorough understanding of the smaller lines scattered throughout the system. This accomplishment capped a lifetime of study by Harrison, who had published an exhaustive legal history of the Southern in 1901, long before he rose to the presidency.

In 1926, when the federal government condemned the Southern's headquarters building on Pennsylvania Avenue in Washington, forcing the railroad to move, the irate Harrison threatened to relocate in Atlanta, a transfer that would have been painful for the capital, since Southern was one of the few large employers, rivaling or surpassing even the federal government in size. In fact, Harrison moved only the accounting department to Atlanta, but this meant a loss of some five thousand jobs to the District of Columbia. At this time, Southern built a new headquarters on McPherson Square, a $2 million structure upon which Harrison left his mark—he had a separate lobby alcove leading to a private elevator, which served only the tenth and eleventh floors.

Harrison's singular tastes were also evident in the executive dining room, to which he summoned key staff members by presenting them with blue chips, each bearing an assignment in the form of a conversational topic—usually intellectual in nature. Luncheons with the president, as a result, were like nothing else in the history of railroading.

Harrison's eccentricities became legendary among Southern's people. He habitually insisted on paying his train fare as he commuted between Washington and Manassas to his Northern Virginia home. He disdained the use of his pass, a perquisite cherished by every other railroad man ever known. The president's home, as old Southern men remembered fondly, had once been known as Swampoodle, but had been endowed with grandeur by Harrison, and became known as Belvoir.

Harrison was rather humorless, an "all business" executive where Southern's welfare was concerned, a trait he revealed on numerous occasions. When the Pullman Company built a plant in Birmingham, Alabama, and began producing freight cars with much fanfare from regional interests, Pullman was widely hailed as a benefactor of the local economy. But Harrison, displeased with Pullman's prices, placed an order for one thousand boxcars

"How Many Blisters Do You Have?"

elsewhere. When angry company officials demanded to know the cause for such an unpatriotic move, Harrison told his longtime business associates, "The Southern Railway is not an eleemosynary institution," a pointed reminder that the railroad's interest was always uppermost in his mind. The breach was quite temporary, however. In the forty-one years after this plant opened, Southern bought almost fifty thousand cars from Pullman, most of them from the Alabama plant.

The Southern had occupied its handsome new headquarters building only two months before the disastrous stock market crash. Until that moment, the public had assumed that all was well with America and with Southern itself. The System's stock sold in a range from $146 to an all-time high of $151 3/8—until Black Thursday, 28 October, when a wave of selling deflated stock prices and created panic throughout the nation. Thousands of firms went bankrupt. Credit lines all but disappeared. Factory orders were cancelled and building projects were scrapped, some of them in a half-finished state. Unemployment reached epidemic proportions.

Conditions only worsened in the following months, until, by 1932, the United States faced a major economic crisis from which recovery appeared difficult indeed. Southern's freight traffic dropped from 8.4 billion ton-miles in 1929 to 4.4 billion in 1932, and passenger miles also decreased by about 50 percent. Gross operating revenues were sliced in half. Harrison and his officers faced an unprecedented financial problem. Many railroads were being forced into bankruptcy. Drastic steps were needed to save the Southern, but it was essential to operate daily schedules of freight, passenger, express, and mail service. Even now, and inexplicably, Harrison and his directors continued to pay common dividends through the first two years of the debacle, rather than conserving funds to help meet the emergency.

This was done in the face of the heaviest debt load in Southern's history. By 1930 the funded debt (long-term bonds and equipment trust certificates outstanding) had reached almost $296 million, and in that year bond interest and other fixed charges reached a record high of about $18 million, taking fifteen cents of every dollar of operating revenues.

In 1931 the Southern operated at a loss for the first time, which it would continue to do for five more years as its management grappled with apparently insoluble problems. In 1932, when the deficit reached $11,219,000, dividends were suspended on both

"How Many Blisters Do You Have?"

preferred and common stock. The officers took voluntary salary cuts and the railway brotherhoods and unions agreed to a temporary wage cut of 10 percent in order to save the railroad, with the understanding that wage levels would be restored when conditions warranted.

But Harrison had only begun to prepare Southern to weather the storm. Latter-day critics were to charge that he failed to perceive the proportions of the crash and the ensuing depression, but there were no half measures in Harrison's second wave of economies. Officers who felt that expenses had already been cut to the utmost were ordered to curtail costs further in an all-out effort to reduce expenditures below income. Drastic and sweeping reductions were made throughout the company, regardless of sacrifices entailed. Officers combed their budgets anew, studying every facility, even the smallest branch lines, in quest of prospective cost cutting. This study resulted in elimination of numerous branch lines, side tracks, stations, sidings, and shops over the next few years.

Consolidation of operating divisions, track section gangs, and shop maintenance facilities created savings; improved signal systems and the use of chemically treated ties aided the cause. Since purchase of new locomotives was out of the question, men in the shops struggled to maintain the system's power by pampering those on hand—including some pre-1914 Americans, Moguls, and Tenwheelers. Somehow, they pampered the aging engines long enough to perform the work of the railroad, and these old-timers always seemed to have fresh, gleaming paint, often the president's favorite Virginia green.

By 1932 the corporate debt had swollen to some $301 million and gross operating revenues were down about 40 percent from the previous year. Fixed charges now took twenty-four cents of every earned dollar, a record high.

On 16 May 1932 Southern stock hit an all-time low of $2.50 per share, having fallen almost $150.00 since the day of the crash. On that day Southern had 1,298,000 shares of common and 60,000 shares of preferred outstanding. Thus, at the quoted price of the day, control of the Southern Railway Company, with an asset value of $556 million, could have been acquired for less than $2.4 million, assuming that the stock had been available.

Fortunately for Southern, the great majority of stockholders retained their stock, confident that the company would flourish again under better conditions. Though he appeared to be su-

"How Many Blisters Do You Have?"

premely confident, Harrison himself was aware that perilous times lay ahead. Major railroads in all sections of the country were going into receivership. Bankers declined to finance railroad issues except at steep discounts, and refused to lend money to the lines at normal rates of interest. Like many another corporation, Southern was in desperate need of financial aid.

In January 1932 the Reconstruction Finance Corporation (RFC) was created by Congress at the request of President Herbert Hoover, to provide emergency financial aid to industry and agriculture. Within a month after the RFC opened its doors, Southern applied for a short-term loan of $10 million and received one of $7.5 million secured by $18.75 million in mortgage bonds. By virtue of this loan, combined with one of $2 million from the Railroad Credit Corporation (owned and financed by the railroad industry), the Southern escaped bankruptcy by the narrowest of margins in 1932. So threatening was the situation that company lawyers prepared for the worst by keeping a bankruptcy petition in a desk drawer.

In these days, Harrison called on an old friend to become his chief lieutenant—and heir apparent. Ernest E. Norris, who had been operating two Southern properties, the Mobile & Ohio and the Columbus & Greenville railroads, was transferred back to headquarters as vice-president, Operations. Norris had served as assistant to Harrison during World War I, after a sixteen-year career with Southern.

Bright, resourceful, and energetic, Norris had shown positive signs of his capacity for leadership during his climb up Southern's ladder, beginning as a car service agent in 1902. He had served through every phase of the company's development and knew its operating problems intimately from service as trainmaster, assistant superintendent, superintendent, and general superintendent, before joining Harrison as his assistant in 1918. Increasingly, Harrison came to depend upon Norris as the hardships of the Great Depression grew more threatening.

The dark years of the depression must have seemed endless to Harrison and his beleaguered executives, but the tide began to turn at last. In 1936 the Southern finally showed a profit for the year's operation—the first in six years. The modest net income of $4,308,000 inspired Harrison to declare, somewhat grandly, "There are no financial difficulties facing the Southern Railway."

The depression dragged on but Southern's future was perceptibly brighter with the passing months, and it seemed clear that the

"How Many Blisters Do You Have?"

System had weathered the worst of the storm. Harrison chose the moment to announce his retirement, ending a quarter-century of presidential service, during which he had led the company through war, high prosperity, and grinding depression. On 21 October 1937, the sixty-eight-year-old Harrison asked his directors to relieve him of his duties, saying that a chief reason for the request was "the satisfaction it would give him to see his officers move up while he was still there."

Harrison thus gave his younger executives an opportunity to cope with the lingering recession which had proved such a challenge to him. He planned to retire to Belvoir and resume his study of Greek and Latin classics, French literature and southern history, but Fairfax Harrison did not live to enjoy a scholar's life in retirement. He died on 2 February 1938, three months after leaving office.

Harrison had made notable contributions to Southern, but despite his efforts, he had been unable to secure sufficient capital to modernize its physical plant. He had failed to develop a cohesive management structure to carry on after his departure, and his fiscal policies had resulted in the accumulation of a heavy load of debt. The System was still operating numerous unprofitable branch lines and passenger trains. An infusion of fresh capital was essential. There was an equally pressing need for a firm hand on the throttle. Ernest Norris filled that need.

SEVEN

"We Have an Abiding Faith"

Ernest E. Norris, the supersalesman of Southern, was a thirty-seven-year veteran of railroading when he took office as president on 1 November 1937. Virtually all of his experience had been with Southern or its subsidiaries, and most of this was in the field of operations.

Norris was now fifty-five, a slender, red-haired man of medium height, sharp-featured but handsome. He was voluble and volatile, fond of laughter and given to colorful language. Colleagues long remembered the way in which he expressed his abiding love for railroads: "There are only two things a man will turn his head for—one is a pretty woman, the other is a train."

Norris walked with a limp, the result of a train accident, but moved vigorously despite his handicap. He made friends easily and quickly, and was equally at home with national political leaders and ranking business executives, or children and dogs. As Southern's magazine *Ties* once observed, "Walking is his favorite exercise, and that's where the dogs come in; Mr. Norris never passes one by; he knows how to scratch a dog in those special spots guaranteed to produce canine delight. He probably has a scratching acquaintance with more dogs than any other individual in the country."

It was this warm, affable man whom Fairfax Harrison had urged his directors to name as his successor in a time of trial. The first nonsoutherner to head the System, Norris was a small-town youth from Hoopeston, Illinois. He had shown initiative from boyhood, first as a ten-year-old agent for a steam laundry in Kokomo, Indiana, which required him to collect and deliver the town's laundry each week, pulling his burden on a homemade sled. A few years later, fascinated with railroading, he persuaded a local Western Union operator to teach him the Morse code and telegraphy. Since there was slight chance of landing a job in his new field near home, the resourceful youngster read out-of-town newspapers avidly. One day in 1900 he read of the suicide of a telegraph operator in Arlington Heights, Illinois. Norris wrote the station to offer

"We Have an Abiding Faith"

his services. He was surprised to land the dead man's job, and even rented the room in which his predecessor had lived.

Arlington Heights, thirty miles outside Chicago, a small out-of-the-way station on the Chicago & Northwestern Railway, did not hold the ambitious Norris for long. Telegraphy was not enough for Ernest. He swept floors, filled and replaced switch lamps, and helped the older and less active agent with milk cans, the baggage room, and ticket office. One day when the agent told him that a traveling auditor of the railroad was due on a periodic inspection, Norris determined to make a good impression.

The auditor came, completed his work, and asked for a sheet of carbon paper. Norris gave him a fresh sheet, which the auditor left behind a few moments later. When he had gone, Ernest read from the carbon paper: "There is a young man here by the name of Norris who seems to be very capable. I suggest that you might keep him in mind."

That was enough to speed Ernest on his way, for someone at headquarters did take note, and Norris was soon offered the post of agent at Reidsville, and asked if he would agree to go.

"I'd have gone to New Guinea for a raise," Norris said later. "That job was paying only $35 a month."

From that point he climbed rapidly. A train dispatcher in Chicago before he was twenty, he landed a job with Southern in Washington through the influence of a friend in the headquarters offices. After two years as a car record clerk, he became trainmaster at Norfolk in 1904, and then moved to Greensboro, North Carolina, in the same post. His rise continued—assistant superintendent at Knoxville in 1906, superintendent of the Coster Division at Knoxville in 1907, and superintendent, Atlanta Division, in the same year. By 1917 he was general superintendent of the Middle District, and the following year became assistant to President Harrison and the headquarters expert on System operations.

At the end of the war, Harrison sent Norris to serve as vice-president of the Southern-controlled Mobile & Ohio. In 1932, when the road succumbed to the depression, Norris served as its receiver. A year later Harrison summoned him back to Washington, where he served a four-year term as vice-president, Operations, before ascending to the presidency.

The Southern had adequate notice that Norris would be a vigorous leader, but many of his associates were sometimes taken aback by his volatile manner. Harry DeButts, the new vice-president, Operations, who admired him greatly, recalled the lightning

"We Have an Abiding Faith"

changes of mood in the presidential office: "My, but he'd fly off the handle. He'd get mad quicker than anybody I ever saw, but five minutes later everything would be all right and he would be his charming self again. He got things off his chest in a hurry."

But Norris quickly demonstrated his inspirational leadership and the application of his full attention to the most demanding problems. Despite long service in operations, Norris was quite aware that Southern's major problems were still financial: on 1 September 1938, he must meet the System's obligation to the RFC, a loan totaling $24,270,000. There was no money in the treasury to pay such a sum, and prospects of a bank loan were still bleak. Southern's fiscal position was hardly less perilous than it had been in Harrison's time of trial.

After suffering losses for five years ending in 1935, the railway had moved slightly into the black in 1936 and 1937, but traffic and earnings declined once more in 1938 and Southern's losses mounted. Receivership was once more a threatening possibility.

To his despondent staff Norris preached optimism and hope. "Courage! Courage!" he said. "Let us not lose faith in our ability to meet the crisis. We shall find a way. If the banks will not come to our aid, what about the RFC? Let us go back to them and lay our cards on the table and see if they will not help us out." For six weeks during the summer of 1938 Norris and his financial officers negotiated with the RFC and were finally successful in refinancing the debt with a new five-year loan of about $29 million, at 5 percent interest. As collateral, Southern pledged securities valued at $80 million. Norris and his officers celebrated the salvation of the System, but their joy was short-lived.

A deteriorating fleet of freight cars, operated for years without replacements, had dwindled so alarmingly that car rental payments were beginning to drain the treasury. Merely to restore the fleet so that rental payments and rental collections balanced would cost about $20 million. No bankers could be interested in a new loan with Southern mortgaged heavily, and some $80 million of its securities in the hands of the RFC.

As a last resort, Norris returned to the office of Jesse Jones, the big Texan who headed the RFC. As Jones recalled the visit, "Norris . . . came to see me and told me he'd pay us every cent he owed us if he had to do it with dollar bills."

Norris made his case tersely: "Jesse, I owe you about $30 million. We haven't bought a freight car in eight years and we can't get any money anywhere else. Half the car-making plants in the country are shut down. The only men they've got working are the guards at the gates. We badly need some new freight cars. I'd like to order about eight or nine thousand of them. I can save enough money on rent that I'm paying other roads for the use of their cars to pay for them."

"How much would the cars cost?"

"About $20 million—but I can't pay anything down."

Jones did not hesitate. "O.K., Ernest," he said. "Have equipment trust certificates issued at 4 percent and we'll buy them."

The entire conversation lasted barely a quarter of an hour, but, as Jones said later, "The result was that many men were put to work building the cars and we helped the railroad at the same time.... Mr. Norris got his nine thousand freight cars, and we made $800,000 on the deal."

Jones also noted that Southern met its certificate payments promptly—and that when World War II came to America some three years afterward, Southern's new cars were rolling. "After the war," Jones added, "such cars would have cost twice what [Norris] paid in 1938."

With the aid of a business upturn, Southern was able to pay a first installment of $2 million on its RFC loan in November 1939, and to make other payments in 1940. It was probably the most satisfying day of Norris's career as president when, on 15 May 1941, Southern sent the RFC a check for the $10 million balance, erasing the debt and redeeming its $80 million collateral. With that step, Southern entered a far more favorable financial climate than it had known since the Roaring Twenties.

Throughout trying times, Norris managed to maintain the traditions of Southern's passenger service. A welcome innovation in 1935 was air-conditioned sleeping cars; public response was so favorable that coaches were also air-conditioned. As flagship of the System, the Crescent Limited continued to operate with the best equipment, but it was discontinued in 1934 and revived as the Crescent. In 1941 the trains received their first diesel equipment, which Norris had painted a striking green and light gray with gold striping.

On the eve of World War II, Southern operated one of the nation's largest passenger fleets. With the Frisco, it operated the Kansas City–Florida Special and the Sunnyland from Kansas City to Georgia and Florida. The Memphis Special linked the Tennessee city with Washington, the Royal Palm and the Ponce de Leon served Florida from the Midwest, and the Queen and Crescent ran

"We Have an Abiding Faith"

from Cincinnati to New Orleans. In May 1941, within a few days of his settlement with the RFC, Norris had the satisfaction of seeing two stainless steel streamliners enter his passenger service—the Tennessean, running from Washington to Memphis, and the Southerner, from New York to New Orleans. Traffic on these crack trains began to swell steadily as the nation approached Pearl Harbor, and after the fall of 1941, the passenger department found itself taxed to the limit by the vast expansion of military posts in the System's territory.

Norris said wistfully, "I never thought I'd live to see the day when I had to beg folks to please not ride our trains unless the trip was absolutely necessary." The pressure was to continue throughout the war. Southern's loss of key personnel and the effects of food rationing added to the woes of the dining-car department. In 1939 it had been serving 70,000 meals monthly; by 1943 this total had zoomed to 350,000.

The vast increase in civilian traffic seemed to augur well for a revival of passenger business after the war, and, as a result, Norris placed a large order for streamlined equipment of stainless steel in anticipation of postwar passenger business exceeding the record levels set in early 1929. This judgment—soon to be proven erroneous—was shared by most American railroad executives at the time; the vast expansion of air and automobile traffic could not be foreseen.

The last half of 1939 brought a boom to railroads. Southern's ton-miles of freight reached levels it had not achieved in a decade and passenger traffic, gross revenues and net income also rose sharply. It was a trend that accelerated as the war in Europe grew more intense, and the United States became increasingly involved as "the arsenal of democracy."

Norris himself had a substantial effect upon the road's operations in these days. Previous presidents had seldom gone off on extended tours to visit shippers, but as Harry DeButts recalled, "Norris burned the wheels off those cars of his. He knew everybody—he made it a point to know presidents and chairmen of the leading corporations everywhere—and he was welcome everywhere. He was particularly effective with chief executive officers of the larger companies like Alcoa and Reynolds, and he always was out to talk business with the top man." Norris prepared thoroughly for these interviews, however. Another associate recalled: "When he was out visiting a plant, he'd make a beeline for the loading dock and talk with the supervisor there, to get an idea of

"We Have an Abiding Faith"

just what he wanted and needed, and what problems existed—and then he'd go in to the president of the firm fully armed with knowledge of everything involved, and in great detail." He often made fifty calls a day.

DeButts, who worked closely with Norris on a daily basis, never forgot his vivid personality: "Norris was a character. He could do or say anything and get by with it, where no one else could. Everybody would laugh with him. He had jokes for all occasions and was enormously popular on the railroad and elsewhere. Norris was absolutely tops in dealing with people, our customers and prospective customers, and I tried to emulate him."

Norris spent more than two weeks of each month on the road, and Southern employees came to know him as an early riser. Many of these men were his guests for coffee or breakfast in the first hours of the presidential day; he was gaining valuable insight into the workings of the System at lower levels. Thousands of Southern men learned to recognize their chief by the sight of him, walking briskly through yards, shops, and offices. But others were also welcomed by Norris. As the Southern's house organ reported, "No one can tell the number of children and their mothers who have been guests on his office car, mostly at breakfast time. Fruit bowls and candy dishes were sure to be emptied if there were children around."

The affable Virginian DeButts felt that Norris made a substantial contribution to Southern through his personality alone, especially in making peace with the System's connecting lines, which had been sources of irritation in the past. "Norris made the best contacts with these lines that could have been made. In the old days there was always fighting between us, in the courts and out. But Norris made friends of all of them. He was a pretty tough bargainer, but he dealt in a friendly sort of way, and was never at a loss for a joke. He didn't make many speeches, but in man-to-man talks he was superb."

But with competing lines in his region, Norris was quite another personality. As DeButts said, "He was in more lawsuits and fights and fusses with the Atlantic Coast Line and Seaboard than you can imagine."

The fresh, candid, disarming approach of Norris was a distinct asset to Southern, since his impressive personal magnetism was always evident, whether in charming prospective customers or warring on the enemy.

Bill Brosnan, a newly promoted trainmaster who was to win

"We Have an Abiding Faith"

fame as a Southern executive, met Norris in 1938, when the president passed through Oakdale, Tennessee, enroute to the Kentucky Derby with a number of directors, customers, and friends.

Brosnan went aboard the special train, located Norris, introduced himself, and said he would be on call in case of need.

"Sit down," Norris said, and introduced him to his friends. "How long have you been trainmaster, son?"

"Two days."

Norris roared with laughter and fell into an animated discussion with Brosnan and the guests. Brosnan liked him from the start: "He was vigorous, forceful, stimulating and positive. I had found the Southern somewhat stultifying under Harrison, and I could not have stayed there long if Norris hadn't come in."

"What are your duties as trainmaster?" one of the guests asked Brosnan.

When Brosnan began a lengthy explanation Norris broke in: "The trainmaster's job is out here between the rails checking train movements. The only equipment he needs is a pair of good shoes, a timetable and lots of guts."

Brosnan came to know Norris well in later years, and admired him: "He really turned Southern around in the minds of the public. The line had not been too popular in the South for years, with the public, shippers or employees. Norris changed that. He was a dynamo. I did not consciously make him a model—but I couldn't have found a better one."

This was the age of the New Deal, whose policies stirred Norris to wrath—but Southern found an ardent admirer in President Franklin D. Roosevelt, who was a dedicated railroad buff. Roosevelt made frequent trips over the Southern in his special armor-plated car, the Magellan, which was rented from the Association of American Railroads at the rate of $1 per year. Southern's operating people had reason to know when the president was on the lines, since he enforced a train speed limit of 35 miles per hour, so that he might enjoy the scenery. The Roosevelt trains were enabled to keep to their unique schedule whatever complications that might involve, for the anti-New Deal policy did not operate in this case.

Norris presided over the care of special cars of other well-known Americans in this era, including the Ranger of Cissie Patterson, the colorful publisher of the *Washington Times-Herald.* The Ranger was kept in Southern's Washington yards, fully staffed around the clock, ready for its owner's possible departure in any direction. The car was celebrated for its elaborate fittings, which included seven complete sets of slipcovers for the furniture, "so that passengers might not become fatigued with the same decor on successive days."

Other special cars became familiar on the road, including Doris Duke's so-called Doris, and the Jomar of John Ringling North, the circus heir.

The year 1939, in which Norris made his historic decision to enter the diesel-powered era, was not only history making—it spawned a number of public relations problems new to railroading. When the approach of World War II prevented further dieselization of the road beyond the tentative start made by Norris and DeButts, both men realized that it was merely a question of time before the steam locomotive disappeared from the tracks. They were better prepared for that than for the almost insatiable demand which later arose for the old brass bells from Southern's retired steam engines as they were displaced by diesels.

This began in 1946 in Bethania, North Carolina, where a Moravian church had risen on the site of an earlier building destroyed by fire. The building was complete except for a bell to summon worshipers who lived in the village. Recalling the sweet tones of the old locomotive bells, members of the congregation asked Southern to provide one for their belfry. Norris sent a bell from a scrapped locomotive, and his public relations staff published an ad telling the story under the headline: "A Bell for Bethania." Results were unexpected.

Requests for bells poured in from churches, orphanages, boys' and girls' camps, schools, and colleges all over the South. Southern was to donate hundreds of these bells before the supply gave out some years later. Among these bells still ringing some forty years later is one inscribed: "It used to serve the Southern, now it serves the Lord."

"A Bell for Bethania" was one of the more attention-getting aspects of a public relations and advertising effort that hit its full stride under Norris and his assistant, Bernard E. Young, in the 1940s. Southern Railway's concern for corporate citizenship and the good opinion of its neighbors dates back to the railway's beginnings, and has been expressed in various ways over the years.

Attracting farm families to the sparsely settled South in the 1890s led to interest in crop diversification and the promotion of the dairy industry. Southern was involved in the good roads move-

"We Have an Abiding Faith"

ment of the early twentieth century and sponsored numerous agricultural fairs and exhibitions, in addition to furthering the industrial development of the South. Presidents Samuel Spencer, William W. Finley, and Fairfax Harrison were frequent spokesmen on behalf of the company and the industry. Under Harrison the public relations effort became more formally organized, with a publication for employees called the *Southern Railway News Bulletin* and an occasional newspaper advertisement. But it was Ernest Norris and Bernie Young who really began to shape Southern's public image.

Young, a native of Martinsburg, West Virginia, who began his railroad career with Norfolk & Western Railway at Roanoke, Virginia, came to Southern from the Association of American Railroads in Washington, where he had helped set up and administer the railroads' first industrywide public relations program. He joined Southern Railway in 1942 and three years later became assistant to the president in charge of public relations, advertising, and related activities.

For almost a quarter century, Bernie Young was at the side of three successive presidents, as the spark plug of the railway's public relations and advertising efforts. He helped launch a successful and long-running series of newspaper advertisements highlighting the railroad's contributions to its region in war and in peace. The magazine campaign urging industry to "Look Ahead—Look South" helped boost the region's growth year after year. To replace the *News Bulletin*—which had disappeared during the early 1930s, a victim of the Great Depression—Young produced a new magazine, *Ties*, to reach not only Southern's employees but its customers and friends as well.

The Roosevelt administration, against stout opposition, launched a vast expansion of national defense programs in 1940, and Southern once more became a major carrier of construction materials for posts, camps, training centers, aviation schools, supply bases, defense plants, and shipbuilding yards. Troops and military equipment flooded in a few months later, in an ever-expanding stream. The strains were felt throughout the System.

It was now that the talents of Bill Brosnan, a hard-driving Georgian, first came forcibly to the attention of Southern's top management, reinforcing the favorable first impression he had made upon Norris. Here began one of the System's most remarkable

"We Have an Abiding Faith"

eras of growth. Brosnan's rise had already been rapid, but it was in the confusion of the national defense effort that his resourcefulness won the attention of Harry DeButts and Ernest Norris.

As superintendent in Macon, Georgia, Brosnan learned that the army planned to build Camp Blanding in northern Florida, in an area served only by a light line of Southern's subsidiary, the Georgia, Southern & Florida (GS&F)—a line already slated for abandonment. But F. Hamlin Brown, an energetic young salesman of the GS&F, persuaded Brosnan that Blanding offered Southern a major opportunity, and the two discussed prospects of building a new line into the camp site. Word of this reached Elmer R. Oliver, Southern's vice president of sales, who hurried to Macon and queried Brosnan about Blanding.

"We have a good chance to get in there, but Keister [O. B. Keister, Brosnan's superior] told me not to touch the project, because the line is to be abandoned."

A few days later Brosnan had a call from DeButts, to whom he reported the facts. DeButts replied, "Go ahead and build that line anyway, as diplomatically as possible, and avoid antagonizing Keister if you can."

Brown and Brosnan soon made a proposal to Major Larson, a hard-bitten Quartermaster Corps veteran, who told them that Seaboard had also made a proposal, but wanted to delay for several months. "I want service," Larson said, "and I want it in a hurry. This country's going to war."

Brosnan hurriedly wrote a proposal, estimating costs of extending a ten-mile line into the camp using sixty-pound rail laid on new ties. He offered to find a grading contractor, and he made the entire contract price at cost plus ten percent. He agreed to complete the line within thirty-two days after signing of the agreement.

Brosnan awakened a stenographer one Saturday night to have his proposal typed and took it to Major Larson the next day. "By God," Larson said, "you people mean business!" and scrawled across the bottom of the agreement, "Accepted, Larson, Chief Quartermaster, USA." The document became the only contract. DeButts approved, but Keister called Brosnan and shouted angrily, "I thought I told you not to touch that."

Brosnan explained that DeButts had ordered him to undertake the project and that he had been forced to oblige. Soon afterward, Keister told DeButts, "I'm afraid I'll have to fire Brosnan."

"I wish you wouldn't do that."

"We Have an Abiding Faith"

"Why not?" Keister asked.

"Because I've got him in line to succeed you."

Keister's mood was not improved by Brosnan's success in pushing the project to completion one day before his deadline, by standing over the workmen, aiding the contractor in winning state approval for a crucial highway crossing (which was accomplished despite stout opposition from local property owners), and generally supervising the work. "We practically paved that line with ties," Brosnan recalled. "We hoped to keep the light line from breaking and it never did break, despite many years of heavy traffic." Brosnan claimed little credit for himself. "When DeButts approved, we put large crews to work. They're the ones who did it, and not me or Ham Brown. We were out there pushing and prodding every day, but the men deserve the credit, and especially John Walker, who was the division engineer."

This project opened a working relationship between Brosnan and DeButts that was to culminate in the revolutionizing of the Southern System, as well as railroads in many countries.

Brosnan's next assignment was in Birmingham, where inadequate yard facilities had been overwhelmed by the flood of oil cars, tanks, munitions, and troops—crude oil was now moving from Louisiana and Texas to refineries in New Jersey, and old tank cars had been rescued from retirement. Clark Hungerford, who was then general manager, western lines, sent Brosnan to end the chaos developing in the yards.

The trouble, as Brosnan quickly discovered, was largely due to gangs of "boomers," refugees fired from other railroads, and to the inept efforts of new employees hired to replace departing veterans. Brosnan lived most of the time out on the line and in the yard, keeping an eye on "the boomers, loafers and drunks who were causing the trouble."

He hired a number of young women to hand train orders up to the passing trains. These women were required to stand quite near the trains as they came past at high speeds, and the wind often blew their skirts over their heads, presenting Brosnan with a delicate problem: "I was afraid that their clothing would catch on trailing wires or grab irons and they'd be killed—or else that a brakeman would fall off the train while looking at the sights, and break his neck."

Brosnan ordered that the women be required to wear trousers in the name of safety. His supervisor was reluctant, "I don't want to do that."

"We Have an Abiding Faith"

Brosnan laughed. "It's an order—and you're old enough to be their grandfather." The problem disappeared. It was one of the few moments of relief in a time of round-the-clock struggle to keep pace with the demands of approaching war.

The unusual concentration of military posts in the Southern territory, where climatic conditions were favorable, imposed heavier burdens on Southern than on most railroads. Southern's military traffic was probably a record, for it was to operate nearly 16,000 troop trains carrying over six million service people—exclusive of millions of soldiers, sailors, and Marines who traveled singly or in small groups.

The System's most dramatic accomplishment in moving troops came during severe weather in December 1941, soon after the Japanese attack on Pearl Harbor plunged the nation into war. Within seven days after Pearl Harbor, while the targets of attack still smouldered on Battleship Row, Southern's operating crews had made an emergency movement of an entire division from its post in the Southeast, hurrying it on its way to the West Coast. The move involved 69 trains and some 12,000 men, but was complete in three days and nights: 54 Pullmans, 289 coaches, 1,024 flat cars, 124 box cars, 52 baggage cars—1,543 in all. Of these 69 trains, Southern handled 52 exclusively and turned the others over to its competitor, the L&N. The trains were loaded and dispatched at intervals of less than an hour and went through "with hardly a minute of delay."

After Pearl Harbor, caught in a swirl of unprecedented growth, the System strained the resources of its 8,000-mile network to provide links between the industrial North and Midwest and the spreading defense facilities of the Southeast—and to connect the vital oil-producing areas with eastern ports. The Southern was to carry almost 70 percent more traffic than it had during World War I—with 29 percent fewer locomotives, 14 percent fewer freight cars, and 41 percent fewer passenger cars than it had owned during the Great War. Southern executives never understood how this record was accomplished.

Nothing that the System contributed during the war was of greater strategic importance than the movement of gas and oil from the Southwest to eastern ports and refineries. German submarine packs cut off normal deliveries by tankers passing through the Gulf of Mexico and the Atlantic coastal waters. Existing pipelines could not carry the load, and railroads became the only hope of keeping the oil flowing, and the war machine run-

"We Have an Abiding Faith"

ning. Southern became a key element in this effort. Harold Ickes, the self-styled "Old Curmudgeon" who was secretary of interior and had now become federal petroleum coordinator, was responsible for supplying oil to the eastern seaboard and American forces in Europe without the use of ocean shipping along the American coast. Ickes had been assured earlier by John J. Pelley, president of the Association of American Railroads, that railroads could do the job in an emergency. Pelley claimed that rail carriers could move two hundred thousand barrels of petroleum daily if the need arose. Ickes had scorned Pelley's claim in his emphatic manner, saying that the railroads were incapable of such a feat with the inadequate tanker fleet of the day.

Within a few weeks of the initial shipments, the volume of crude oil moved by rail exceeded the two-hundred-thousand-barrel quota and Ickes declared that he was happy to "eat crow" in light of "a perfectly amazing achievement" by the railroads.

Southern's role in this accomplishment had been crucial. The System moved 13,650 tons of crude petroleum in 1941, 226,000 tons in 1943, and 560,777 tons in 1944, a new record. The movement of refined petroleum products in this period almost doubled in volume. Most of these wartime movements of petroleum over Southern lines were accomplished in solid trainloads from point of origin to destination. These movements began the flow through complex and often imperiled lines of supply that powered the aerial bombardment of Germany, the D-day assault in Normandy, and the final thrust into Nazi Germany itself.

Southern's war effort was impressive in light of its contribution of manpower to the military services, just as was the case on other railroads. The first employees to enter service left long before Pearl Harbor and by war's end some seventy-six hundred of Southern's men and women had left for military service. Southern also trained army railroaders for overseas service. As the first railroad chosen for on-the-ground training of railway operating battalions for the Transportation Corps, Southern began its program in 1942 on the New Orleans and Northeastern Division between New Orleans and Meridian, which was made available to the government at no charge. About six thousand officers and men of four of these battalions used Southern's "classroom" to learn railroading from practical experience that prepared them well for the campaigns in Europe and North Africa.

The first such unit trained was Southern's own, most of its ranks filled by the System's employees and commanded by Lt. Col. Fred-

"We Have an Abiding Faith"

erick W. Okie, who left his post as superintendent of the Birmingham division. The 727th Railway Operating Battalion was sent overseas to a career of wartime railroading in North Africa, Sicily, and Italy, and to the climactic assault on Germany.

Southern's equipment was often strained beyond the limit in these days, and maintenance men struggled with mounting problems, trying to keep aging locomotives and cars in service. Dining cars came out of long retirement to be refitted as passenger coaches. Locomotives were rescued from the scrap heap to resume service.

For the first time, with the support of Norris, the System launched an advertising campaign to persuade civilians to stay off the trains except in emergencies. To neutralize the negative aspects of this campaign a new series of advertisements was published, underlining the mutual interests of the railroad and the southern people in the development of the South, particularly in the postwar world. A typical advertisement said in part: "We are learning—the hard way—how to do our job better. That's why, when victory has been won, there will be a better Southern Railway System to better serve the new South that is expanding so tremendously ... commercially, industrially, and agriculturally. That's why we say, 'Look Ahead—Look South'."

The theme, and the new slogan, echoed the railroad's campaigns that had begun with Samuel Spencer, and the slogan was to become familiar to generations of southerners as the railroad expanded this advertising program, stressing the superior advantages of the Southeast in terms of raw materials, growing markets, labor sources, and fields for industrial expansion.

In 1947 Norris approved *Ties*, a magazine designed to improve communications between management and employees, which were not always satisfactory. The monthly publication became a major factor in the company's efforts to inform the work force of its prospects, problems, and resources. The cover of the magazine's first issue carried a 1941 photograph that became a classic in railroad lore: America's first diesel-electric locomotive, Southern's 6100, crossing the Cumberland River Bridge near Burnside, Kentucky. Leaning from the cab window was fireman Charles F. Denny, who would later die as a Marine private in the American conquest of Okinawa.

President Norris discovered that company morale was almost too high in some respects. His retired officers refused to remain at

"We Have an Abiding Faith"

home and continued to come into the headquarters building daily just as they had during their working days. Norris provided them with a room on the second floor, complete with desks, typewriter, conference table, telephone, and couch. The old-timers made themselves at home immediately. When a photographer appeared to take pictures for *Ties*, there was a scramble to snatch photographs of pin-up girls from the walls.

Norris understood the reluctance of the veterans to leave the scene of action, since he devoted almost every waking moment to the company. His only hobbies were walking and swimming. "No time for anything else except my two red-haired granddaughters," he once said.

As the war progressed shortages and restrictions on private business led to rapidly advancing prices and wage increases, a foretaste of the inflationary waves to come. Southern was forced to apply to the ICC for periodic rate increases. The average compensation of railway employees rose by about 42 percent during the war, prices of fuel doubled, and costs of other supplies rose across the board at rates of 40 to 75 percent. To offset these advances, there was an increase of only 1 percent in freight revenues. In 1942, the first year of America's involvement in the war, Southern's revenues topped $200 million for the first time since 1926, and the road then managed a return of only 6.1 percent on capital investment and 10.7 percent on equity. Taxes soared with the levy of an excess-profits tax, taking all profits over a stipulated percentage of earnings. As a result, Southern paid in federal, state, and local taxes more than 21 percent of its gross operating revenues—in contrast to about 2 percent during World War I. In the five-year period 1941–45, Southern paid more than $237 million in taxes. Only the enormous volume of traffic and reduction in costs per carload enabled Southern to meet these tax burdens, and this advantage vanished when business returned to normal in 1946.

Southern emerged from the war with the first major income tax problems in its history; the government claimed the road owed some $30 million in taxes, including excess-profits levies. The company employed Charles M. Davison, Jr., a tax expert from the Washington law firm of Covington and Burling, to handle its case. As Davison recalled the situation, "Southern had done a good job of filing returns for the war years, for despite numerous amendments in the statutes and the imposition of the excess-profits tax, the government claimed an error of only 17 percent. The chief problem was that no one knew what the proper tax should have been.

"During the war, naturally enough, the government had refused to say what was in its freight cars, and Southern had to guess what was military freight, with its lower rate, and what was not. It made its charges the best it could. There was a question as to how charges of the half-rate for military goods were to be computed in light of the excess-profits tax imposed for the duration of the war."

Further complications were raised by the ICC, which did not use a depreciation formula—so that railroads were writing off capital expenditures as they were made. Since there were no capital outlays of importance during the war, the ICC and the railroads agreed to adopt depreciation accounting for the period. To get the accustomed deductions, Davison said, "we had to work out a formula between the ICC and IRS positions, and the IRS imposed a 30 percent reserve formula on the railroads. We had to fight it out from that point."

With many millions involved, Southern's chief executives took a lively interest in the case. Ernest Norris had been advised by Davison's predecessor to pay the IRS $8 million in advance, but Norris replied with a flash of his steel-blue eyes, "I think I understand, but I'll stand pat." In his turn, President DeButts was also resolved to fight out the case on its merits. Davison advised DeButts that the claim would cost Southern from $1 million to $8 million, since government agents had invested so much time in preparation of the case, and the issues involved important precedents. In the end, the case was settled by Southern's paying $5 million of the $30 million claim, a victory for Davison and his staff.

Davison's most notable service to Southern in this field was his negotiation with the government when the road adopted the diesel engine and wrote off its huge investment in steam locomotives and their support—coaling and watering stations, roundhouses, maintenance shops, and all else pertaining to steam operations. Davison's first task was to convince old-time railroaders of the seriousness of the problem, and of the fact that the steam era was actually over. Without their cooperation, he could hardly have assembled pertinent data to support Southern's claims for the substantial write-offs. He was successful only after he had won Bill Brosnan's confidence, and then information flowed freely into the legal offices.

In 1954, when Davison approached the IRS with his problem and staked a claim for all steam operations costs back to 1941, a

"We Have an Abiding Faith"

startled agent said, "Oh, come on! Nobody had even heard of diesel engines in 1941."

After long negotiating sessions, and the presentation of a detailed affidavit from Ernest Norris on the birth of the diesel era, the government agent agreed: "O.K., let's say steam equipment became obsolete in 1944—and we'll let you charge off ten years." The elated Davison took back word of his triumph, only to hear an explosion from his superior, Thomas H. Seay: "Hell, no. You did a good job, all right, but I'm a poker player. Go back to the IRS and get another year's depreciation for us. If they gave you ten years, they'll give you one more."

To Davison's surprise, the government agreed to this, and Southern was allowed to write off more steam losses for 1943, to the extent of about $1 million. Davison sent Seay a telegram, reading: "Orchids to thee for '43."

At war's end, Norris prepared for the expected boom. He invested in a Centralized Traffic Control (CTC) system to improve safety and increase train speeds through continuous movement. A system of trackside signals and remote-controlled switches permitted operators at consoles to guide train movements on hundreds of miles of track, with greatly increased efficiency and safety. In 1948 the first nineteen-mile test showed fifty-nine hundred fewer stops than in 1947; thirty years later more than two thousand miles of Southern were equipped with the new CTC. Meanwhile, the process of installing heavier rail, longer passing sidings, crushed rock ballast, long-life ties, and other housekeeping chores resumed. More new steel bridges were erected, tunnels were eliminated, and curve reduction removed many sections with low-speed restrictions. In addition, Norris added more than thirteen thousand new freight cars between 1945 and 1952.

He did not neglect passenger service, which he still believed would boom with the war's end. In 1946 he ordered 141 passenger cars from Pullman-Standard, E. G. Budd, and American Car & Foundry, though forty of these were to belong to other railroads over which the streamliners operated. Norris announced the purchase with an expression of great optimism that the sleek new trains would attract record traffic.

Unfortunately, his order went out at a time when builders were swamped with similar demands from other railroads, and the streamlined cars were not received until 1949, when airline and automobile traffic had begun their period of phenomenal growth. The new equipment gave Southern's crack trains even more luxurious accommodations. The Crescent assumed new grandeur, with a shower in its master suite in the lounge car, a radio in the buffet lounge, the traditional southern-style cuisine, and complimentary coffee and orange juice for passengers.

Investments in such crack trains did not prove profitable, and Southern, like other lines, faced rising deficits in passenger operations. Competition from expanding highway and air travel was too great. New equipment, reduced fares, and promotion campaigns availed little; traffic and revenues went into a steady decline. Passenger service, it appeared, was a lost cause. Based on 1946 receipts, Southern experienced a drop of 57 percent in passenger revenues in 1948, and 80 percent in 1949. Receipts were then only two and a half cents per passenger mile, and since Southern logged 818 million passenger miles in 1948, and accountants calculated that 460 million of these miles went to pay for the new equipment, the road was obviously losing money on its passenger business. In 1947 the System began an intensive campaign to discontinue passenger trains on branch lines, and pressed it despite vigorous opposition from the public.

Consistent gains in freight service, however, coupled with the benefits of dieselization, were providing a satisfying reduction in Southern's operating ratio—from 81 percent in 1946 to 70 percent in 1950. And, though ton-miles of freight were almost the same in 1951 as they had been in 1946, freight train–miles had been reduced by almost 40 percent.

A significant index of operating efficiency, gross ton-miles per train hour, rose from 27,500 in 1946 to 44,500 in 1952, and it became obvious that Southern was reaping dividends from the heavy investments made by Norris.

Norris had not forgotten the lessons of the depression. He followed a conservative fiscal policy throughout, using a substantial part of earnings to reduce the railroad's debt. His achievement went unnoticed by the public, but Wall Street began to note his streamlining of Southern's financial structure and his ability to reduce funded debt while making extensive improvements.

Largely as a result of the Norris policies, Southern's debt was reduced by almost 50 percent between 1930 and 1960, and fixed charges dropped from nearly $18 million to $12 million in the period. By contrast with Fairfax Harrison's burden of 24 cents of every dollar for fixed charges, this ratio was to fall to 4.6 cents by 1960.

"We Have an Abiding Faith"

Southern's major debt obligation of $200 million, the Development and General Mortgage dating from 1906, would not mature until 1956. The entire issue had never been sold, but by 1942 the public held more than $111 million of these bonds. Beginning in that year, Norris reduced this mortgage piecemeal as conditions permitted, gaining greater flexibility in his dividend policy. Southern resumed payment of dividends on its preferred in 1942, and on its common a year later.

The conservative fiscal policies of Norris gave the Southern reason to hope for a prosperous future, but the recession of 1948 demonstrated that the System's basic financial structure must be improved over the long term, and that the road was not yet out of trouble. The uncertain demands of future years concerned Norris and his staff. With the postwar lull in the nation's economic growth, Southern's experts could see that the ratio between costs and income was unfavorable.

In February 1948, when its average freight rate was just over 1 cent per ton-mile, Southern's financial officers calculated that the System must move one ton for fifty-seven miles merely to earn a 69-cent tie plate—and more than thirty-six hundred miles to pay for a $43 switch stand. Since its Charlotte roadway storehouse was then shipping some $250,000 in maintenance supplies each month, the road was obliged to carry one ton about twenty-five million miles to finance that outlay.

By autumn of 1949 the outlook was once more so bleak that company lawyers had prepared bankruptcy papers in case that contingency arose. Bill Brosnan, who saw them, resolved to change conditions on the railroad so drastically as to remove the threat forever. In addition to the twin plague of low rates and declining traffic volume, costs mounted substantially during the year, with the advent of the forty-hour week. This reform added some $640 million annually to American railroad payrolls, and increased the burden on Norris and his financial officers—but it was a great boon to rail workers and their families.

Since Southern then had about thirty-five thousand employees, massive shifts were made to accommodate the new working schedules. Wages and payroll taxes consumed about half of Southern's revenues, with most of the rest going for materials and equipment and some 12 percent for taxes. As management pointed out, there was little margin for profit. Norris insisted that the company must earn 6 percent on its investment or remain in

"We Have an Abiding Faith"

danger. The stage was set for Brosnan and a spectacular cost-cutting campaign that was unprecedented in American railroading.

Southern had almost lost Brosnan several years earlier. Clark Hungerford, as general manager, wanted the ebullient Georgian in Cincinnati as chief engineer, a "staff" job that would keep Brosnan out of the field as a line officer. Brosnan insisted that he would not make the move and said finally, "If you order me to take it, I'll have to quit."

"You'll have to tell that to the vice-president," Hungerford said. Brosnan liked and respected Hungerford, but he clung stubbornly to his position.

Harry DeButts sent for Brosnan: "What's this about your not wanting to report to Cincinnati?"

"I'm a line officer and I want no part of staff work. I've seen enough of that."

"But you've been ordered to go."

"If that's a serious order I'll have to quit."

"Why?"

"Because I want to be on the side of the railroad that runs it, and none of that sterile staff business."

"You know, I have to like that," DeButts said. "You're serious, aren't you?"

"I am, sir. I mean no threat. But I'll have to go if you insist."

DeButts broke him down at last: "I'm asking you personally to take this job for the time being. I'll see to it that you don't stay on it. You won't be stuck there."

When Brosnan protested that he'd heard such promises made to others, DeButts continued to press him, and Brosnan said, "Mr. DeButts, many promises have been made by others on the railroad, but if you'll shake hands on it, I'll do as you say."

The two agreed and Brosnan went to Cincinnati as chief engineer. DeButts rescued him a year later, sending Brosnan to Knoxville as general manager of central lines, moving him toward the threshhold from which he would climb to the presidency.

Ernest Norris was nearing the end of his career. He had won national attention for his leadership at last. *Forbes* magazine said in July 1947, "Ernest Norris, energetic, capable and articulate president of the Southern Railway System, has made both himself and his road a potent factor in the upbuilding of the South." *Kiplinger's* magazine cited Norris's reputation for spending

"We Have an Abiding Faith"

more time out on the tracks than any other American railroad president.

Norris took advantage of his national attention to speak on issues affecting Southern and the industry. He once assailed critics who depicted railroads as parasites that had grabbed vast areas of government lands. "Land grants to a few pioneer railroads were the best horse trade the U.S. ever got," he said. "They granted 181 million acres worth about $123 million—but there were some strings attached: railroads had to haul government property at reduced rates. By 1946 the government estimated it had saved $1 billion in freight rates on these deals. That's to say nothing of the greatly increased value of government lands because of railroad development—or of the soaring tax income to U.S., state, and local governments."

His response to charges that railroads had been guilty of profiteering was equally trenchant. "It's all loose talk," Norris said. "The railroads have earned an average return of over 3 percent in only three of the last thirty-five years, and then it was under 6 percent. In 1946, when we had a record peacetime traffic, the average profit was only 2¾ percent." Like other railroads, Norris said, the Southern wanted not only an adequate return—6 percent—but also an end to public subsidies of air, truck, and barge lines that wore "the false whiskers of cheap transportation."

He warmed to his subject when he spoke of the contrast between railroad operations during World War I and World War II: "Taxpayers lost $1.5 billion while the government operated the railroads in World War I—and even that after freight rates had been increased by 80 percent.

"But in World War II, under private management, the railroads made profits of $4.5 billion—and freight rates remained the same they were at the beginning of the war." To this object lesson in the economics of railroad nationalization, Norris added a warning that was unusual in the afterglow of the Franklin Roosevelt era of big government: "If we trade self-reliance for government aid, individual initiative for collectivism, and thrift for public subsidies—we stand to lose the freedom and blessings of our American way of life."

His speeches revealed Norris's philosophy and colorful approach:

"If the railroads are constantly to improve their services ... there must always be something in the 'kitty' to encourage inves-

"We Have an Abiding Faith"

tors to put their savings in railroad securities. For too many years the private investor ... has been the 'forgotten man.' He must be given more than the present 'heads I win, tails you lose' break. If that isn't done, the invigorating stream of private capital will dry up and the railroads' plans for continued modernization and improvement must reluctantly be packed away in moth balls."

He once explained the System's vigorous campaign of regional promotion: "Why do we advertise the territory we serve? Because we are part and parcel of the South; because we share its ups and downs; because we have an abiding faith in its bright future; and because we know that we can prosper and progress only as the territory we serve prospers and progresses."

He was apt to pound the podium or his desk top as he became caught up in a favorite theme. He was especially enthusiastic about his dream of the South that was to be—almost a generation before the widely publicized immigration to the Sunbelt burst upon the public consciousness: "As we go farther into this bright new era which stretches so invitingly before us, let us remember that, great and rapid as our progress has been in the past, we are only in the kindergarten of our ultimate development. For the Southland *is* a land of unlimited opportunity—and we may confidently expect it to become the most prosperous region of all—if we have vision, if we have courage, if we have faith ... *and if we work together*."

From 1937 to 1951 Ernest Norris guided Southern through the final phases of the Great Depression, into the diesel era, and through the hectic days of World War II. By 1951, Southern owned a fleet of 847 diesel-electric units, representing an investment of almost $200 million. By the end of that year these locomotives were performing 92 percent of the System's freight service and 86 percent of its passenger service.

Forbes said of the System at the close of the Norris era, "Perhaps no other railroad is more representative of the section it serves than the Southern. Its 8,000 miles of rails cover every state south of the Potomac and Ohio rivers and east of the Mississippi—except West Virginia. The lines reach into every southern city of any size except Nashville, Tennessee, and Montgomery, Alabama."

The growth of the postwar South foreseen by Norris had resulted in great gains for the System. Newly scheduled freight trains now carried cargoes that altered the traditional traffic patterns: the Clipper, the Southern Flash, the Jack Pot, the Spark Plug. Before Norris, major traffic categories had been in lumber,

"We Have an Abiding Faith"

pulpwood, and agricultural products, but his regime had seen the flowering of industrial growth in the region to such an extent that new types of cargoes assumed major importance. The System passed on by Norris to his successor hardly resembled the road he had inherited from Fairfax Harrison fourteen years earlier.

Norris retired in December 1951 at the age of seventy, to be succeeded by Harry DeButts. Norris became chairman of the Board, an office created for him.

Fellow directors presented Norris with a silver plate to express Southern's gratitude for his service:

> ERNEST EDEN NORRIS
> President of Southern Railway Company
> Undismayed by difficulty
> Unspoiled by success
> He has brought to the discharge of his responsibilities
> the vision of a president for his company
> and the devotion of a patriot to his nation
> The Empire of the South bears witness to his power
> as a creator and the transportation of America
> is a debtor to his genius as an executive.

Equally telling was a tribute from an officer who had traveled often with Norris in his busy office car: "Everybody will miss him. But I think the children and dogs will miss him most."

Now a little more than half a century old, on the threshold of the diesel era and an era of unprecedented growth, the Southern could look back to a past unique in the industry. The new president, Harry DeButts, could appreciate as well as anyone the significant history of the System and its antecedents. The heritage of the Southern Railway had its roots in virtually every state of the Old South and was intimately linked with the social and economic development of the region. DeButts began his career as president with the determination to capitalize on the strengths inherent in the colorful, creative past of the System.

EIGHT

"What a Bold Conception!"

The tradition of innovation within the Southern System began in 1830 with the birth of its earliest predecessor line, the South Carolina Canal & Rail Road Company (SCC&RRC) of Charleston. On Christmas Day 1830, a historic date in railroading, a tiny locomotive known as the Best Friend of Charleston made its first scheduled run, carrying passengers and freight over a six-mile track on the nation's first regularly scheduled steam railway service.

An excited passenger wrote that this first American train, "flew on the wings of the wind at the speed of fifteen to twenty-five miles per hour, annihilating time and space and leaving all the world behind." The locomotive, he reported, "darted forth like a live rocket, scattering sparks and flames on either side—passed over three salt-water creeks, hop, step and jump, and landed us all safe . . . before any of us had time to determine whether or not it was prudent to be scared."

The initial run of this miniature train marked the culmination of a bold speculation by a few South Carolina investors, for the railroad was to surpass in mileage and cost all of the railroads then existing in England and Europe. The South Carolina railroad project was thus one of great magnitude, undertaken by men whose faith in the steam locomotive and the American future was limitless.

The chief promoters were Charleston businessmen who were prospering from the boom that the invention of the cotton gin had brought to South Carolina and its thriving port city—but foresaw the loss of profitable traffic to Savannah, Georgia, and other competitors. These men turned to the railroad as their salvation. Two of them, Alexander Black and William Aiken, were natives of Ireland who had served in the South Carolina legislature. The resourceful, twenty-eight-year-old Black assumed a leading role in the venture, supported by a remarkable group of fellow entrepreneurs. Aiken, a cotton merchant and owner of a large plantation, was a local capitalist whose town house at King and Ann streets is thought to have been the site of meetings which formulated plans

"What a Bold Conception!"

for the nation's pioneer railroad. This house now contains Southern Railway Company offices.

Another promoter who made vital contributions to the project was Ezra L. Miller, a merchant, wagoner, lumberman, cotton ginner, and tanner who was also an accomplished self-taught mechanic and inventor. He patented an upright boiler and a set of driving wheels for a locomotive, perhaps inspired by his operation of one of the South's first steam-powered lumber mills. Miller's enthusiastic support became a key to the railroad's success.

Fortunately, these pioneers discovered Horatio Allen, a brilliant young engineer, who agreed to leave the Delaware & Hudson Railroad of Honesdale, Pennsylvania, to survey a route for the South Carolina line, over a projected route from Charleston to the neighborhood of Augusta, Georgia. Allen had recently returned from England, where he had studied operations of the world's first railroads. He had also purchased four steam locomotives, the first to reach America. In August 1829 he had driven one of these engines, the Stourbridge Lion, on the first run of a full-scale locomotive in the New World. Shortly after this feat, Allen arrived in Charleston to become chief engineer of the SCC&RRC. He found plans for the new road far advanced.

Black's influence had resulted in a legislative charter and a state loan of $100,000 for the railroad, and the company had been formally organized on 12 May 1828, with Aiken as president. The Charleston Chamber of Commerce had named a Committee of Ten to help promote the railroad, and citizens of the city had subscribed for the original thirty-five hundred shares of stock.

Horatio Allen urged the use of steam power at his first meeting with the road's directors in the spring of 1829, and the enterprising Ezra Miller, who had also visited England to inspect early locomotives, offered to design and build an engine at his own expense, which he would sell to the company if the directors approved its performance.

Miller drew plans and built a model and contracted with Gouverneur Kemble and his West Point Foundry Association of New York City to produce his locomotive. Miller himself supervised construction. Within three months the New York *Journal of Commerce* hailed the new ten-horsepower locomotive as an improvement over English models, as "lighter and less complex." Miller pledged that the locomotive would be able to draw three times its own weight at a minimum speed of ten miles per hour.

"What a Bold Conception!"

With an eye to the prospects of providing new outlets for shipments from the interior, Miller named his locomotive the Best Friend of Charleston. It was hoped the new marvel would halt the slow decline of shipping from Charleston's port and enable the city to keep pace with Savannah, whose growth was based on cheap, easy barge traffic on the Savannah River.

Miller had the tiny locomotive shipped to Charleston, where it arrived in October. Earlier experimental runs over the newly laid tracks already had Charlestonians in a state of excitement. The first spectacle was provided by a sail-powered car, "high sport" enjoyed by fifteen passengers until a gust took mast, sail, rigging, and several crewmen overboard. The next novel experiment, a car known rather grandly as the Flying Dutchman, was powered by a horse walking on a treadmill. The company then unveiled the Pioneer, billed as a "pleasure car" for twenty passengers and standing room for as many more. Though the loaded car weighed some twenty-five hundred pounds, two Negro men propelled it along at speeds of from six to ten miles per hour.

It was the Christmas Day run of 1830, when the road began a daily published schedule between Line Street and a point six miles distant, that America's first regular steam railway service began. The locomotive was piloted by Nicholas Darrell, who thus became the nation's first steam locomotive engineer. The company's schedule was maintained despite numerous handicaps. Most serious of these was the refusal of the city of Charleston to permit locomotives within the city limits—or to allow tracks to be extended from the terminal to wharves and docks.

Original schedules were limited to daylight trips, but Chief Engineer Allen found that accidents and delays made night operations desirable, and he began a search for some means of illuminating the path of the engine. His simple and somewhat unsatisfactory solution produced the first "headlight" in history: Allen merely attached a small flatcar ahead of the engine, covered it with a thick layer of sand, and built there a bonfire of pine knots.

Allen became a fertile source of innovations that were to make the South Carolina road a model for the infant industry. He built his line on stilts, supporting the tracks with pilings. His strap-iron tracks, fastened on timbers nine inches square and fifteen to twenty feet long, were laid on a gauge of five feet, at least three inches wider than any rails then in use. This was America's first five-foot gauge. Allen's plans for the longest railroad of the day set

"What a Bold Conception!"

a pattern for later southern roads and influenced others throughout the world.

The route was surveyed from Charleston to Hamburg, South Carolina, on the Savannah River opposite Augusta, Georgia, in hope of diverting river traffic to Charleston. Landowners along the route donated or sold right of way. When completed, some ninety-seven miles of the line rested on pilings, thirty-three miles on sills, and five miles on trestles or bridges.

The progress of the road was spectacular, and its pioneer leaders established many "firsts." On the first anniversary of commencement of construction—15 January 1831—the railroad celebrated by running an excursion train from the Charleston terminal to the end of the track and back. Among the party of some two hundred guests was a detachment of United States troops with a small cannon—the first military body to travel on an American railroad. Later, during the Creek and Seminole Wars, the railroad was to carry soldiers to the troubled frontier. The military potential of railroads thus became apparent to management and to the federal government, a factor that was to enhance appeals for future subsidies and land grants for American railways. The SCC&RRC was also the first to use chemicals to prolong the useful life of crossties, by treating timbers with turpentine. Later, in 1838, the road became the first in America to use the Kyanizing process of preserving wood, a method developed by Dr. John M. Kyan of England. By August 1831, tracks reached Summerville, South Carolina, twenty miles from Charleston, and the company built a station, laid out streets, and became the first American railroad to promote a townsite. In November the line became the first to carry U.S. Mail. Somewhat later an inadvertent "first" was recorded when some unknown scofflaw fired on a South Carolina train, putting a rifle slug through the hat of a Mr. Sears of Baltimore. *Leslie's Weekly* declared, "Such uncouth practices should be abated."

But 1831 was also a time of tragedy and trial for the South Carolina enterprise. President William Aiken was killed in a carriage accident and was succeeded by Elias Horry, an energetic Charleston businessman who guided the railroad to completion. Soon after Aiken's death, the Best Friend of Charleston was put out of service by an explosion—when the fireman tied down the safety valve and sat on it in order to silence the sound of escaping steam. The engine blew up, fatally injuring the fireman and scalding the

"What a Bold Conception!"

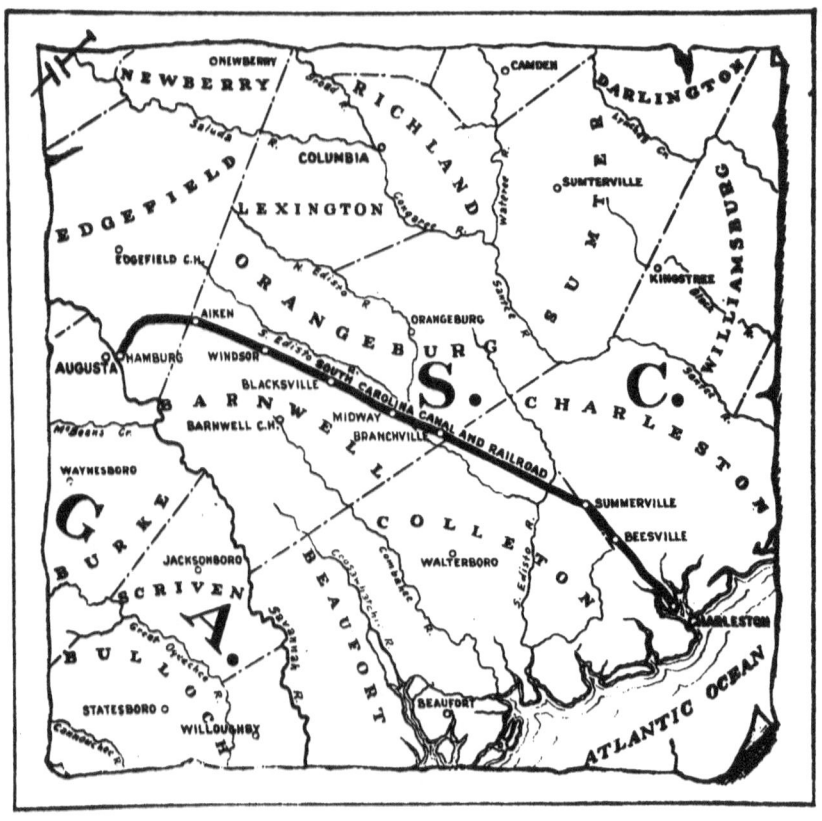

Map 1. *South Carolina Canal and Railroad*

"What a Bold Conception!"

engineer. After renovation, the locomotive returned to the tracks and served several more years, bearing a new name, the Phoenix. Tracks were pushed ahead rapidly and by October 1833, some forty-five months after the first pile was driven at Charleston, the last rail was laid at Hamburg, completing the world's longest railroad and the first in America of more than one hundred miles in length.

The event was celebrated in Charleston and a few villages along the route with parades, barbecues, and speechmaking, and the completion of the line was hailed by newspapers in the North, and even in Europe, as a milestone in transportation history. Patrons were quick to appreciate the advantages of railroad travel, which reduced journeys of several days of uncomfortable jolting to brief, smooth passages of a few hours. One Charleston woman wrote of her journey during the early days of the line, "We not only had no accident, but no tendency to one in our 136-mile flight between sunrise and sunset; and it was like magic to be seated with a dear circle of friends in Augusta, sipping a quiet cup of tea at twilight."

Hamburg bustled with activity as some farmers who had been shipping their cotton to Augusta shifted to the railhead across the river. The new line sought to attract them with reasonable rates. Passenger rates of five cents per mile were less than half those charged on stage coaches and the authorized freight rate of thirty-five cents per hundredweight was about one-third of prevailing wagon rates.

As was usual in the South in that period, the line had been laid and was maintained by black laborers. Most of these were slaves owned by planters living along the route; the railroad owned only sixteen slaves and preferred to hire its workmen—at the rate of $8 to $12 per month and keep.

In its first flush of prosperity the road invested heavily in new equipment. The E. L. Miller, probably the first American locomotive to be named for a person, went into service in 1834. The company purchased forty-one new locomotives during the 1830s at an average cost of $6,500. Six of these were built in Charleston, twenty-five by northern manufacturers, and ten were imported from England. The railroad's progress remained limited, however, chiefly because of regional competition and local jealousies. The city of Charleston continued to bar locomotives from the city limits and refused to allow tracks to be built to its docks (it was only in the 1880s that trains reached the Charleston waterfront). The

"What a Bold Conception!"

city of Augusta was equally uncooperative, refusing to permit a railroad bridge over the Savannah to connect the South Carolina line with the Georgia Railroad, then being built westward from Augusta. In both cases municipal resistance to railroads was inspired by local draying, hacking, and hotel operators. The South Carolina line suffered serious losses of traffic as a result, since river traffic to Savannah was much cheaper than ferrying the river to Hamburg, shipping to Charleston, and then unloading cars and draying goods to the docks. Still, the line prospered and became a model for others in the region.

In 1834 President Horry was succeeded by John Ravenel, a Charlestonian whose improvements in the railroad included the elimination of stilted sections by the use of fills and embankments. Ravenel also placed the company upon a firmer financial basis. The energetic new president was to become known as the father of the North Eastern Railroad, which forms the modern main-line link of the Seaboard Coast Line between Charleston and Florence, South Carolina. After three years Ravenel was succeeded as president by Tristram Tupper, a Charleston merchant who had served as a director since the formation of the SCC&RRC. A native of Maine, Tupper was the last president of the company. He served until 1843, when the road was merged with the Louisville, Cincinnati & Charleston Railroad to form the South Carolina Railroad. This consolidated road was to merge into the South Carolina & Georgia Railroad in 1894, and five years later, on 29 April 1899, was to join the Southern Railway System, bringing to the emerging regional giant a rich heritage of railroad tradition that had begun with the Best Friend of Charleston.

The South Carolina line, popularly known as the Charleston & Hamburg, not only served as an inspiration to visionaries in other states. It became a working laboratory where innovation in equipment and service was tested in daily operations on a basis of trial and error. Officials of the line also looked far beyond their own neighborhood, since it was clear that it was possible to build railroad lines almost anywhere, and that vast American regions might be linked by ever-swifter and more efficient trains. The company's leaders were especially drawn by prospects of building a line to the west, hoping to tap the resources of the rich new areas now being settled by migrants from the eastern states and Europe. The growing production of grain, livestock and animal products in the newly settled region foreshadowed the develop-

"What a Bold Conception!"

ment of major trading centers and drew the attention of the ambitious planners in Charleston.

By 1831, when his line was only a year old, Chief Engineer Horatio Allen told a railroad convention in Virginia that the South Carolina road was definitely interested in a line to the north and west. In the following year a convention was held in Asheville, North Carolina, to promote interest in a new western railroad along the French Broad River, following an ancient Indian pathway through the mountains.

Committees from Tennessee and the Carolinas began studying the possibilities, basing much of their work upon an investigation and report by President Horry of the South Carolina line. A few leading western businessmen and political leaders then proposed a line between Charleston and Cincinnati, a challenging prospect whose benefits were championed by two U.S. senators, Gen. William Henry ("Old Tippecanoe") Harrison of Indiana and his friend Robert Y. Hayne of South Carolina. These were joined by a distinguished group of "founding fathers": John C. Calhoun, the South's leading statesman; Joel R. Poinsett, diplomat, botanist, and world traveler; Christopher G. Memminger, a future treasurer of the Confederate States of America; and Col. James Gadsden, who was to become U.S. minister to Mexico and negotiator of the Gadsden Purchase, which added vast southwestern lands to the United States.

Not only would the new railroad proposed by these men be four times the length of the South Carolina line, but it would have to cross forbidding mountain terrain and would involve vast investments in heavy bridges and tunnels. To further the effort, the president of the United States appointed Col. Stephen H. Long, a leading engineer-explorer, to survey a route from Columbia, South Carolina (the terminus of a proposed branch of the South Carolina line), to the confluence of the Tennessee and Nolichucky rivers in East Tennessee.

Enthusiasm in Charleston was so great that the Chamber of Commerce named a Committee of Fifteen to organize a new company to build the railroad. The Charleston *Courier* declared in October 1835, "What a bold conception! What a magnificent project. There is inspiration in the very thought—inspiration ... to surmount every obstacle, and achieve the great, the auspicious, the glorious consummation."

The promoters were never to realize their dream despite strong

"What a Bold Conception!"

support from many sources. The South Carolina legislature granted a charter to the Cincinnati & Charleston Railroad in December 1835, with unlimited authority to build needed branches. The Tennessee and North Carolina legislatures also granted charters, but Kentuckians, anxious for the future of their own river ports in rivalry with Cincinnati, insisted upon changes in the plan: There must be branches to Louisville and Maysville, Kentucky; the line must be called the Louisville, Cincinnati & Charleston; and six, rather than three, Kentuckians must be named to the Board of Directors. The other states bowed to these demands and a regional effort was launched to create the east-west line linking the Atlantic with the Mississippi.

Many prominent southerners joined the effort, rallies were held, stock was sold, and the state of South Carolina offered a provisional loan of $1 million. General Hayne, who was elected president of the road, had several routes surveyed, including lines along the French Broad and through the Rabun and Cumberland gaps. This only stirred controversy. John C. Calhoun insisted upon a more southerly route through Augusta and Athens, Georgia, or through Abbeville and Anderson, South Carolina, thence through northern Georgia into the valley of the Tennessee west of Muscle Shoals, with a goal of reaching Memphis and the Mississippi. As leaders of South Carolina opinion, both Hayne and Calhoun grasped the enormous social, political, and economic implications of the route's location.

This controversy raged for years, even after the death of Hayne in 1839. Calhoun went so far as to finance a survey of his route and to walk the rough country as a rodman. Calhoun's eloquence won influential friends for his proposal, but all efforts were to end in frustration. By the following year, in fact, work was begun on a line from Columbia to Branchville, South Carolina, on the original Charleston-Hamburg line. But the unexpected deaths of Hayne and Colonel Blanding, president of the railroad's banking arm, blighted prospects in 1839, and hopes of a passage through the mountains began to fade.

But in June 1842 the first train ran into Columbia, setting off lively celebrations in Piedmont South Carolina and prompting demands for rail service into several growing cities of the region.

It was to be fifteen years before South Carolina's dream came to pass, and rails finally linked the Atlantic and the Mississippi from Charleston to Memphis. And South Carolinians were to wait almost sixty years to see a unified rail route from Charleston to

"What a Bold Conception!"

Cincinnati become a reality—when the South Carolina and Georgia Railroad became part of the Southern Railway System.

But by 1842 the American railroad era had definitely begun. Lines in other regions had expanded rapidly, and by the end of this year more than 4,000 miles of track had been laid in the United States, of which almost one-fourth—965 miles—was in the ten southern states in which Southern Railway was to operate. Tracks now extended from Fredericksburg, Virginia, via Richmond and Petersburg, to Wilmington, North Carolina. North of Richmond a line reached Gordonsville, and from Norfolk, Virginia, another ran to Weldon, North Carolina. Scattered through Kentucky, Mississippi, Alabama, and Louisiana were a few short, disconnected lines of iron-capped wooden rails on which passengers were pulled by horse- and mule-power.

Though these western beginnings held great promise for promoters of the proposed Charleston-Mississippi routes, developments in Georgia were of more immediate importance. In December 1833, only three months after completion of the Charleston-Hamburg line, the state of Georgia had chartered three railroads in a single week—and by the close of 1842 the 104-mile Georgia Railroad line reached from Augusta to Madison and was moving toward White Hall, the future Atlanta, where it would connect with the state-owned Western & Atlantic, then building toward Chattanooga. These two roads, though they were natural extensions of the South Carolina road leading westward, would not be connected with the pioneer line until 1853 when the city of Augusta relented and permitted the bridging of the Savannah River for railroad use. Elsewhere in Georgia the Central Railroad & Banking Company built a line toward Macon—and the Monroe Railroad was building from Macon toward White Hall.

Meanwhile, up-country South Carolinians began expanding their own infant network of lines. The Greenville & Columbia Railroad Company, chartered in 1845, was inspired by one of the most remarkable of the early entrepreneurs—Joel R. Poinsett, a South Carolinian who had served as U.S. minister to Mexico (and brought home the lovely plant that was to bear his name—Poinsettia), President Madison's special envoy to South America, and secretary of war in the Van Buren administration. A man of parts, Poinsett had also been founder and first president of the National Institute for the Promotion of Science, which evolved into the Smithsonian Institution.

With the failure of promoters to extend the early railroad north-

"What a Bold Conception!"

ward from Columbia, Poinsett turned to the building of the Greenville & Columbia. Under the presidency of Judge John O'Neall of Newberry and the direction of Col. William Brown as engineer, the line reached the Broad River at Alston in 1850, and after the opening of a large, expensive bridge there, went into Newberry in 1851. A flash flood in 1852 washed out bridges and trestles, however, and claimed the life of Colonel Brown, who drowned in the Broad while trying to reach Columbia. Rebuilding the long wooden structure of the bridge was a major trial to Brown's successor: laborers caught "swamp sickness" and fled, and a new crew demanded to be returned to Columbia each night by rail; a stonework contractor was dismissed; and it was December 1853 before the tracks reached Greenville, an occasion celebrated as "the greatest day in the history of the 'Uplands.' " At last, the rich agricultural lands of the South Carolina Piedmont were linked with tidewater, and commerce from Charleston flowed into the back country.

Branches of the Columbia-Greenville line were built from Hodges to Abbeville and from Belton to Anderson. The 164-mile road was then complete, at a cost of $12,200 per mile. President O'Neall noted with pride that many single-track railroads had cost four or five times as much.

Two other antebellum lines were closely associated with the Greenville & Columbia: the thirty-four-mile Blue Ridge Railroad, between Anderson and Walhalla; and the thirty-mile Laurens Railway, between Newberry and Laurensville. The Blue Ridge line, proposed in 1836 by John C. Calhoun and a few associates as an alternative route to the West, was chartered only in 1852, after an extended political battle. The line was planned to serve as South Carolina's link in a chain of railroads extending from Anderson, South Carolina, across the northeastern tip of Georgia, thence across western North Carolina to connect with the Knoxville-Charleston route, then under construction. It was 1859 before the little Blue Ridge reached Walhalla, in the rugged foothill country, and it was here that Calhoun's project foundered.

Crews of workmen labored for six years, with much loss of life and expenditure of almost $1 million, in an effort to bore a one and a half mile tunnel through the solid stone of Stump House Mountain. This, the most ambitious railroad project undertaken in the South in that era, was abandoned with the coming of the Civil War. The unfinished tunnel was to stand for many years as "a costly memorial to South Carolina's early progressive spirit." Pri-

"What a Bold Conception!"

vate investors and the state of South Carolina poured $2.5 million into the thirty-four-mile line (an average cost of $73,500 per mile—one of the most costly lines built in the region).

The Laurens Railway, chartered in 1847 and completed seven years later, provided a connection between Laurens and the Greenville & Columbia, and was to operate as a branch of the larger line until the Civil War, when it was dismantled by the Confederate government, and its rails were used on more important links in the Southern rail network.

Intimately associated with South Carolina's rail development, and largely dependent upon it, Georgia's early lines were built more slowly. By 1845 Atlanta existed only as a remote railroad station, which the Georgia Railroad line from Augusta had reached with its first locomotive drawn by oxen, an ignominious beginning for the future rail center of the Southeast. The Georgia Railroad was for years only an extension of the South Carolina line ending at Hamburg, but grander plans were afoot.

One of the engineers surveying for this line was young Lemuel P. Grant, a native of Maine. As "the father of Atlanta," Grant was to play a leading role in the building of the city, and in the history of Southern Railway. Grant and his friend Jonathan Norcross, a Maine lumberman, became the first promoters of the great city Atlanta was to become. Norcross had set up a trading post at Five Points, now the heart of modern Atlanta's business district, where he operated the region's first sawmill. Norcross became mayor when Atlanta was incorporated in 1850. With Grant, he began to dream of a railroad which would take advantage of the city's strategic location: it lay on the most direct route between Washington and New Orleans, just at the point where it was intersected by the much-discussed Thirty-second Parallel Route to the Pacific. When the Richmond & Danville and the North Carolina railroads were building in states to the north, the Atlanta promoters realized that an unbroken line of rails would soon connect northern cities with the South, on a line that approached within 260 miles of Atlanta. To the south, other lines already linked Atlanta with Montgomery, Alabama, with plans for an extension to New Orleans.

Norcross and Grant and a few associates acted to close the gap in these railroads in the winter of 1855–56, by organizing the Georgia Air Line Railroad Company. Norcross was named president and began the task of raising funds for an expensive line through north Georgia into Chester, South Carolina, and a link

"What a Bold Conception!"

with the Charlotte & South Carolina line. But, as was the case in most Southern states where development was late, economic depression and the approach of the Civil War doomed the effort. As the war approached, north-south passengers and freight still had to make a roundabout approach to Atlanta from North Carolina.

Other Georgia projects met similar fates. The Georgia & Western, chartered in 1854 to run from Atlanta to Carroll and a connection with other roads to Jackson and Tuscaloosa, Alabama, expired in 1860 without a foot of track having been laid.

The Southern Railway's modern line from Atlanta to Brunswick was the brainchild of Congressman Thomas Butler King, a wealthy planter and entrepreneur who lived at Retreat Plantation on St. Simons Island. King and his wife entertained many eminent visitors, including Thackeray, Audubon, and Fanny Kemble—and he also entertained visions of expansive railroad development. In 1835 King organized the Great Western Railroad, to run from Brunswick on the coast to Macon, with branches to Columbus and to the Tennessee or Alabama line in the northwest corner of the state, "in Cherokee country." King made his enthusiastic beginning when there was not a piece of track in Georgia, but his political career caused continual delays to his rail project, and when he left Congress in 1850 to become collector of the Port of San Francisco and continue his brilliant social life, the charter of his line was allowed to expire.

King's idea was revived in 1857 as the Macon & Brunswick Railroad, with Judge A. E. Cochran of Brunswick as first president. The little line was disrupted by Georgia's secession in 1861 and was fated to struggle through the war as a short line in constant danger of being dismantled.

In the vast region of South Carolina and Georgia the oft-projected network of rails remained in embryo.

NINE

FFVs and Tar Heels Take to the Rails

South Carolinians were not alone in their enthusiasm for railroads. Infant rail projects sprang up in almost every state east of the Alleghenies. In fact, Virginia's first railroad was operating by 1831, when the Best Friend of Charleston was in its first year of operation. The Virginia entry, a puny twelve-mile line serving some coal mines, operating by a combination of gravity and mulepower, was also destined to become part of the Southern Railway System.

The little Chesterfield Railroad, chartered in 1828, ran downhill from coal pits at Midlothian, Virginia, to the south bank of the James River opposite Richmond. Nicholas Mills, a Richmond businessman, had joined a few mine owners to build the Chesterfield line. Mills used ordinary farm wagons to cruise over the route, riding on iron-capped wooden rails. To celebrate completion of his railroad, Mills took a group of his friends for an inaugural ride. The wagons were pulled from the river to the coal pits by two-mule teams, and for the return journey, the mules were loaded on a flat car, and the train coasted down the long slope to Richmond.

The Chesterfield road, built with an investment of $150,000, was profitable to its owners, and the cost of moving coal over the route dropped from about ten cents per bushel to three cents. The success of the tiny road inspired interest in more ambitious projects in Virginia, and may have proved the undoing of the Chesterfield.

In 1838, Whitmell P. Tunstall, a young legislator from Danville, Virginia, proposed the building of a railroad from Richmond to Danville. Tunstall foresaw the opening of a new era for Virginia. His eloquent plea rang through the historic hall in which the voices of Jefferson, Madison, Henry, and Monroe had echoed before him: "Mr. Speaker, let us bring all the resources of our State to bear... penetrate every valley... draw by every artery... to our own seaport those great internal resources which lie dormant from our apathy, but which are the life-blood of our existence ... with the greatest water power on earth and minerals to an extent unequalled ... iron, coal, gypsum and salt, we require others to

FFVs and Tar Heels Take to the Rails

furnish us that with which we should supply the world.... We pay others the immense profits of importation and transportation when we have a harbor at our own threshold upon whose capacious bosom a thousand ships can ride together in safety."

The House was not impressed. Newspapers branded Tunstall's scheme as impractical and "chimerical," and the state's energies were turned instead to a project for improving the James River for navigation. Tunstall persisted for years, making speeches and personal pleas until at last, in March 1847, with the aid of a few influential friends, he won a charter for the Richmond & Danville (R&D) Rail-Road Company. Tunstall resigned from the legislature to become president of the railroad and stumped the state to sell the necessary stock. By the end of the year the Richmond & Danville had qualified for a state loan. Tunstall began construction in the summer of 1848 at Manchester, on the bank of the James opposite Richmond.

Tunstall pushed his rails westward, resisting pressures to connect with towns off his route, such as Nottoway and Petersburg, following "the most direct line." On 4 July 1850, a day of celebration in Richmond, the R&D's first locomotive appeared, the Roanoke, a gleaming new $8,000 American type that weighed 37,600 pounds. Three other locomotives followed during the year, two of which were built by Richmond's Tredegar Iron Works.

The railroad opened a bridge over the James before the end of 1850, and on Christmas Day regular train service opened between Richmond and Midlothian. The old Chesterfield line, now abandoned, retired its mules and sold part of its tracks to the R&D.

Tunstall's road flourished. The tracks pushed westward to cross the Appomattox River, through Jetersville, and in May 1852 made a junction with the new Southside Railroad at Burkeville, creating the most important station between Richmond and Danville. The R&D entered an agreement with the Southside to interchange freight cars and establish joint rates on through traffic—perhaps the first such arrangements of their kind in American railroading.

However, after laying rails about halfway to Danville, the R&D fell upon hard times. Financial and engineering problems and the death of Tunstall rocked the railroad. Tunstall had ordered some six hundred tons of expensive new "U" rail to supplant the thin strap iron then in use, but the ship carrying the rail from England was lost at sea, and Tunstall's successors were further delayed.

Vincent Witcher, an energetic director, assumed Tunstall's role as the driving genius of the R&D; new rails arrived late in 1854,

FFVs and Tar Heels Take to the Rails

and with completion of a long, tall bridge over the Dan River, the line was completed into Danville.

By the end of the year the presidency of the line passed to Lewis E. Harvie, a capable businessman who guided the R&D for ten years, during which the road was linked with a great network of railroads in the upper and middle South, foreshadowing the creation of the Southern Railway little more than a generation later. Harvie spoke prophetically to stockholders in 1857:

"Already our road is a link in a great chain of railroads from Richmond to Memphis. It has but begun to develop the resources of the country through which it now runs. True, the land upon its borders has doubled, if not quadrupled, in value ... has swelled our profits and liberalized our views; has broken down the jealousy between town and country.... it will ... be an artery in the grand system of American roads, pouring ... life-blood into the bosom of our beloved state."

Harvie's dream was delayed, for the outbreak of the Civil War brought construction plans to an end. At its completion in 1856, the R&D represented an investment of $3.5 million, of which nearly $2 million had been raised from stockholders. Both men and women attended stockholders' meetings, which were sometimes lively affairs. One session was held in a Presbyterian church where, to the dismay of the men and the delight of the women, cuspidors were banned. The men evened the score by holding a later meeting in Richmond's Old Ballard Saloon; the ladies boycotted that one and forced President Harvie to compromise by meeting in Odd Fellows or Metropolitan Halls, with cuspidors present, but no whiskey allowed.

The first phase of the R&D's history was to end with the coming of the war, but in the years before the conflict, the far-sighted President Harvie joined with North Carolina's ex-Governor John M. Morehead to plan a north-south link, between Danville and Greensboro, North Carolina, with the new North Carolina Railroad (NCRR). This plan outraged some North Carolinians, who forced through their legislature a charter provision barring "The Danville Connection" from approaching within twenty miles of the NCRR's tracks. The potential blessings of a South-wide network had not become obvious to all.

Other railroad projects were launched by Virginia's pioneer builders, all fated to be halted in their growth and seriously damaged during the Civil War. Several of these survived to become components of the Southern.

FFVs and Tar Heels Take to the Rails

In 1832, perhaps inspired by the efforts of mulemaster Nicholas Mills, Virginia's general assembly chartered the Richmond & York River Railroad, to link the capital with the Chesapeake Bay steamer traffic. Public apathy delayed the project for about twenty years, but in 1853 the company was beginning to build its line from Richmond to the village of West Point, at the head of navigation on the York. By 1859 a locomotive was in service from Richmond to White House, twenty-four miles distant, and it was March 1861 before service to West Point began. The Confederate government was already meeting in Montgomery, Alabama, when the first trains made connections with the line's steamer, *West Point*, which operated to Baltimore.

Similar enterprises in northern Virginia met the fate of the Richmond & York, but only after some remarkable developments during their early years. On 4 July 1832 the aged Revolutionary War hero Charles Carroll of Carrollton turned the first sod for the B&O in Baltimore, and on the same day President John Quincy Adams broke ground for the Chesapeake & Ohio Canal—events that set off a scramble for rail routes in the Virginia region near the District of Columbia. The B&O, under aggressive leadership, reached Harpers Ferry, Virginia, in 1834 and opened a branch to Winchester two years later, to tap the brisk trade of the Shenandoah Valley.

These moves set off a civic explosion in the small town of Alexandria, which was then a part of the District of Columbia. Fearful that the B&O would cut off their lucrative wagon trade with the Shenandoah, Alexandria merchants promoted a legal secession ("retrocession," it was called) from the District to enable the town to build a rail line of its own. With the approval of Congress and President James K. Polk, Alexandria was returned to Virginia in September 1846, and a railroad from the town to Harpers Ferry was soon chartered. But early enthusiasm languished once more, and it was 1858 before trains of the Loudoun & Hampshire Railroad reached Leesburg, which was to remain the western terminus until after the war.

Elsewhere in northern Virginia the Orange & Alexandria (O&A) and the Manassas Gap railroads began operating in 1851 and 1852, adding further links to the South-wide network of the future. By now two other lines had appeared in central Virginia: the Richmond, Fredericksburg & Potomac, operating between Richmond and Fredericksburg, and the Louisa Railroad (later to be-

FFVs and Tar Heels Take to the Rails

come the Virginia Central), running from Louisa Courthouse to Taylorsville (now Doswell).

The first locomotive to turn a wheel in northern Virginia, the Orange, an engine built by the Smith Machine Shop of Alexandria, made its first brief run in May 1851. By October the line reached from Alexandria to Tudor Hall, some twenty-eight miles, ready to form a junction with the Manassas Gap, then under construction. At this point George H. Smoot, the O&A's first president, resigned, and was succeeded by thirty-two-year-old John S. Barbour of Culpeper, who was to be a major figure in Virginia railroading for thirty-five years. Barbour drove the line rapidly southward, reaching Culpeper Courthouse in October 1852. One of the first runs was by an excursion train bearing President Franklin Pierce, the Russian ambassador, John Barbour, and other dignitaries. This was the first known trip of a United States president over rails that were to become part of the Southern Railway.

In March 1854 the road reached Gordonsville to connect with the Virginia Central, which ran from Richmond—and for the next sixteen years, the O&A and the Central formed the only rail route between Richmond and Alexandria.

Barbour offered a variety of services from junction points: a train from Manassas to Strasburg; to Richmond, Charlottesville, and Staunton from Gordonsville—and stagecoach service to Lynchburg from Charlottesville three days a week. When the Potomac froze over in the era's bitter winters, Barbour advertised "No Detention from Ice" and offered Washington passengers an omnibus across the Long Bridge to Alexandria, if they were ready for departure at 6:30 A.M., with the arrival of a train from Baltimore. In the winter of 1855–56 thick ice on the Potomac supported a sixteen-hundred-pound stagecoach, which Barbour had pulled across on a horse-drawn sled.

Barbour also opened an extension from Charlottesville to Lynchburg to connect with the Virginia & Tennessee Railroad to Bristol, and the Southside Railroad, which ran to Petersburg and Norfolk. Work was delayed by the panic of 1857, and it was not until January 1860 that the last spike was driven in Lynchburg, an event of some significance, since this completed the Virginia end of the "Great Southern & Southwestern Mail Route," which passed through Bristol, Knoxville, and Chattanooga en route to New Orleans. The final incomplete section, an eighty-seven-mile gap between Coffeeville and Durant, Mississippi, on the Mississippi

FFVs and Tar Heels Take to the Rails

Central, was closed in the first days of 1860, and then, for the first time, passengers or freight could move by rail from Bangor, Maine, to New Orleans (except for short ferry transfers at New York, Havre de Grace, Maryland, and over the Potomac at Washington).

The O&A, an important link in this chain, had grown under Barbour's leadership from a ninety-seven-mile line capitalized at $457,000 to a 168-mile line with capital of $7.18 million, only five years later. The road's main line became a major traffic artery to the South and was to acquire additional connections in Virginia.

The Manassas Gap, though it served a limited territory, merely linking the Shenandoah Valley and upper Fauquier County to the O&A, had a colorful early history and was to become famous in the campaigns of the Civil War. This little railroad owed its existence to the vision of John Marshall, an early chief justice of the U.S. Supreme Court. When Marshall's son Edward Carrington Marshall was campaigning for the Virginia legislature, the father advised him, "My son, the most pressing problem before Virginia today is that of developing her transportation facilities." That admonition became the theme of Edward Marshall's legislative career and later the "ruling passion" of his life. As a founder of a turnpike company through Manassas Gap, he soon realized that more wagon roads could not fulfill Virginia's need, and he formed a railroad company. After the O&A was chartered, young Marshall planned to link the Shenandoah and his home county with Barbour's larger railroad.

Marshall's charter, granted in 1850, authorized a line to reach from Bull Run through Manassas Gap in the Blue Ridge foothills, thence to Strasburg and Harrisonburg in the Shenandoah. Marshall's prominence and legislative experience attracted investors, and public meetings in the area produced numerous stockholders. Among these was Robert E. DeButts of Fauquier County, whose grandson, Harry A. DeButts, was to become a president of Southern Railway some 102 years later. Success was assured once the state of Virginia pledged to take two-fifths of the stock.

The Manassas Gap bought "T" rail from Welsh iron mills, and in November 1851 work was begun at Tudor Hall on the O&A line, a point to be known thereafter as Manassas Junction. The road ran to Markham on the eastern slope of the Blue Ridge, which remained the western terminus for a year, while crews and engineers toiled their way up heavy grades. At Linden Station, on the crest of the Blue Ridge, workmen removed many tons of earth and

FFVs and Tar Heels Take to the Rails

stone, using the most elementary tools—hand shovels, crowbars, and hand drills. Accidents, sickness, and strikes impeded progress, and in 1853, during the excavation of Summit Cut, rioting crews left the job, prowling and marauding through the countryside, terrifying the mountain communities. Order was restored by a small company of armed horsemen led by young Turner Ashby, a merchant in the village of Rosebank, who guided his Mountain Rangers on patrol for a few days and nights until troublemakers were cleared out. Many rioters failed to return, and those on the job worked under armed guard for several weeks.

The entry of the Manassas Gap line into Strasburg in 1854 moved the sentimental President Marshall to report: "The iron horse of Manassa this day takes its first drink of limestone water." Though Marshall hoped to carry the road on to Harrisonburg, he was handicapped by a prolonged economic depression, and it was March 1859 before the rails reached the settlement of Mount Jackson, short of his goal, but the road's terminus until after the Civil War. Marshall also began building a line from Gainesville toward Fairfax Courthouse, but the depression of 1857 halted work after crews had built up several miles of embankments. The road remained unfinished.

North Carolina was probably the first southern state to hear the call of the railroad age—and one of the last to heed it. As early as 1822 the prophetic Dr. Joseph Caldwell, president of the University of North Carolina, proclaimed the benefits to be had from a rail line linking the port of Beaufort with Asheville in the mountains.

With the aid of Judge Archibald DeBow Murphey, a leading Tar Heel historian, Dr. Caldwell campaigned for a system of canals and improved waterways to reach every part of the state, to be supplemented by railroad lines. Before his death in 1832, Judge Murphey had passed his enthusiasm to a young law student in his office—John Motley Morehead. For the rest of his active life Morehead was to campaign for railroads as a means of overcoming North Carolina's isolation. Soon after he became governor of the state in 1841, Morehead urged the legislature to approve a large network of railroads, canals, and turnpikes, and took up the railroad cause when he left office in 1845.

While he and his colleagues were stumping the state to fan public interest in their railroad projects and other public improvements of "The North Carolina Plan," two distinguished Americans

FFVs and Tar Heels Take to the Rails

visited the state and helped to shock lethargic legislators into action. Senator Stephen A. Douglas of Illinois, one of the most celebrated orators of the day, came on a romantic mission, to court a young woman who lived in Rockingham County. And Dorothea Dix, a well-known reformer, came to promote the establishment of hospitals for the mentally ill. These two visitors found travel over North Carolina roads so trying that they appeared voluntarily before the legislature to brand "the worst-roads state" as a trial to all travelers. Both Douglas and Dix urged building of railroads as an antidote to the isolation and backwardness that gripped the state in that era. By 1849 these combined efforts yielded results. A bill creating the North Carolina Railroad, to run for 223 miles from Goldsboro in the east to Raleigh, Greensboro, and Charlotte, came before the Assembly, where it was hotly debated.

The climax of Morehead's campaign came in January 1849, when the railroad bill, having passed the House by a narrow margin, came before the Senate for its final reading. Presiding over the Senate was a tall, bony Jacksonian Democrat from Caswell County —Calvin Graves, "The Baptist Enigma," whose party stoutly opposed Morehead's program of public works. The bill came to a final vote before a packed chamber.

Graves called for the question, a clerk called the roll, and a tally clerk announced: "The vote is twenty-two ayes and twenty-two nays, a tie." Graves rose slowly to cast his own vote, the fate of the railroad in his hands. Though his Democratic party had consistently stood against railroads, his constituency favored them. Graves had been given an agonizing choice.

Graves pounded his gavel and called in a clear voice, "The vote on the bill being equal, twenty-two ayes and twenty-two nays, the Chair votes 'Yea.'" The chamber erupted in bedlam. By voting against his party, Graves had committed political suicide. He was never again to hold public office. But his vote in the interest of what he felt was best for his state became a landmark in North Carolina history. A new pattern of development grew in the wake of his courageous stand.

Morehead staged meetings in every county and conventions in several county seats along the proposed route. He made short work of raising the necessary capital. A rousing rally in Greensboro raised $190,000, another in Raleigh, $40,000, and during a convention in Hillsboro in 1850, with only $100,000 to go, Morehead announced that he would join with any nine other men to take $10,000 each in stock. Within a few moments the $1 million

FFVs and Tar Heels Take to the Rails

goal had been reached. Morehead was named president of the road and Major Walter Gwynne, former president and engineer of the Portsmouth & Roanoke Railroad, became chief engineer. Ground was broken in Greensboro in 1851, and Senator Calvin Graves turned the first spadeful of earth.

Construction moved rapidly, thanks to Morehead's shrewd management. He contracted with stockholders who lived along the route to clear and grade the right of way and build bridges, or to furnish timber and crossties. These men were paid in both stock and cash. With hundreds of stockholders on the line at work with their slaves, the work force in July 1852 was 1,828 men and boys, 785 horses and mules, and 44 oxen. By September 1854 the road was open from Charlotte to Concord, a twenty-one-mile stretch; the entire eastern end between Goldsboro and Raleigh opened a month later. Rails reached Salisbury and Durham in January 1855, and the road was completed a year later at a point near Greensboro.

Celebration of the event was postponed until 4 July, when an excursion train ran the length of the road, past local parades, barbecues, band concerts, and balloon ascensions. It was more than seven years since Calvin Graves had cast his costly vote for progress, and now all Tar Heels, Democrat and Whig, could take pride in the accomplishment.

With construction complete, the company located its repair shops and supply facilities in western Alamance County, at a spot named Company Shops; townspeople in nearby Graham refused to allow the line to pass through their village, and an ordinance forbade the rails to pass within a mile of the courthouse. Company Shops, later known as Burlington, served as headquarters for the road for many years.

Morehead resigned as president and director, soon before completion of the line, to promote eastern and western extensions of the road. His successor was Charles F. Fisher of Salisbury, an influential legislator who had worked closely with Morehead to improve public schools and promote a new state constitution. Fisher was to serve as the road's president until the Civil War.

The legislature of 1852 authorized the building of branch lines —the Atlantic & North Carolina from Goldsboro to the port of Beaufort; and the Western North Carolina Railroad from Salisbury to Asheville. The state was to bear two-thirds of the cost of construction. Not unexpectedly, rival interests sought to influence the direction of the route to their advantage, but in the case of the eastern branch, first to begin building, Morehead had fixed opinions of his own. Rather than locating the ocean terminus at Beaufort or New Bern, or the proposed Carolina City near Beaufort, as some groups insisted, Morehead chose Shephard's Point, on the Newport River, just west of Beaufort. His decision may have been influenced by the fact that the Shephard's Point Land Company, which he controlled, owned tracts of land in the vicinity. A new town, Morehead City, began rising there even before construction of the Atlantic & North Carolina Railroad had begun.

The new road, to be known as the Mullet Line because of the fish products it hauled, began building in 1855. Morehead himself was the contractor for the western section and W. R. Stanly, a legislator who had aided in the fight to charter the NCRR, contracted to build the division between New Bern and Kinston. This road was one of the first in the South to import large numbers of laborers from the North—Irish, German, and Scandinavian workmen who worked hard, drank heavily, and were frequently unmanageable. Turnover was so rapid that the railroad refused to pay wages for fewer than six days. Progress over the flat, swampy terrain was rapid despite handicaps, and the line was opened to Goldsboro in 1858. Wharves and warehouses, completed on the eve of the Civil War, made possible special fast service between Goldsboro and the port, connecting with steamships to New York.

The route of the Western North Carolina Railroad, begun in 1855, passed through the village of Asheville (population 500), and was planned to connect with the East Tennessee and Virginia line, then building.

In addition to Governor Morehead, the line's backers included Col. William Holland Thomas, white chief of the Cherokee Indians; Thomas had served in the North Carolina Senate, where he fought for improvement in the mountain region. He was to command the famed Thomas Legion of white and Indian troops for the Confederacy. James C. Turner, the chief engineer, was a veteran who had witnessed the laying of the cornerstone of the B&O Railroad, and had worked as an engineer for that line. On Turner's staff also was an energetic and capable young man—Alexander B. Andrews—who was to become president of the Western North Carolina and later first vice-president of the Southern Railway System.

After ground breaking in Salisbury in 1855, the line moved westward, with stockholders and other contractors doing the grading. A major contractor was Colonel Charles Fisher, president

FFVs and Tar Heels Take to the Rails

of the NCRR, who performed many miles of grading and some of the bridge construction. The panic of 1857 delayed construction, and a year later the line had been laid no farther than Statesville, twenty-five miles away. By 1861 when shortages of rail and approaching war forced abandonment of the work, the road was within two miles of Morganton. Fisher entered the Confederate army and was killed a few months later at the first battle of Manassas, or Bull Run.

Meanwhile, the two connecting railroads had built shops in Salisbury equipped to build and repair cars and locomotives and manufacture switches, frogs, bolts, and other items—a facility that was to prove of great value to the Confederacy. The Western North Carolina's annual report of 1860 carried no hint of the chaotic events ahead, but projected an extension westward that Chief Engineer Turner envisioned as transcontinental: "This is only the commencement of this national highway which presents nearly an air line from Portsmouth, on the Atlantic, to San Diego, on the Pacific. Is it more improbable that this whole line should be completed through to San Diego than that within the last 24 years, the 789 miles now in operation shall have been built?" Turner recalled that he had seen the beginning of the B&O thirty-two years earlier, at a time when there had been only three miles of track in the United States—and that in 1860 some thirty thousand miles of track were in service.

But war overwhelmed the North Carolina lines, as it did almost all others in the South. The Western North Carolina's new president, A. M. Powell, wrote, "This great and important enterprise ... is virtually at a standstill, but it is not crushed or beyond resurrection."

TEN

Westward the Rails

The first railroad west of the Alleghenies was a two-mile line for horse-drawn cars operating between the small town of Tuscumbia in northern Alabama and the nearby Tennessee River—a primitive attempt to bypass the rocky barrier of Muscle Shoals and speed the passage of goods on the major traffic artery of the region. The father of the road was Maj. David Hubbard, a Virginia-born lawyer from Huntsville, Alabama, who was to spend many years in Congress and was to serve the Confederacy as both congressman and commissioner of Indian affairs. The Alabama legislature chartered Hubbard's line in January 1830, the first railroad west of the Atlantic seaboard. By 1832 horses were pulling cars over the route, opening the rail era in the Tennessee Valley. The most notable feature of the line was a wooden truss bridge 274 feet long, whose solid floor was covered with cinders to provide a path for the horses. Despite all handicaps, the little Tuscumbia line made vast improvements in the flow of goods around Muscle Shoals and inspired a kindred effort on a much larger scale.

The forty-three-mile Tuscumbia, Courtland & Decatur Railroad, promoted by Major Hubbard and his friend Benjamin Sherrod, a prominent cotton planter, opened in December 1834 offering the first steam-powered transport in the region. But though several locomotives were in service over the next two or three years, horses were in use until mid-1836. The Tuscumbia, Courtland & Decatur was the nucleus of a great trunk-line railroad that emerged in the 1850s and finally connected the lower Mississippi Valley with the eastern seaboard.

The impetus for this ambitious project came from the city of Memphis in 1831. Though their early efforts came to naught, Isaac Rawlings, Nathaniel Anderson, and the city's first mayor, Marcus B. Winchester, led a movement to build a railroad from Memphis to the Mississippi border near the upper end of Muscle Shoals. The projected line won the attention of the federal government, which surveyed a route through northern Alabama and Mississippi into Memphis "as a measure of national defense" as well as a commercial outlet. Pressure to protect the southwestern

Westward the Rails

frontier from Indians led to surveys and the sale of stock in the line, but the road languished.

In 1835, impatient with delays, a few men in Fayette County, Tennessee, launched the LaGrange & Memphis Railroad, and three years later welcomed the first locomotive to Memphis, a Philadelphia-built engine that had been shipped by sea and then up the Mississippi by steamer. A throng gathered atop the bluff of the river to help pull the huge weight up to the city streets, and followed the flower-bedecked locomotive through town to the music of bands. But enthusiasm waned once more; the railroad built only six miles of track. After ten months of serving pleasure riders, the road fell into disuse—and it was not until 1845 that Memphis awoke to the challenge of the railroad era.

By this year, the United States was served by some forty-six hundred miles of railroad, and steam engines were at work in every state east of the Mississippi—except for Tennessee. Only here was there a gap in the growing South-wide network of rails. Other states began to prosper, while Tennessee lagged behind. A fever of railroad enthusiasm that had swept the country now engulfed Tennessee. Some "visionaries" talked of extending rails to Texas and even to the Pacific Coast. In response, Tennesseans staged a Southern and Southwestern Railroad Convention in Memphis in November 1845. Delegates from fifteen states heard orators extol the glories of railroads.

Out of this convention grew the Memphis & Charleston Railroad, incorporated in Tennessee in 1846, empowered to acquire assets of the defunct LaGrange & Memphis and to build a line eastward to an eventual link with Charleston. The road was launched under leadership of Tennessee's Governor "Jimmy" Jones, a popular spellbinder who had twice defeated the formidable James K. Polk for the governorship. Jones stumped the Tennessee and Mississippi valleys to sell stock in the new road with such success that $170,000 worth of stock was sold after two of his speeches in New Orleans, and a speech before a mass meeting in Charleston resulted in the extension of $250,000 in credits from the city of Charleston. Jones soon entered the U.S. Senate and was succeeded as railroad president by Robert C. Brinkley, an energetic Memphis bank president who visited England to buy rails, and there met George Peabody, a financier who was a partner of the banker Junius S. Morgan.

Peabody extended credit to the Memphis & Charleston, and by June 1853 the road reached LaGrange. After prevailing upon re-

Westward the Rails

luctant Mississippians to permit passage through the northeastern corner of their state, the new line pushed on to the old Tuscumbia, Courtland & Decatur and thence to Stevenson, Alabama, to make a junction with the Nashville & Chattanooga at Huntsville. The junction village became a railroad center within a few months, with the building of engine houses, a turntable, machine shops, and a hotel. Lots were sold to encourage railroad employees and others to settle in the town.

Under the vigorous leadership of Sam Tate, a Memphis merchant, the Memphis & Charleston began to flourish. Tate reported to Governor Andrew Johnson in October 1854 that the road owned six new locomotives, forty-five freight cars, four first-class passenger cars, ten hand cars, and six gravel trucks. He added that the equipment was barely equal to the task of handling traffic.

In 1855 the remaining gap in the Memphis & Charleston lay between Pocahontas, Tennessee, and Tuscumbia, Alabama, a distance of seventy-one miles. This was reduced to thirty-seven miles the next year when rails made a junction with the Mobile & Ohio at Corinth, Mississippi. Track gangs worked feverishly in competition. Through tickets to Augusta and Charleston were already being sold, and Tennessee passengers bridged the dwindling gap by fast stagecoaches. Headlines in the Memphis *Daily Appeal* kept pace with the workmen: "Open to Corinth—staging reduced to 40 miles," and "Open to Burns—staging reduced to 12 miles," and finally, on 1 April 1847, "COMPLETED."

The road was already a success. Cotton carried by the line had jumped from fifty-seven thousand bales in 1854 to nearly one hundred thousand bales two years later. Memphis celebrated 1 May and the following day and the jamboree spread to Atlanta, Macon, Charleston, and Savannah. The next day a crowd gathered in Memphis near the riverbank to watch a ceremonial "Marriage of The Waters," as a barrel of salt water brought from Charleston was sprayed into the Mississippi. Soon after, thousands of people from the region traveled eastward on special trains to a companion celebration in Charleston. The dreams of John C. Calhoun and James Gadsden and their associates had been realized.

Passengers could now travel from Memphis to New York City in seventy-nine hours and forty-five minutes by the "most direct, expeditious and comfortable route" and could reach points in the southern mountains and their "springs and medicinal waters" as well. Transportation sped up all along the route. Mails that had spent weeks in transit by stagecoach and riverboat now arrived overnight. The Memphis & Charleston played a similar role in improving the Great Southern Mail Route, which operated from New York and Philadelphia and Baltimore to Washington, Richmond, Petersburg, Wilmington, Augusta, Columbus, and Montgomery by rail, thence by mail coach to Stockton, Alabama, and from that point to Mobile and New Orleans by steamboat. Sixteen contract carriers handled the mail en route, and transit time ranged from seven to twenty days.

By January 1860 an unbroken rail route from New York to New Orleans was in use, and transit time had been cut to fewer than four days.

Though promoters and businessmen of Memphis and Charleston touted the advantages of linking the two cities by mail, the more important role of the Memphis & Charleston was in linking the eastern and western rail networks in the South. This opened vast new farmlands in western Tennessee, northern Mississippi, and Alabama, and created an effective bypass around Muscle Shoals. Memphis gained an edge over competing river towns and could now tap the trade of the interior as readily as New Orleans could. The creation of a single new railroad served to unify the South economically even as it was moving toward political union and civil war.

Still, the Memphis & Charleston was a rather "primitive affair" in the recollection of C. A. DeSaussure, an early officer of the road: "Its engines—scarcely larger than logging engines—carried not more than five cars. Coaches had link-and-pin couplings, and when the engine made an unusually quick stop, everyone in every coach simultaneously bowed ... obeisance.... When the engine started, the passenger felt that the back of the seat was the only thing that kept him from going heels over head backward. There were only the hand brakes with wheels on platforms. Each brakeman had charge of two or three brakes, and after setting up one, would rush madly through the aisle to reach the wheel on the next car. Experienced mothers learned to know the engineer's whistle to set up the brakes and hurriedly gathered their children from the aisles to keep them from destruction in the wild flight of the brakeman."

Like almost all other early railroads in the South, the Memphis & Charleston was financed by southern capital—from states, cities, counties and individuals. Promoters and officials also adopted

Westward the Rails

important new attitudes; they soon abandoned local interests and pressed for through service, not short-haul traffic. No longer parochial, economic concerns became regional and national.

While Memphis was taking the lead in promoting regional rail development, the mountainous region of east Tennessee lagged far behind, though not for lack of leadership. As early as 1831, when the Virginia legislature had chartered a railroad to link the James River Canal and the headwaters of the Kanawha River to connect Richmond with the Ohio Valley, men in Knoxville, Tennessee, began planning a railroad to serve their region, and in June 1831, "an Association of Gentlemen" was formed to push for a rail line between Knoxville and Lynchburg, Virginia. A journal, *The Rail-Road Advocate*, was published to aid the cause, and in December 1831 the Lynchburg & New River Railroad was chartered by the Tennessee legislature. It was the first granted to a road in east Tennessee, but one destined to fail. The *Advocate*, deploring a lack of vision in the legislatures of Tennessee and Virginia for refusal to lend support, wrote sorrowfully of "our loved but neglected, almost ruined, country," and declared in one of its final issues: "Rail roads are the *only hope* of East Tennessee. With them would be everything the patriot would desire—without them ... a depressed and languishing region—too unpromising to invite capital or enterprise from abroad, or retain that which may grow up in her own bosom."

The *Advocate* could not save the pioneer railroad effort, but its appeal was not forgotten. Three years later, in 1835, leaders in Athens, Knoxville, and other towns of the region met in Philadelphia, Tennessee, and organized the Hiwassee Railroad, an ambitious project that was planned to run for 112 miles through the most forbidding section of the Tennessee Valley. The new line was the first to receive financial aid from the state. Gen. Solomon D. Jacobs, a wealthy Knoxville merchant, was named president, and John C. Trautwine of Pennsylvania, one of the best-known engineers of his day, was named chief engineer.

Construction began near Athens in late 1837, with Kenerly Lonergan in charge. The energetic Lonergan advertised in the Knoxville *Register* in 1838:

WANTED 100 NEGROES
To Work on the Hiwassee Rail Road at 200
Dollars per Year

Westward the Rails

WANTED TO BUY: Fifty HORSES
Sixteen Hands High & Stout in Proportion
ALSO
200 BARRELS OF WHISKEY

Not even these stimulants to the local economy could keep the railroad solvent during the panic of 1837 and the ensuing depression, but though work was suspended, President Jacobs never gave up. To provide cheaper rail he proposed producing his own from ore deposits along the road, but he was halted by a court order challenging the line's right to engage in manufacturing. For several years the line was at a standstill, and its tracks were overgrown. By May 1844 the Hiwassee Railroad appeared to be doomed, as reflected in a report by the Chattanooga *Times:*

TENNESSEE MONEY
Tennessee Banknotes, Par;
Morgan, Allison & Company's Tickets, Par;
All Other Tennessee Tickets, Uncurrent;
Hiwassee Railroad Scrip, Bursted.

The state of Tennessee sued in 1845, seeking to annul the Hiwassee's charter. The road was saved by resolute citizens of McMinn County, who had subscribed for three-quarters of the original stock. Judge T. Nixon Van Dyke, who was elected to succeed General Jacobs, was so persuasive that principal creditors agreed to accept half the amount due them in stock and the other half in state bonds. Within a year Van Dyke reduced the road's debt from $235,000 to $42,000, and public confidence returned.

With the consent of the legislature, Van Dyke and his directors made changes in the Hiwassee charter, changing the name to East Tennessee & Georgia, increasing capital stock, postponing the completion date to 1860, and obtaining consent to make a junction with the Western & Atlantic at Dalton, Georgia. From that point the road began to prosper. Construction began at Dalton in early 1851 and ten months later rails reached Athens. By summer of 1852 trains operated between Dalton and Blairs Ferry on the Tennessee River.

Thomas H. Callaway of Knoxville now took over the presidency. For three years Callaway pushed the rails toward his home town before he retired in favor of Campbell Wallace of Knoxville. Wallace electrified the town in the early days of his regime by announcing that Knoxville would be linked with Atlanta, Augusta, Savannah, and Charleston on 4 July 1855. The first train arrived more than a week early and the town gave itself over to celebration. The Knoxville *Whig* greeted crowds: "On the whole it will be a great day, and all the world, and the rest of mankind, will be here. Come one, come all, and see how we do things in the Queen City of East Tennessee."

As the East Tennessee & Georgia neared completion an equally important project was underway to the east of Knoxville: twin railroads were approaching—the Virginia & Tennessee, building from Lynchburg to Bristol, Virginia, and the East Tennessee & Virginia, building from Bristol to Knoxville. The latter road was the inspiration of Dr. Samuel B. Cunningham, a Jonesboro surgeon of remarkable capacity for leadership. The road was pushed through Greeneville and Jonesboro on a route whose steepest grade was eighty feet to the mile, and whose shortest radius of curvature was thirteen hundred feet.

Cunningham and his associates in Washington County solved the inevitable financial crisis in decisive action. When stock sales lagged and the legislature seemed unlikely to renew the road's charter, thirty citizens of Washington County pooled resources to subscribe for $500,000 in stock, pledging their personal fortunes as collateral, a response that set off a brief boom in stock sales. The state joined the effort with a loan of $8,000 per mile and an extra appropriation of $300,000 for bridging.

The most distinguished of the East Tennessee & Virginia stockholders was Andrew Johnson, seventeenth president of the United States. The native North Carolinian had begun his career as a tailor in Greeneville, Tennessee, and served as the town's mayor when the first railroad promotion began in the region. Johnson was a vigorous supporter of the rail lines as a state legislator in 1830 and as governor during the 1850s. He remained a stockholder of the East Tennessee & Virginia until the 1860s, including the period when he was president of the United States.

The new line began construction at McBee's Ferry on the Tennessee River in March 1851; grading and bridging were complete early in 1855, but the line awaited completion of the East Tennessee & Georgia so that rails could be hauled in. By early 1856 the first passenger train operated over the western portion of the line and the following year, with completion of the Virginia & Tennessee from Lynchburg to Bristol, rails were brought in for the com-

Westward the Rails

pletion of the eastern end of Dr. Cunningham's line. In 1859, when he resigned as president, Dr. Cunningham reported with satisfaction on the ten-year struggle to create the railroad, which had cost $2.5 million, a substantial investment in the new era of progress for east Tennessee.

Except for the tiny road in the north, railroad building in Alabama was to be delayed. The rich frontier, with its "Black Belt" farmlands and huge deposits of coal and other minerals, its two great river systems—the Alabama and the Tennessee—and its outlets to the Gulf of Mexico, all awaited the coming of rails for development. The dream of a north-south rail line to tap Alabama's natural resources actually began in the 1830s, with the formation of the Selma & Tennessee Railroad—the genesis of the Southern Railway line of the future from Selma to Rome and Dalton, Georgia.

James C. Calhoun, nephew of John C. Calhoun, championed this pioneer effort by pushing its charter through the legislature. But though Selma's citizens pledged $500,000 for the project and Senator William Rufus King, Alabama's leading statesman, solicited federal aid, all ended in failure and no track was ever laid. The inevitability of further development had been foreseen during the 1840s when John C. Calhoun, speaking before a railroad convention in Memphis with the aid of a huge map, had pointed to the future site of Birmingham as the spot where trunk lines would meet some day, creating a vital center for a deep-South rail network.

But in 1848, as Alabamians saw their state falling behind its neighbors, the legislature chartered the Alabama & Tennessee Rivers Railroad, to run from Selma through Montevallo, Talledega, and Gadsden to the Tennessee River at Gunter's Landing (now Guntersville). The line was well begun by John W. Lapley, the first president, and Colonel Lewis Troost, his chief engineer, who though forced to buy rails from Wales, produced their own timber with a company sawmill. The road progressed under a succession of presidents until Judge Thomas A. Walker took over for a ten-year period. With the aid of federal land grants and a state loan of $225,000, the line was completed to Talladega, a distance of 110 miles, before the coming of the Civil War.

In 1852 another line had been chartered—the predecessor of the Alabama Great Southern of the future, which was to run diagonally across the state from Chattanooga to Meridian, Mississippi,

Westward the Rails

a distance of some 300 miles. The pioneer line was the Wills Valley Railroad, begun when only two other lines were actually in service in Alabama—the little Tuscumbia, Courtland & Decatur, and the new eighty-eight-mile Montgomery & West Point Railroad in east-central Alabama.

In nearby Louisiana there was only one trunk line when war came: the New Orleans, Jackson & Great Northern, which skirted the western shore of Lake Pontchartrain and ran on to Jackson, Mississippi, with connections to Vicksburg, Meridian, and Memphis. A few minor roads also served the area, among them the Mexican Gulf, which ran for twenty-nine miles around the southern shore of Lake Pontchartrain through the historic plantations of Chalmette and Bienvenue, where Andrew Jackson had conquered the British invaders—and thence to the Gulf. Among the commissioners of this little road was Jacques Toutant de Beauregard, father of the future Confederate general Pierre Gustave Toutant Beauregard.

Another early road was the New Orleans, Opelousas & Great Western, running from Algiers to Brashear; one of its contemporaries was the little Louisiana Southern, which began in 1834 when the United States boasted only six hundred miles of track, and the only line operating in Louisiana ran for four miles from the foot of Elysian Fields Street in New Orleans to Milneburg on Lake Pontchartrain. Despite all these efforts, Louisiana remained isolated from the southern rail network at large; there were no direct lines to Montgomery, Alabama, to the northeast, or to Mobile in the east.

In other areas of the vast territory that was to be served by the Southern Railway System there was little railroad development in the prewar era. In Kentucky, there was one thirteen-mile route from Lexington to Nicholasville, and in Illinois there was the six-mile Pittsburg Railroad & Coal Company, which began in 1837 as the Coal Mine Bluff Railroad—the first line in the Mississippi Valley. This line hauled coal from pits along the river to Illinoistown—later East St. Louis.

Illinois, however, had dreams far grander than those of other states. With young Abraham Lincoln, a representative from Sangamon County, working industriously on the project, the Illinois legislature passed a remarkably ambitious public improvements project in 1837. This called for a network of 1,341 miles of state-owned railroads, lines which would have exceeded in length the total mileage then in existence on the continent—in order to serve a population of fewer than three hundred thousand people. The cost was estimated at $20 million for the project, but the fantastic scheme soon collapsed, leaving the state heavily in debt—and resolved to stay out of the railroad business forever.

Horatio Allen, a young civil engineer, built the South Carolina Canal & Rail Road Company line from Charleston to Hamburg, S.C., and helped steer it toward locomotive power rather than horse power. The SCCRR was Southern Railway's earliest predecessor, opening its first section of track in 1830.

The wood-burning Best Friend of Charleston made the nation's first regularly scheduled steam passenger run on Christmas Day, 1830, on the South Carolina Canal & Rail Road.

The E. L. Miller, the second locomotive built by the Baldwin Locomotive Works, went into service on the South Carolina Canal & Rail Road in 1834.

John Motley Morehead, governor of North Carolina, 1841–45, was president of the North Carolina Railroad, 1850–55.

Dr. Samuel Cunningham served as first president of the East Tennessee & Virginia Railroad. A well-known physician, he gave up his medical practice in 1849 to see the railroad through difficult early years.

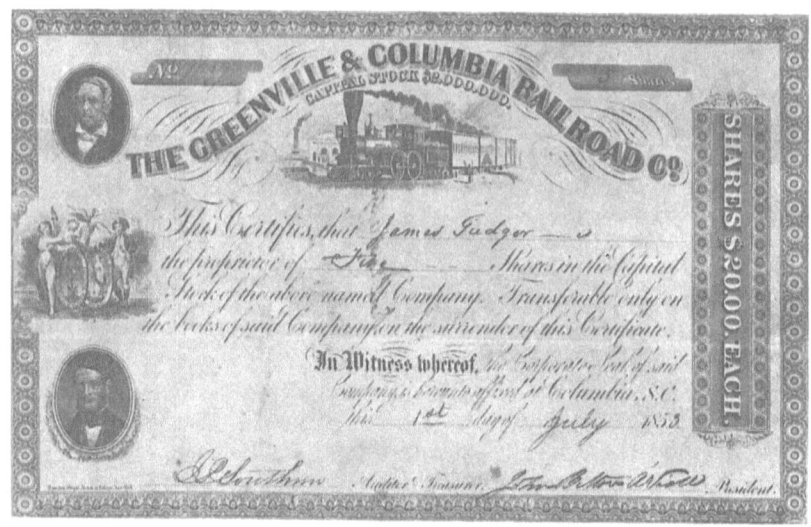

An early stock certificate, dated 1853, of the Greenville & Columbia Railroad, now part of the Southern Railway system. President John Belton O'Neall not only signed the certificate but also appears in the upper-left-hand corner.

During a two-day celebration at Memphis in May, 1857, water from the Atlantic Ocean was sprayed into the Mississippi River to represent completion of the Memphis & Charleston Railroad and a through rail route from river to ocean.

The War between the States marked the first use of railroads in a war effort. Rail-carried mortars, like this one used in the Virginia campaigns, offered maneuverable and well-protected artillery power.

Both Confederate and Union raiders made railroads a primary target for destruction. A favorite method was setting ripped-up rails atop burning stacked crossties. Heated rails would bend out of shape by their own weight.

This scene at a Richmond railroad station in April 1865 was typical of the destruction suffered by railroads throughout the South during the course of the war.
(Courtesy of the Library of Congress)

Joseph E. Johnston, a Confederate general in the War between the States, began the postwar rehabilitation of the Southern predecessor Selma, Rome & Dalton Railway when he became its president in 1866.

Scrollwork, fancy gold lettering, and the distinctive diamond stack marked this wood-burning locomotive and tender, built by Baldwin in 1874 for the South Carolina Rail Road.

An employee's pass issued by the Richmond & Danville Railroad shortly before its reorganization as the modern Southern Railway.

A gaily fringed, festooned, and flag-bedecked locomotive and tender of the Richmond & Danville Railroad at the old Windser Street turntable in Atlanta in 1894.

Samuel Spencer, first president of the Southern Railway System, 1894–1906.

Southern Railway's first headquarters in Washington, D.C., which was remodeled in 1899, then gutted by fire in 1916. Southern's last headquarters building, erected in 1928, still stands at 15th and K streets, N.W., in Washington.

Immortalized by song as one of the most famous train wrecks, "Old 97" plunged to the bottom of Stillhouse Trestle north of Danville, Va., on 27 September 1903.

The described excursion, over Southern Railway lines, cost a mere ninety-five cents for the round trip.

William W. Finley, second president of Southern Railway (1906–13), continued the expansion and improvement of the young rail system.

The luxury of turn-of-the-century train travel can be seen in the sumptuous appointments of this club car.

The Vulcan, one of Southern's first diesel-powered motor car/passenger combinations, was acquired in the mid-1930s.

The Carolina Special was one of Southern's first named trains, beginning operations between Cincinnati and Charleston in 1911.

The South was dotted with picturesque passenger stations, such as this one in Orangeburg, S.C.

Washington, D.C.'s Union Station, a Beaux Arts masterpiece of public architecture opened in 1907, was the northern terminus for Southern Railway passengers traveling from the South through to New York.

The famous Crescent Limited, long the South's premier train, carried an all-Pullman consist that included the latest sleeping, dining, and lounge cars.

Southern's great green-and-gold Pacifics pulled named passenger trains for a quarter of a century before being replaced by diesel-electric units in the late 1940s and early 1950s. No. 1401 today resides in the Smithsonian Institution's Museum of American History in Washington, D.C.

Fairfax Harrison, Southern Railway's third president (1914–37), presided over an eight-thousand-mile, thirteen-state system.

The Tennesseean was one of the last totally new passenger trains put into service before the start of World War II. Pictured is the streamlined diesel Tennesseean, which made its debut in 1941.

Southern's fourth president, Ernest E. Norris (1937–51), made it a personal crusade to develop the South and strengthened Southern Railway to serve it.

The world's first diesel-electric road freight locomotive served Southern Railway customers. Bought in 1941, the four-unit 5,400-hp. locomotive operated for nearly twenty years before taking up residence in the National Museum of Transportation in St. Louis.

Southern rose to the challenge of mobilizing men and machinery as World War II approached. Here, a trainload of tanks is loaded at Wiggins, Miss., for return to their base after field maneuvers at DeSoto National Forest in 1938.

Flags flew at half-mast throughout the nation when this Southern train arrived in Atlanta in 1945, carrying the body of President Franklin D. Roosevelt from Warm Springs, Ga., to Washington, D.C.

While Harry A. DeButts was president of Southern (1951–62), it became the first major railroad to switch to all-diesel service.

Inman Yard in Atlanta, opened in 1957, was Southern's fourth modern electronic freight classification yard. Modern technology helps all seven "hump yards" speed freight car movement across the railway.

Sheffield Yard in Alabama (opened in 1973) was Southern's first completely computerized freight classification and forwarding yard.

The Southern Crescent, Southern's last passenger train, remained independent of the Amtrak system, but succumbed to declining ridership in 1979. Here, the Crescent passes the Masonic Temple in Alexandria, Va.

The distinctive stainless-steel passenger cars introduced by Southern in 1941 were used on the Southern Crescent until it was discontinued. Some of this equipment is being used today in Amtrak passenger service.

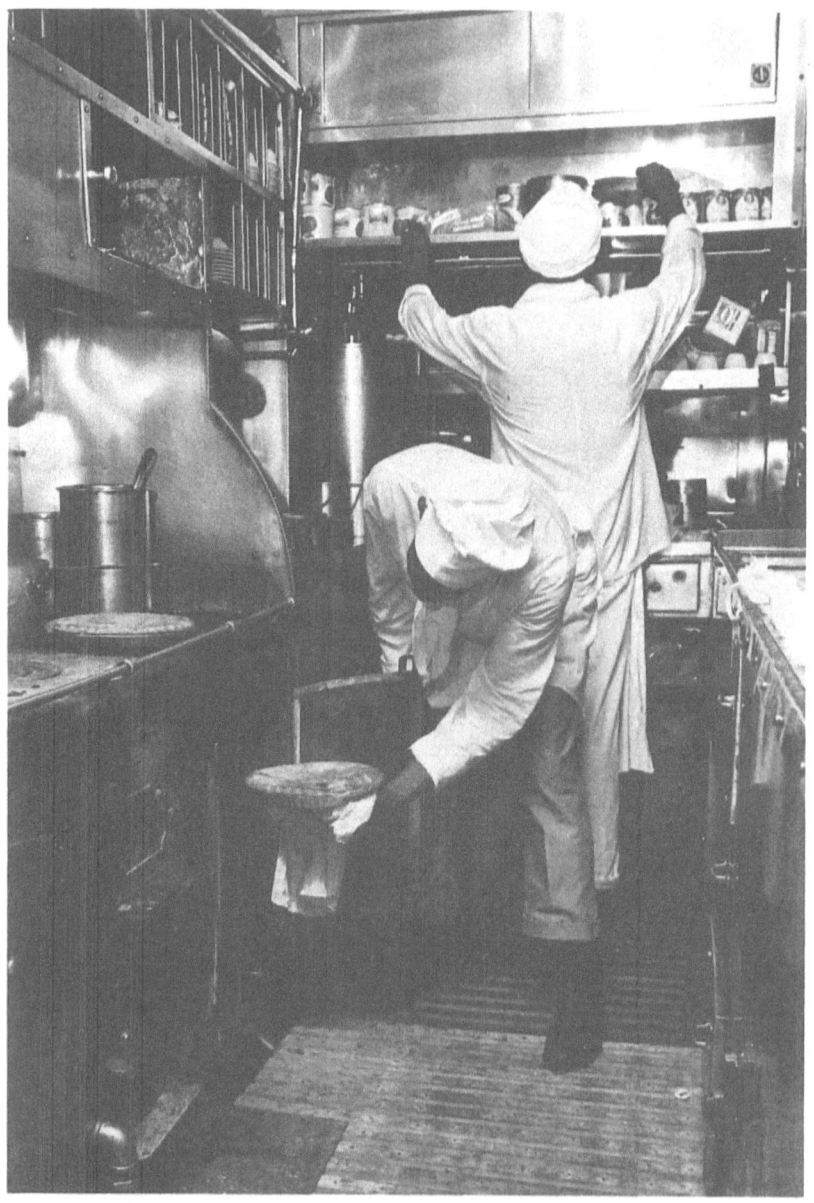

Incredibly crowded and equipped with old-fashioned wood-burning stoves, Southern's dining-car kitchens nevertheless turned out some of the best southern cooking available anywhere.

This ninety-seven-car unit coal train nearly meets itself coming the other way. Southern Railway introduced the unit train concept for coal traffic in 1959, offering fast turnaround between coal source and electric generating plants.

D. William Brosnan, Southern's chief executive from 1962 to 1967, presided over the modernization of the railroad's physical plant and computer applications to rail operations.

The Southern Railway–developed "Big John" oversized grain hopper car, coupled with reduced rates for grain traffic, revolutionized the rail market for grain traffic.

A relatively large portion of Southern's lines are now continuous welded rail—quarter-mile-long rail segments that have silenced the familiar "clickety clack" of rail movements.

Southern Railway was the first industrial user of the IBM 705 computer in 1956. Today, computers are used in everything from market analysis to train dispatching.

W. Graham Claytor, Jr., chief executive from 1967 to 1977, instituted a variety of management techniques and processes that led to Southern's selection by Dun's Review *as one of the five "best-managed companies" of 1974.*

Southern's R-1 (Research-1) track test car measures and records various track conditions—such as variation in gauge and super-elevation of track—as it rolls across the system. This helps pinpoint sections of track that require special maintenance work.

Intermodal, or "piggyback" traffic—truck trailers or containers on railroad flatcars—was a rapidly growing part of Southern's business by the last years of its independent existence. Here, a trailer is hoisted by a giant crane at the expanded intermodal terminal in Jacksonville, Fla.

L. Stanley Crane, Southern's chief executive from 1977 to 1980, strengthened the railroad's commitment to research and use of advanced technology.

Solar power was tapped for a variety of uses on the railroad. Here, solar panels provide power for railroad signals at a remote location near Lake Pontchartrain, La.

One of Southern's modern freight locomotives makes a "service station" stop at the Sheffield, Ala., electronic yard.

Harold H. Hall, the last president of the independent Southern Railway System, was the driving force behind Southern's emphasis on safety and its resulting excellent safety record.

On 1 June 1982, the day Southern Railway joined Norfolk & Western Railway to form Norfolk Southern Corporation, engineers from each railroad shake hands as a symbol of the new partnership.

ELEVEN

Casualties of War

On a February day in 1861, after Jefferson Davis had been notified of his election as president of the Confederate States of America, he left his plantation home near Vicksburg, Mississippi, and boarded a train for Montgomery, Alabama, the temporary capital of the new government.

Montgomery was only 280 miles distant, but Davis was forced to travel 700 miles to reach his destination—via Jackson, Mississippi, to Grand Junction and Chattanooga, Tennessee, thence via Atlanta to Montgomery.

Within a few weeks the Confederate government moved to a new capital in Richmond, Virginia, in a procession of trains bearing officials and clerks of the infant bureaucracy on a heroic hegira. The movement was to be secret, but almost everyone in the South knew of it before the last cars reached Richmond, many days after departure. The journey was by the West Point Route to Atlanta; thence to Dalton, Georgia, over the Western & Atlantic; to Bristol, Tennessee, over the East Tennessee & Georgia and the East Tennessee & Virginia; to Lynchburg over the Virginia & Tennessee; to Burkeville over the South Side Railroad; and finally into Richmond over the Richmond & Danville. The new government could scarcely have had a more pointed reminder of the deficiencies of its rail network on the eve of hostilities.

In fact, one Confederate state had already acted to take control of its railways. After seceding from the Union in December 1860, South Carolina made plans to seize fortifications in Charleston Harbor. On 2 January 1861, a company of eighty-six artillerymen from Columbia arrived in Charleston aboard two trains of the South Carolina Railroad, ready to help bombard Fort Sumter and other Federal posts. This was the first known movement of troops by railroad during the Civil War. It was followed in the next ten days by the arrival of other state troops from inland South Carolina, gathering to take part in one of the most momentous events in American history.

As war approached, the United States had thirty thousand miles of railroad in use, of which about nine thousand miles were in

Casualties of War

Confederate territory. The South's railroads consisted of 144 separate lines, about two-thirds of which were of 5-foot gauge—but some were of 4 feet 8½ inches, and one, in Mississippi, was of 4 feet 10 inches. Through traffic would be difficult, if not impossible.

Of the lines within reach of the Confederates, 2,483 miles belonged to roads that were later to be merged into the Southern Railway System—about one-third of the South's total mileage at this time. This trackage was controlled by twenty-nine companies. The wartime lines later incorporated into the Southern were:

Alabama
    Alabama & Mississippi Rivers, 78 miles
    Alabama & Tennessee River, 110 miles
    Cahawba, Marion & Greensboro, 13 miles
    Northeast & Southwest Alabama (also in MS), 27 miles
    Memphis & Charleston (also in MS, TN), 291 miles

Kentucky
    Lexington & Danville, 13 miles

Louisiana
    Mexican Gulf, 27 miles

North Carolina
    Atlantic & North Carolina, 95 miles
    Atlantic, Tennessee & Ohio, 45 miles
    Charlotte & South Carolina (also SC), 110 miles
    North Carolina, 223 miles
    Piedmont (built during war), 48 miles
    Roanoke Valley, 22 miles
    Western North Carolina, 84 miles

South Carolina
    Blue Ridge, 34 miles
    Greenville & Columbia, 166 miles
    Kings Mountain, 23 miles
    Laurens, 30 miles
    South Carolina (also GA), 242 miles
    Spartanburg & Union, 40 miles

Tennessee
    East Tennessee & Georgia (also GA), 139 miles
    East Tennessee & Virginia, 130 miles

Casualties of War

Rogersville & Jefferson, 10 miles
Wills Valley (also GA), 12 miles

Virginia
Alexandria, Loudoun & Hampshire, 42 miles
Manassas Gap, 87 miles
Orange & Alexandria, 157 miles
Richmond & Danville, 143 miles
Richmond & York River, 39 miles

Though these rail lines were a network in theory only, they inevitably drew the attention of military strategists north and south.

Oddly enough, there were no physical connections between northern and southern railroads when war came. All traffic transferred by ferryboats at points of interchange in Washington, D.C.; Cincinnati; Louisville; Evansville, Indiana; and Cairo, Illinois. Thus, even if gauges on both sides had been the same, direct interchange of railway cars between the warring sections would have been impossible.

The "first Railroad War" was not long in coming, and the first action took place on a segment of what was to be the Southern Railway System. Within a few hours of Virginia's secession from the Union on 17 April 1861, state troops boarded a special train under sealed orders to attack the U.S. Arsenal at Harpers Ferry. Their train from Richmond ran to Staunton and then back to Gordonsville over the Virginia Central, thence to Manassas Junction over the Orange & Alexandria, and finally over the Manassas Gap to Strasburg. From that point the troops completed their march on foot, only to find that the Federal troops had burned the arsenal and most of its contents a few hours before their arrival. This was the first use of railroads to carry troops in a direct assault upon an enemy post. Many people now began to understand the military potential of railroads.

Since northern Virginia railroads were some of the South's most vulnerable, the three roads based in Alexandria were first to become involved in the fighting. The Orange & Alexandria and the Manassas Gap, in fact, were to be fought over with greater intensity and for longer periods than any others, north or south.

Confederate plans to carry all railroad equipment southward to safety were thwarted on 24 May 1861, when Maj. (later Gen.) Wil-

Casualties of War

liam T. Sherman led the first Federal troops into Virginia and seized the Orange & Alexandria properties in Alexandria. Sherman's artillery battery galloped into town as a train loaded with Confederate troops pulled off toward Manassas Junction. Despite all Confederate efforts, Sherman captured locomotives and cars in repair shops and much equipment. Most important, he seized eleven hundred tons of rail recently imported from England.

Rebels were quick to strike back. From his post at Harpers Ferry, Col. Thomas J. (soon to become Gen. "Stonewall") Jackson watched the heavy double-line traffic of the B&O Railroad. One day when the railroad was at its busiest, he struck with his troops, catching all east- and westbound trains and taking them to Winchester. Col. Thomas R. Sharp of his staff supervised the ingenious theft. This thirty-two-mile run was only the beginning of the journey, however. From isolated Winchester, by the superhuman effort of his troops and farmhorses from the vicinity, Jackson dragged the locomotives and cars over twenty miles of dirt road to Strasburg and the tracks of the Manassas Gap Railroad. The heavy loads were drawn by forty-horse teams—ten teams pulling four abreast. These engines and cars provided desperately needed rolling stock for southern railroads and crippled the B&O for months to come.

Both Lee and Jackson were quick to appreciate the importance of railroads in modern warfare. Jackson became the first to make use of the new military weapon in a major engagement.

The Confederates opened the war by concentrating a large army under Gen. P. G. T. Beauregard at the strategic point of Manassas Junction, where the Orange & Alexandria met the Manassas Gap Railroad. Beauregard was ready to attack Washington or defend Richmond. A second Confederate army under Gen. Joseph E. Johnston was sent to the upper Shenandoah Valley. When Federal troops advanced from Washington, prepared to strike Beauregard at Manassas, seize the railroads, and move on Richmond, Confederate headquarters telegraphed Johnston to move to the relief of Beauregard. Colonel Jackson led the advance of the relief expedition.

Jackson marched his men through Ashby's Gap and put them aboard trains of the Manassas Gap Railroad at Piedmont station, some thirty-five miles west of Manassas. The first train, carrying Jackson's brigade, left Piedmont at dawn on 19 July, and by its swift movement saved Beauregard's army from savage Federal

Casualties of War

assaults. The battle of First Manassas, or Bull Run, raged throughout 20 and 21 July, with Johnston's army arriving in time to send Federal forces reeling back to Washington in a rout.

The telegraph and the railroad, introduced into military use, had proved decisive. New possibilities of rapid communication demonstrated at First Manassas would mark the conduct of this war to the end, and greatly influence all wars to come.

This bit of history was recalled one hundred years later when a diesel-powered Southern Railway train carried two thousand "Confederate" troops to the centennial reenactment of this important opening battle—the men clad in authentic uniforms and carrying weapons and equipment designed in the Civil War period. The North Carolina contingent aboard the five-car train was led by Col. W. Cliff Elder of Burlington, a textile executive who was the commander of the reborn 6th North Carolina Regiment, CSA, whose predecessors had been mustered into service by Charles F. Fisher, president of the North Carolina Railroad, a vital link on Southern's main line between Washington and Atlanta. Most of the men of this original Civil War regiment were North Carolina Railroad workers from Company Shops—modern Burlington.

The Confederacy had scant time to rest on its laurels from First Manassas. A few months later contending armies in the western theater fought for possession of the Memphis & Charleston, the great trunk line from Memphis to the Atlantic. For a few days the rural village of Corinth, Mississippi, became one of the most vital military posts in the Confederacy, for it was here that communications between the eastern seaboard and the Mississippi Valley, and between the Ohio Valley and the Gulf of Mexico came together. The army that controlled the crossing of the two long railroads held a decisive advantage.

A large Federal army led by Gen. U. S. Grant, pushing southward toward Corinth, was attacked at Shiloh on the Tennessee River by General Beauregard, who had been hurried west to meet the threat. The battle of Shiloh, fifteen miles northeast of Corinth, was bloody, and though it was a draw, tactically, it resulted in Confederate disaster. The Southern army withdrew, after a loss of ten thousand men (the Federal loss was fifteen thousand), and on that day lost control of the Memphis & Charleston Railroad, the trunk line connecting east and west. Never again did a Confederate train run over this line from Memphis to Chattanooga. Beauregard had given up what his secretary of war called "The Vertebrae of the Confederacy."

Casualties of War

Even as these movements were taking place, fresh disasters fell upon the Confederacy to the east. On the day after the battle of Shiloh, the Federal general Ormsby M. Mitchel marched an army south from Shelbyville, Tennessee, and seized Huntsville, Alabama, the major shop and supply center on the Memphis & Charleston east of Memphis.

This Federal raid was among the most destructive of the war. Repair shops were wrecked and all company books were destroyed. When Confederates drove bluecoats from a section of the road, they found it in ruins. Of the 155 miles of rail within Alabama, 140 miles were torn up, the rails heated and twisted until useless. Virtually all the road's machinery was destroyed.

The invaders staged a more dramatic raid at this time in hopes of cutting rails east of Chattanooga and isolating the western Confederacy. General Mitchel sent twenty-five soldiers, most of them in civilian dress, into Georgia under command of James J. Andrews, a Secret Service agent. Andrews was to steal a train on the Western & Atlantic Railroad, on the line between Atlanta and Chattanooga, and then steam westward, setting fire to bridges and tearing up track as he went. Though Andrews's Raid, or "the Great Locomotive Chase," became famous in American folk history, it ended in tragedy for the Federals.

On 12 April 1862 Andrews and his men came upon a locomotive, the General, at Big Shanty (Kennesaw Mountain), Georgia. The engine and its train were waiting on the tracks while passengers and a three-man crew were eating breakfast inside the station. Andrews and his men unhitched the General and chugged off northward on their mission of sabotage. The three trainmen gave chase at once. They borrowed a handcar at nearby Moon's Station and at Etowah boarded a locomotive. Though slowed by barricades and a few missing rails ripped up by the fleeing Yankees, the three trainmen hung on the heels of the thieves by running and engine-hopping. Another locomotive, the Texas, picked them up and they then ran backward, past Resaca, Tilton, Dalton, and Ringgold. They found the General abandoned at Graysville, near Chattanooga.

Within a week all the raiders had been captured. Andrews and seven of his men were hanged in Atlanta, eight others escaped prison there in October 1862, and the remaining Federals were paroled the following spring.

Loss of the Memphis & Charleston link between east and west forced the Confederate government into action. In October 1862 the Confederate Congress approved issuance of bonds to finance a railroad between Blue Mountain, Alabama, and Rome, Georgia, "as a military necessity." The new line connected the remaining Alabama lines with the Georgia and East Tennessee system and saved the Confederate cause for many months to come.

Meanwhile, reacting to the loss of Huntsville and other shop and supply centers, Confederates built Selma, Alabama, into a major railroad and manufacturing center, second only to Richmond as "the arsenal of the Confederacy." In addition to its large arsenal, Selma's military complex included iron mills, a naval factory and shipyard, a horseshoe factory, and a gunpowder plant.

The Alabama & Tennessee River Railroad was an important adjunct, carrying coal to these factories from Montevallo mines. Selma's industrial output continued until March 1865, when the Federal general James Harrison Wilson burned all facilities there, and destroyed the Alabama & Tennessee River Railroad, including almost every station between Blue Mountain and Selma.

But the most telling raid of all was the seizure of Memphis & Charleston, whose tracks east of Tuscumbia remained in Federal hands for the rest of the war. The major battles of Iuka, Corinth, and Grand Junction were fought on the road between Tuscumbia and Memphis, and parts of the road were fought over and changed hands frequently as the armies surged back and forth. It was a pattern to be repeated in Virginia, where the growing conflict was virtually endless.

In response to Northern public opinion, which raised a clamor for ending the war, Lincoln ordered a general advance of all forces against the Confederates, adding a special order for seizure of the Orange & Alexandria Railroad south of Manassas, Virginia, where Confederates were still concentrated. Gen. George McClellan disagreed with the president, insisting upon moving his army by sea to Yorktown, Virginia, for an advance against Richmond from the east. Lincoln relieved McClellan of overall command, but gave him the Army of the Potomac, to conduct his move on the Confederate capital.

McClellan's line of supply during the desperate fighting of 1862 was the tiny Richmond & York River Railroad, whose eastern terminus, West Point, was at the head of navigation on the York River. Confederate attempts to cut this line precipitated heavy battles, and when advancing rebels captured a nearby station, McClellan was forced to retreat to the bank of the James River and there open new communications and supply lines. McClellan's cam-

Casualties of War

paign ended in disaster for the North, incurred terrible casualties on both sides, and brought Robert E. Lee to the command of the Army of Northern Virginia. The wounding of Joseph E. Johnston and the rise of Lee meant hardships for the Federal cause.

One of Lee's first moves as a field commander revealed his appreciation of the military value of railroads. He ordered his staff: "The only way by which the enemy can convey heavy artillery from the Chickahominy is the York River Railroad.... I am very anxious to have a railroad battery.... I propose ... a railroad flat, with one of your Navy aprons adjusted to it to protect gun and men. If I could get it in position by daylight tomorrow, I could astonish our neighbors." Lee's large gun was soon blasting away at the enemy—an advance apparently inspired by the North Carolina Railroad, whose shops at New Bern were credited with building the first railroad gun, an armored car carrying a huge cannon.

Just as Richmond was saved by Confederate capture of a railroad, so the tide of war in northern Virginia was turned by rail lines. The second battle of Manassas in the late summer of 1862 reached its climax on 30 August when thousands of men fought hand-to-hand along a railroad cut of the unfinished Manassas Gap Railroad. Stonewall Jackson's men used the cover of this cut to beat off waves of Federal assaults, using bayonets, musket butts, knives, stones, and fists.

This battle had been brought on by the wily Jackson, who led his troops on a stolen march from the Shenandoah to Manassas Junction, where they fell upon vast stores of Federal supplies. Jackson's loot included ten locomotives, eight heavy cannon, and supplies sufficient to sustain Lee's army on the invasion of Maryland, which followed a few days later.

In the west, the city of Chattanooga had been recognized as the key to railroad operations in the South, because of its location in the Tennessee Valley at the junction of the lines connecting Richmond and Memphis, and Nashville and Atlanta. Federal strategists made plans to seize the city.

In June 1862, a few days after the hanging of the raider Andrews, the Federal general O. M. Mitchel wrote, "In my opinion, the great struggle is to take place for the mastery of the railroad from Richmond south to Atlanta." By the opening of the next year it was clear that this struggle was to center instead upon Chattanooga, with its roads extending in several directions throughout the Confederacy.

By the fall of 1863 major armies were contending for control of

Casualties of War

Chattanooga and its railroads. On the approach, these armies fought the battles of Lookout Mountain, after which the Federals occupied Chattanooga; the battle of Chickamauga; the capture of Cumberland Gap by the Federals; and finally the battle of Chattanooga.

Some of the war's most remarkable rail movements took place during this extended campaign. The most extraordinary feat of transport was accomplished in September 1863, when Gen. Braxton Bragg, retreating southeast of Chattanooga, called on Lee for reinforcements. Lee sent to him Gen. James Longstreet's corps of the Army of Northern Virginia—two divisions of infantry and an artillery battalion, almost twenty thousand men, plus hundreds of horses and vast stocks of supplies.

Ten railroads took part in the movement, including three lines that were to become part of the Southern Railway System: the North Carolina Railroad, from Raleigh to Charlotte, North Carolina; the Charlotte and South Carolina, from Charlotte to Columbia, South Carolina; and the South Carolina Railroad from Columbia to Augusta, Georgia. The movement began in Virginia on 9 September at the Rapidan River station of the Orange & Alexandria and was completed on 25 September at Catoosa and Ringgold in northwest Georgia, a few miles from the Chickamauga battlefield. The several thousand men who arrived and went into battle on 20 September saved the day for Bragg, enabling him to retain possession of Missionary Ridge and Lookout Mountain the next day. Some of Longstreet's troops, however, were still straggling in five days after the battle was over.

G. Moxley Sorrell, Longstreet's chief of staff, wrote: "Never before were so many troops moved over such worn-out railways, none first-class from the beginning. Never before were such crazy cars—passenger, baggage, mail, coal, box, platform—all and every sort, wobbling on the jumping strap-iron—used for hauling good soldiers."

The only comparable movement of troops during the war took place during the same campaign, with the seven-day transfer of Gen. Joseph Hooker's army of fifteen thousand Federals during August and September 1863. The Federals moved this army 1,168 miles from a point on the Orange & Alexandria in Virginia, then running through Maryland, West Virginia, Ohio, Indiana, and Kentucky to Bridgeport, Tennessee, 30 miles west of Chickamauga. Following these spectacular moves, Federal troops occupied the

Casualties of War

valleys of the Tennessee, Ohio, and Mississippi, and the centers of operations shifted to Georgia and Virginia.

Throughout the latter stages of the war economic conditions were as devastating to railroads as were invading armies. The ravages of inflation consumed railroad property as they did all other in the beleaguered South. A typical indication of the ruinous effects of inflation and the collapse of the Confederate currency late in the war was the fate of a locomotive of the Wills Valley Railroad in Tennessee. This engine was described as "a painted scrap heap" when purchased for $7,000 in 1861—and was sold three years later to the Macon & Brunswick for $75,000, payable in cotton at $1 per bale.

There were kindred problems, many of them political—especially the rigid political philosophy of States' Rights to which the Jefferson Davis government clung throughout the war. When a Confederate judge ruled that the welfare of the South at large took precedence over state control of railroads, Davis opposed and condemned the decision, declaring that it undermined the sacred cause for which the South was fighting. This unrealistic attitude prevented government control of railroads even in the direst of emergencies. For example, when the War Department insisted that Virginia railroads discontinue civilian passenger service during peak demand by the Confederate army, the railroads declined to comply, and the Davis government refused to force the issue.

It was in these days that General Lee wrote Davis, "I cannot see how we can operate with our present supplies. Any... disaster to the railroad would render it impossible for me to keep the army together.... We have rations for the troops to-day and tomorrow.... All pleasure travel should cease, and everything devoted to necessary wants." But the Confederate government was unable to bring itself to face these realities and its attitude hastened its end.

That end approached in 1864 as Gen. U. S. Grant came east to take command in Virginia, leaving General Sherman in the west with orders to drive southward and seize Atlanta, which he besieged and burned, and then moved eastward toward the sea. Sherman destroyed Georgia's railroads as he went. The Central of Georgia and lesser roads were taken up, their crossties burned and rails heated and twisted into " Sherman's neckties." After occupying Savannah, Sherman's army turned northward, striking the South Carolina Railroad at Midway, Branchville, and Black-

Casualties of War

ville. Many miles of this pioneer line were destroyed by the burning of stations, bridges, shops, enginehouses, and tracks. In Columbia, South Carolina, which he left in flames, Sherman wrecked the South Carolina Railroad and the Greenville & Columbia Railroad for many miles outside the city.

Turning northward again toward the North Carolina border, Sherman destroyed the Charlotte & South Carolina line. The railroad's president, William Johnston, wrote that all the road's Columbia property was "annihilated as far as practicable except the boarding house. The machine and car shops, engine and depot houses and sheds, foundry and offices were consumed.... Several hundred car wheels, with a number of cars and some machinery ... were all destroyed. A portion of the army followed the line of road to above Blackstock's, over 50 miles, entirely destroyed. The superstructure ... of about half the road."

Sherman moved rapidly into North Carolina. At Goldsboro, the junction point of the North Carolina Railroad, the Atlantic & North Carolina, and the Wilmington & Weldon Railroad, Sherman turned the rails to his own use by ordering his engineers to repair lines, bridges, and equipment, and to improve the line from the port of Morehead City so that it could bear a traffic of three hundred tons daily—supplies for his army.

Meanwhile, Confederate troops under Generals Johnston and Beauregard were concentrating near Smithfield, North Carolina, in hopes of halting Sherman's advance. Johnston's attempt to bring the battered Army of Tennessee eastward by rail came to naught this time—for lack of adequate telegraph service and efficient railroads. The transfer failed to deliver enough troops to fill Johnston's ranks, and he was forced to meet Sherman with an inferior force, and was defeated at the Battle of Bentonville. In the aftermath, frightened railroad officials and clerks and crews fled the state capital, Raleigh, and Confederate transport was near complete disintegration.

It was during this time that Lee's army collapsed in Virginia, forcing the evacuation of Richmond. President Davis and his cabinet, carrying the archives and the gold treasure of the Confederacy, prepared to flee over the Richmond & Danville, the only westward rail route out of the city. On 2 April 1865 rickety trains began moving westward over the single track, hoping to escape the approaching Federal army. The siege lines had been broken, and the enemy was near the city.

Col. Lewis Harvie, president of the Richmond & Danville, real-

Casualties of War

ized that the race against the enemy would be close. His war-worn road was in ruins, and derailments had been daily occurrences for months. Most of the rails and crossties were at least fifteen years old, and on one stretch of line, the original strap iron was still in place. Most locomotives and cars were ready for scrapping, and numerous bridges were dangerously frail. Thus, for several hours during 2 and 3 April the last hopes of the Confederacy and the lives of thousands of refugees hung upon the two thin iron ribbons that led westward from Richmond to Danville.

The first special train to depart was loaded with records of government departments, and with eight wagonloads of gold coins—the specie of the Confederate Treasury, as well as deposits of Richmond banks. The president's train stood ready in the station by 8:30 P.M., but it was not until 11 o'clock that Davis went aboard with his cabinet, and "the train moved in gloomy silence over the James River," leaving the doomed capital of the Confederacy. Two hundred picked troops were riding on a car between the engine and the presidential car, their leader wearing spurs. Horses were carried in a nearby car, in case an emergency called for a cross-country flight. There was a variety of other cars amid the "scattering of ruined coaches," all carrying officials and clerks of the government, plus a weird assortment of personal belongings.

John Wise, an eighteen-year-old Confederate soldier, saw the Davis train pass Clover Station at 3 A.M. The president sat at a window looking composed, waving to a small crowd at the trackside. But Wise thought he looked exhausted. The train soon pulled away, heading west, and at 5 P.M. the relieved passengers reached Danville, temporarily safe from the oncoming enemy.

But more trains followed past Clover Station, where Lieutenant Wise watched: "I saw a government on wheels. It was the marvelous and incongruous wreck of the Confederate capital . . . trains bearing indiscriminate cargoes of men and things. In one car was a cage with an African parrot, and a box of tame squirrels and a hunchback. Everybody, not excepting the parrot, was wrought up to a pitch of intense excitement."

The last train crept past, bringing woeful news. A man shouted from the rear platform: "Richmond's burning. Gone, all gone."

By now the Federal army had occupied the flame-swept city and bluecoat cavalrymen had cut the Richmond & Danville line at several places, attempting to halt Lee's army. Over the James, the railroad bridges had been burned by retreating graycoats.

Lee's army had found no rations at Amelia Courthouse; when

Casualties of War

he heard that the Burkeville and Jetersville stations had been captured, Lee knew the end had come. He changed his route, which lay toward Danville, and bore toward Lynchburg, but his weary column was cut off by swift Federal cavalry, and was surrendered to General Grant on 9 April 1865, at Appomattox Courthouse, ending the war in Virginia.

Soon afterward, Sherman pressed for the surrender of Johnston's army in North Carolina. In the midst of these negotiations President Davis and the cabinet fled once more, this time turning south on the Piedmont Railroad, a new link between Danville and Greensboro, which had been known as "the jugular vein of the Confederacy." The Davis party reached Greensboro the morning of 12 April and the president made headquarters in "an old, leaky car on the railroad tracks," where he held several conferences of state.

Complying with the views of his cabinet majority, Davis ordered Johnston to ask for a meeting with Sherman, who was then in Raleigh, North Carolina. The delighted Sherman rode over the North Carolina Railroad to Durham's Station behind an engine pulling a single coach, and then rode horseback a few miles westward and met General Johnston. In the nearby farmhouse of James Bennett, the generals reached an agreement that led to final Confederate surrender in the east a few days later. The end of the war was at hand.

Two days earlier, on 15 April, Jefferson Davis had resumed his flight, hurrying southward to Charlotte over the broken North Carolina Railroad, now riding the rails, now riding horseback or jouncing along in a carriage over the rutted road. One of the last official acts of Davis before he left Charlotte was to give his reluctant consent to Johnston's surrender. Davis and his cabinet then moved on, making their final railroad journey from Laurens to Abbeville. From Abbeville southward, until he was captured near the village of Irwinville, Georgia, on 10 May, President Davis traveled on back roads by carriage, wagon, or horseback.

Ten days after Appomattox, Federal troops committed one of their last hostile acts against southern rail lines by burning the 1,125-foot bridge of the Charlotte & South Carolina Railroad over the Catawba River, a loss that was to handicap the road until the bridge was replaced in 1868. On the day the big bridge was burned, another Federal detachment destroyed 13 locomotives and 147 cars of the South Carolina Railroad, which had been run for safety to the Camden branch. These last violent acts symbol-

Casualties of War

ized what southern railroads had suffered during four years of war—but despite their deplorable condition, they were called upon immediately for heroic service, without pay.

Anarchy gripped the South in the absence of a government. Confederate currency was worthless, and there was none to take its place. In the bright, spring weather thousands of ex-soldiers were streaming southward toward their homes, some as far distant as Texas. Many of these men were sick and wounded, in dire need of transportation. Most of the burden fell upon the crippled railroads, which, though impoverished themselves, furnished passage homeward for uncounted thousands of troops. The Charlotte & South Carolina Railroad, for example, carried more than fifty thousand Confederate troops on their way home—and many of these had with them horses, wagons, and other property.

Throughout the war, from the day South Carolina soldiers rode the rails to Charleston to aid in the bombardment of Fort Sumter, until defeated Johnnies returned home, rail lines that were to join the Southern Railway System played major roles. They had been destroyed, rebuilt, and used by both Blue and Gray, and now, though almost in ruins, with empty treasuries and bleak prospects, they still looked to the future. Railroad managers and employees, unheralded in the Confederate war effort, believed that the South's greatest railroad-building era lay ahead.

Lack of capital was to dim their dreams and hamper efforts in every southern state, but this very factor was to prevent the orgy of construction that was to plague other regions in later years. The South was forced to build slowly and economically, but even so, the recovery of its railroad system in the next thirty years was almost miraculous.

TWELVE

Out of the Ashes

The plight of the desolate South was to be seen in the wreckage of its railroads—stripped of rails and crossties, the rails twisted into fantastic shapes; shops and stations, bridges and trestles burned. Among the dilapidated locomotives and cars, few were fit for rehabilitation.

The condition of the pioneer South Carolina Railroad was typical: of the line's 62 locomotives, 18 were condemned as beyond repair, 10 were isolated on the Charlotte & South Carolina line, and almost all the rest were wrecked, burned out, or otherwise unfit for service. Only 27 of 50 passenger cars had escaped destruction, and of 612 freight cars that had begun the war, there were 252 decrepit survivors.

Auditors listed the road's losses as $541,000 for loss or damage of track and bridges, $410,000 for rolling stock, $360,000 for materials and machinery, and $126,000 for shops and depots. Almost $2.8 million in transportation charges owed by the government were unpaid, and uncollectible—and the road owned some $235,000 worth of Confederate securities, now worthless.

In this crisis the road's president, William J. Magrath, went to New York seeking funds. He returned empty-handed to Charleston, for the best price he had been offered for bonds was 66⅔ cents on the dollar, with interest at a stiff 8 percent. Magrath began his own program of restoration by stripping rails from the Camden branch and attempting to straighten some of the twisted rail. The branch was to remain in disuse for two years, until a $2 million loan had been secured in England.

Other roads were in worse straits, since the federal government demanded payment for improvements made to roads it had seized during the war. The United States had operated more than 2,100 miles of railroad in the South, more than half of which—1,088 miles—were to become parts of the Southern Railway System. The following roads, used by the Federals and returned to their owners after hard usage, were to join the Southern:

Orange & Alexandria, 77 miles; Alexandria, Loudoun & Hampshire, 15; Richmond & York River, 20; Richmond & Danville, 140;

Out of the Ashes

Manassas Gap, 62; East Tennessee & Georgia, 139; East Tennessee & Virginia, 110; Rogersville & Jefferson, 12; Memphis & Charleston, 155; Atlantic & North Carolina, 95; North Carolina, 223.

Some of the roads, already ruined by war, had been extensively repaired and improved by the United States, and much new rolling stock was furnished. The government claimed it had spent $1.5 million on the two mountain roads in East Tennessee, and had relaid fifty miles of their track. Protracted, often bitter, negotiations between owners and the federal government slowed the return of such roads to private control. Charles B. Thomas, president of the Atlantic & North Carolina line, discovered that Washington held the upper hand. Thomas sent the government a bill for $319,500 for use of his road and warned that the debt would increase by $50,000 per month so long as the bluecoats held the road. The government ignored these demands and held the line until it had completed moving military supplies from North Carolina ports.

But there was soon a lively trade between the penniless railroads and the government. The roads, heavily in debt and without credit, desperately needed new cars and locomotives and supplies; the War Department was eager to dispose of the thousands of engines and cars accumulated during the war—a dilemma solved by President Andrew Johnson in an executive order, directing sales of this equipment to roads whose officers had taken loyalty oaths. The government disposed of more than $5.5 million worth of railroad property in this way, selling without down payment, on a monthly installment basis—with deferred payments at 7 percent interest.

Under pressure of the need to revive old roads and build new ones, state governments began offering aid to railroads. Northern and foreign bankers made few loans, and the federal government was encouraging railroad construction in the West through land grants, leaving southern lines at a disadvantage. Many railroads fell into the hands of speculators, many were taken over by northern or foreign interests, and few weathered Reconstruction with sound reputations or securities. Almost all of them, including future components of the Southern System, found their way into bankruptcy courts or receivership.

But there were men of vision and courage to direct the postwar economic rehabilitation of the South, many of them ex-Confederate soldiers. Several of the most celebrated Rebel generals turned to railroading after the war. Among these were Nathan Bedford Forrest, James Longstreet, Joseph E. Johnston, and the fiery Georgian John B. Gordon. All faced formidable obstacles, but they and their cohorts built so effectively that southern roads led the nation in growth during the 1880s, with an astonishing increase of 93 percent in mileage.

The most spectacular growth—and the most romantic associations—unfolded on the western borders of the old Confederacy. Early in the war Jefferson Davis had sent two former U.S. senators to London and Paris to serve as commissioners. James M. Mason of Virginia and John Slidell of Louisiana were traveling aboard the British steamer *Trent* when a U.S. Navy vessel halted and boarded the ship to arrest the Confederate diplomats. Mason surrendered at once, but when a U.S. lieutenant grasped Slidell to lead him away, Slidell's daughter Matilda clung to her father's neck and repeatedly slapped the young officer. A Marine squad subdued the spirited Matilda and took Mason and Slidell to their own ship.

The *Trent* Affair caused an international sensation and moved England to the brink of war as an ally of the Confederacy. It also made Matilda Slidell into a heroine and took her to England a few months later, when her father was freed from prison and joined his family in London. In England, Matilda was wooed and married by the young German-born Baron Erlanger, the scion of a wealthy and aristocratic banking house that invested in railroads, mines, and other projects in many nations. The Slidell-Erlanger marriage attracted international attention—and at the end of the Civil War resulted in the investment of some $25 million in southern railroads, including the lines from Cincinnati to New Orleans known as the Queen & Crescent Route. The towns of Erlanger, Kentucky, and Slidell, Louisiana, near the extremities of this line, recall the romance of the 1860s and the financial role played by Emile Erlanger and Company of London in the development of the modern South.

The Queen & Crescent Route, which was to join the Southern System in 1895, was composed of three distinct properties: the Cincinnati Southern Railway between Cincinnati and Chattanooga; the Alabama Great Southern between Chattanooga and Meridian, Mississippi; and the New Orleans & Northeastern, between Meridian and New Orleans. Except for two short segments, all of these were built during the 1880s, though their beginnings were much earlier. On the northern end of the route the most important of these were the Lexington & Danville, in Kentucky,

Out of the Ashes

which opened in 1856 as the nucleus of the Queen & Crescent Route, and the Cincinnati Southern Railway, "The greatest undertaking ... ever achieved by an American city." The Kentucky line was built without undue difficulty, but the construction of the Cincinnati Southern became one of the epic enterprises in the nation's railroad history.

Edward A. Ferguson, who became known as the father of the road, was a young Cincinnati lawyer who drafted legislation to circumvent Ohio's constitutional ban against the city's lending aid to private enterprise, by having the city build the line itself. Local businessmen were enthusiastic over the prospect of regaining trade lost to other river towns served by rail, but Ferguson and his associates met determined opposition elsewhere. When Chattanooga was chosen as the southern terminus for the line, both Kentucky and Tennessee had to consent to the passage of the road through their territory. Tennessee did so after a brief legislative debate, but Kentuckians resisted for two years, succumbing only to the suasion of Gen. John C. Breckinridge, "the handsomest man in the South," a former vice-president of the United States, and late secretary of war in the Confederacy.

The 336-mile road, an engineering wonder of the day, ran almost due south from Cincinnati to Lexington, thence through Kings Mountain—whose tunnel was 3,984 feet in length—then across ridges and defiles into the valley of the Tennessee River, crossing the river to enter Chattanooga. The line's 27 tunnels aggregated 5 miles in length, and crews built 105 bridges and viaducts, including huge structures spanning the Ohio, Kentucky, Tennessee, and Cumberland rivers—more than 5 miles of iron bridges. The Ohio River Bridge, more than 5,100 feet long, had a channel span of 519 feet, the world's largest. The Kentucky River Bridge, the first cantilever bridge on the continent, had a deck 375 feet above low water, the world's highest at the time; the cantilevers of the bridge were in use until replaced in 1911. The line was finally opened in February 1880, after six years of work.

The road was leased the following year to representatives of Emile Erlanger and Company. Rental fees ranged from $800,000 annually for the first five years to $1.25 million for the last five. The lessee, a new firm known as the Cincinnati, New Orleans & Texas Pacific Railway, maintained the line and paid taxes and assessments. Within two years the line was carrying 600,000 passengers annually, and owned 54 locomotives, 2,274 freight cars, and 42 passenger cars. Business improved even more rapidly after

Out of the Ashes

1886 when the line changed its 5-foot gauge to the standard 4 feet 8½ inches, conforming to the width of standard roads reaching Cincinnati from the north. Following months of preparation, this change was made in one day, during a thirteen-hour period; during the night trains were running once more along the 446 miles, including sidings.

In 1890, when the road's trustees and the lessee disagreed over road conditions and the lack of terminal facilities in Cincinnati, the case went to arbitration. President Charles Schiff of the railroad named as arbitrators ex-President Grover C. Cleveland and Clarence A. Seward, son of William H. Seward, secretary of state under Lincoln. Arbitrators decided in favor of the trustees.

Largely as a result of the fraudulent issue of stock by Secretary George F. Doughti, the road went into receivership in 1893 and Samuel Felton, the line's able and experienced new president, served as receiver for six years before resigning. He was succeeded by Samuel Spencer, the president of Southern Railway, and control of the line passed to Southern.

Meanwhile another Erlanger rail investment, the Alabama & Chattanooga, acquired in 1877, had been reorganized as the Alabama Great Southern, operating between Chattanooga and Meridian. In 1890 this line, which owned ten thousand shares of Cincinnati, New Orleans & Texas Pacific Stock, was sold to the East Tennessee, Virginia & Georgia Railroad. When the East Tennessee fell into the hands of the expanding Richmond Terminal System, the Virginia holding company was near collapse, and in the ensuing reorganization Southern Railway was born. Thus Southern acquired the Cincinnati, New Orleans & Texas Pacific, which has been operated as part of Southern since 1897. The farsighted investment urged upon his city by Edward Ferguson had proved to be an ever-increasing bonanza.

The Alabama Great Southern, the second link in the Erlanger network, had grown out of the Wills Valley Railroad in Tennessee and the companion Northeast & Southwest Alabama Railroad. These two tiny roads had come under control of two brothers from Boston, John C. and Daniel N. Stanton, vigorous managers who combined the roads into the Alabama & Chattanooga and built that into a 295-mile line running diagonally across Alabama from Chattanooga to Meridian.

Despite scandals and other difficulties of Reconstruction the Stantons made progress. Unable to hire Negroes after advancing wages from the usual $.75 daily to $1.75, they imported three thousand Chinese coolies from California, where they had helped to build the Central Pacific and Union Pacific. These Chinese, proud and difficult to manage, liked to live in tents and spent wages freely on whiskey, chickens, cheap goods, and gambling. The Chinese bested Negroes in dice games so consistently that the camps were swept by riots, which the Chinese always managed to subdue. John Stanton's coolies created Birmingham from a rail crossing in cotton fields; Stanton's partner John T. Milner laid out the town and, with Stanton and Col. Sam Tate, controlled much of the rich mineral lands nearby, through ownership of the Elyton Land Company.

Even at this moment of great promise, however, the expanding railroad was near disaster; it defaulted on its bonds in 1871, setting off a bitter debate in the Alabama legislature as to whether the state should pay interest on the bonds or default. Though the state paid the bonds, it seized the road, and chaos followed. Laborers revolted. Unpaid hands in Chattanooga imprisoned a watchman, disabled locomotives, and ruined machinery. Another mob halted passenger trains and seized them.

After some years in receivership, the railroad was sold to the Erlangers at a price of $600,000, and reappeared as the Alabama Great Southern in 1877, with $10 million in fresh capital. The line grew rapidly until, in 1890, the Erlangers sold it to the Richmond & Danville and the East Tennessee, Virginia & Georgia. The Southern acquired the latter properties in 1894, and the Alabama Great Southern the following year.

Development of the Queen & Crescent Route to Mobile followed a similar pattern. The energetic Francis B. Clark of Mobile founded a new line in 1866—the Mobile & Alabama Grand Trunk Railroad, to run from the Gulf into middle Alabama. He hired an exceptionally able engineer in Col. Alfred L. Rives, who had designed improvements of the Potomac and designed and built the celebrated Cabin John Bridge over the Potomac, the largest single-arch stone bridge of the era. Rives saw the potential of central Alabama mineral deposits and routed his road with a view to making Mobile the great coaling port of the Gulf. Anticipating heavy traffic, the tracks he laid were T rails weighing sixty pounds to the yard, then the heaviest in general use in the South. The line opened in 1871 but, after a prosperous beginning, failed in 1873 and was acquired and reorganized by the expanding East Tennessee, Virginia & Georgia—which now controlled fifteen hundred miles of railroad in Tennessee, Georgia, Alabama, and Mississippi.

Out of the Ashes

The new management completed the line from Marion to Mobile, but fell in the crash of the Richmond Terminal System in the early 1890s. When Southern emerged from this wreck, it rejected the Mobile & Birmingham line because of its poor condition; it was not until 1895 that Southern purchased control of its stock and proceeded to develop it to serve the steadily growing port of Mobile.

The final link in the great north-south line built by the Erlangers reached New Orleans on a direct route of 195 miles from Meridian, a line conceived by Captain William H. Hardy of Meridian, a lawyer and Confederate veteran. With the aid of the former Confederate general James Longstreet and Engineer George Ingham, Hardy obtained a charter for the New Orleans & Northeastern Railroad, but a depression intervened, and in 1877, when the Erlangers took a controlling interest, prospects of success grew bright for the first time. Work began in 1882 and was complete within a year.

One of the wonders of American railroad construction was a spectacular feature of the New Orleans & Northeastern. The Lake Pontchartrain Bridge, twenty-one and a half miles long, was Hardy's so-called moonshine bridge, dismissed by critics as fantastic. But the $1.3 million structure soon stretched across the lake, shortening the run from Meridian to New Orleans by several miles, and paying for itself in lower operating costs. The approaches, fifteen miles long, were built of untreated pilings and timbers, but the six-mile span over the lake itself rested on creosoted pilings. Two steel swing drawbridges rested on stone piers. During months of construction, crews drove 9,600 pile bents (six piles to a bent, or a total of 57,600 piles).

The route to Meridian crossed a most sparsely settled country, without a town or hamlet on the route. Captain Hardy rode the route in a buggy to select sites for new towns. At a spot where a projected line northward from the Gulf would cross his line, the Captain laid out a town which he named for his wife Hattie. Thus was Hattiesburg, Mississippi, born in 1884.

On Sunday, 18 November 1883, "the Day of Two Noons," the cities of New Orleans, Birmingham, Chattanooga, and Cincinnati celebrated both the opened road of the Queen & Crescent, and the adoption of Standard Time in the United States. The Queen & Crescent Limited, Number 1 and Number 2, a superb train equipped with Pullman compartment-buffet cars, began regular schedules. Settlers flocked to the newly opened territory and

Out of the Ashes

small towns began to evolve. Land values doubled. In July 1889 circumstance brought into this back country the most exciting event in the history of "the Old Northeastern"—the world's heavyweight championship boxing bout between John L. Sullivan and Jake Kilrain—the last bare-knuckle battle for the crown. "The battle of the century" was fought in a pine woods near Hattiesburg. The bout had been scheduled for New Orleans, and vast crowds had gathered, ready to pay $10 and $15 for tickets; prize money was an unheard-of $50,000. But irate citizens protested that this brutal display was contrary to state law, and obliged officials to ban the fight. The New Orleans & Northeastern came to the rescue, running two trains of two thousand fight fans each to an undisclosed destination in Mississippi, where a prize ring had been hastily erected within a natural amphitheater, and there Sullivan and Kilrain pummeled each other for seventy-five rounds, the longest fight in prize-ring history. Sullivan emerged the victor.

Though the Southern entered New Orleans in 1895 when it acquired control of the New Orleans & Northeastern, it did not have actual ownership until 1916, when the Southern began developing larger terminal facilities and a passenger station, preparing for its role in the modern development of the Crescent City and its port.

A small road developed by the Erlanger interests in this period was the New Orleans & Gulf, a successor to the Mexican Gulf, whose predecessor dated from 1834. The line from New Orleans ran along the east bank of the Mississippi to the Gulf of Mexico. By 1887, after several changes of name and management, the line had grown to seventy-one miles and became the New Orleans & Gulf.

But though it more than doubled its investment in the first four years and revenues trebled, expenses and debt load increased more rapidly and the Erlangers bought the road at auction in 1890. The new road that emerged, the New Orleans & Southern, survived until 1933, when it went into receivership. In May 1945, only three years after emerging from receivership, the Louisiana Southern paid off the last of its mortgage bonds and was entirely free of debt, a position enjoyed by few American lines. In 1953 the doughty Louisiana Southern became part of the Southern System, when the New Orleans & Northeastern purchased its stock. The Louisiana Southern has continued to operate under its own name.

In neighboring Alabama, lines that failed to attract the sharp eyes of the Erlanger managers did not fare so well. The Alabama

Out of the Ashes

& Tennessee River Railroad, seeking a man of talent and wide reputation to guide the company through Reconstruction, chose as president Gen. Joseph E. Johnston, "the Old Gray Fox" of the Confederacy. Johnston's first task was to raise money to rebuild the line from Blue Mountain to Selma and to push the road on to Dalton, Georgia. A merger with two small roads—the Dalton & Gadsden and the Georgia & Alabama—produced a consolidated line known as the Selma, Rome & Dalton, of which Johnston remained president. Johnston secured a loan of $5 million to complete his road to Dalton, but at that time control was gradually passing from men of the region to northern interests. Dissatisfied with "outsiders" who imposed their will on management, Johnston resigned in 1867. He was succeeded by Frederick H. Delano of New York, which prompted the Selma *Times & Messenger* to deplore "strange names" now listed by the railroad.

The fresh capital completed the railroad, a link which gave, for the first time, a direct rail route from New York to New Orleans. But even as the new line reached Dalton the company defaulted on its bonds and went into receivership. In 1881 it emerged as part of the giant East Tennessee, Virginia & Georgia, and operated as such until 1894, when it became a link in the Southern's system.

Nathan Bedford Forrest, the only man in the Civil War who rose from the rank of private to that of lieutenant general, was little more fortunate in his railroad career than Joe Johnston had been. A wealthy trader in cotton, livestock, and slaves before the war, Forrest had freed forty slaves during the conflict and returned to his Delta plantation in Mississippi to make a fresh start in 1865. His interest in railroads led him to plan a new road from Memphis into central Alabama, which was destined to become the South's first great industrial region.

From Memphis, Forrest planned a route into rich cotton country, through Holly Springs, Pontotoc, and Columbus, Mississippi, thence into the heart of Alabama through Selma to Birmingham. He plunged into railroad promotion with the same zeal with which he had organized and led his celebrated cavalry corps during the war. He enlisted the support of regional leaders, including Judge Porter King and Dr. Alexander W. Jones of Selma and his own wartime engineer, Gen. Edward W. Rucker of Tennessee, as well as ex-Governor Jacob Thompson of Mississippi.

The new road, the Selma, Marion & Memphis, acquired the old thirteen-mile line of the Cahawba, Marion & Greensboro, and un-

Out of the Ashes

der the leadership of Forrest, began construction of its western portion in Tennessee and Mississippi in 1869. Rails came from a new plant in Chattanooga, the region's first large iron mill, and the first train of the road began service in 1870.

Early efforts at financing went smoothly. The forceful, persuasive general announced the sale of $400,000 in bonds at 92½ cents on the dollar, a remarkable feat for such a small southern road. The state of Alabama and counties and towns on the route joined the effort. When the line opened from Marion to Greensboro in November 1870, an Alabama newspaper hailed Forrest as "the most energetic and enterprising railroad man the country has yet produced." But Forrest realized that his rails were outrunning the line's resources. He became so irritable that he quarreled with several associates, including Chief Engineer Meriwether, a friend of long standing. When Meriwether declined to certify the railroad as complete in order to obtain a state loan on a section in Alabama, he and Forrest came near a duel.

By March 1873, though rails reached as far west as Sawyersville, Alabama, Forrest saw his road drifting to ruin. The numerous bankruptcies of the depression of that year forced investors to liquidate holdings, bond prices fell, and the Selma, Marion & Memphis defaulted on its bonds despite all efforts of Forrest to save it. The aging general, afflicted by chronic dysentery, a wartime ailment, went along the route once more, preaching of the economic benefits that a completed line would bring; he sank his personal fortune into the project, but in vain. The road went bankrupt in 1876, and Forrest now neared the end of his active, frequently violent, life. He resigned as president of the line at the end of 1874, in poor health and heavily in debt. He died in 1877, mourned by his thousands of veterans and many others of his region who had shared his hopes in the ill-starred rail venture that would long be known as General Forrest's Railroad.

Bondholders bought the property in 1878 for $75,000 and it was reorganized twice before emerging as the Cincinnati, Selma & Mobile. It was acquired by the ubiquitous East Tennessee, Virginia & Georgia and eventually made its way into the Southern Railway System in 1894, as a valuable branch through the rich "Black Belt" of Alabama.

The end of the war in east Tennessee brought the region's twin railroads toward consolidation. The merger of the East Tennessee & Georgia and the East Tennessee & Virginia in 1869, under the leadership of Thomas H. Callaway, opened the way for an almost

Out of the Ashes

incredible expansion throughout the South. Callaway not only shepherded his line through the war; he achieved the merger and conducted difficult negotiations with federal authorities to keep the road alive, on terms that made possible almost immediate expansion.

Callaway's death in 1870 brought to the road's presidency his energetic partner in a New York banking and cotton brokerage firm, forty-year-old Richard T. Wilson. A native Georgian, Wilson had become a leading Tennessee merchant and during the war had served the Confederacy as commissary general. He was to direct the East Tennessee line until 1880, leading it to regional prominence through resourceful management and a gift for mergers and acquisitions. He led the East Tennessee to a fivefold expansion by 1882, with 1,453 miles of railroad in four states.

Among his early moves, Wilson acquired majority stock of the Memphis & Charleston and leased its lines to the East Tennessee for ten years. He then purchased the Selma, Rome & Dalton and Alabama Central roads, with trackage rights over the Mobile & Ohio to Meridian. Moving south and east, Wilson bought the Macon & Brunswick line in Georgia, and then, by building several short links, created a direct line from Chattanooga to Brunswick via Atlanta.

In 1882, after Wilson retired and E. W. Cole took over, financial troubles overtook this large system, too. The East Tennessee, Virginia & Georgia went into receivership. The company was sold for $10.25 million in 1886 and reorganized a month later under the same name, then known as "the New Georgia." Even now, fresh acquisitions were made: the Mobile & Birmingham, and, of vital importance to later managers, the Alabama Great Southern—which controlled the Cincinnati, New Orleans & Texas Pacific. The new line also leased tracks into Cincinnati and Louisville. In the same year—1890—the New Georgia struck a blow at its old rival, the Louisville & Nashville, by purchasing the Louisville Southern, placing it in the Louisville & Nashville's headquarters city. On the eve of its demise, Wilson's overgrown system had won its way into two great gateway cities on the Mississippi.

The East Tennessee, Virginia & Georgia was taken over by the Richmond Terminal Company, so that the old Tennessee roads shared the financial disaster of the holding company's losses in the 1890s. In 1894 the Southern purchased the New Georgia for about $1.5 million.

This doleful and now-familiar pattern was repeated in railroad

Out of the Ashes

development throughout the South. In Atlanta, where hopes were bright, the founders Lemuel Grant and Jonathan Norcross, having survived the war with ambitions intact, planned to create a Piedmont Air Line Route to connect their city with Carolina's roads. Ground was broken in Atlanta in 1869, but the state of the regional economy handicapped financing. Even as trains began running from Charlotte to Atlanta, providing shippers with their first direct service to Atlanta and New Orleans, a financial crisis brought ruin. The line went into receivership in 1874.

Another colorful Civil War figure, the ex-U.S. general Herman Haupt, tried to save the Air Line, but his two-year struggle as its general manager ended in failure. The 269-mile road was sold at auction for a little less than $6 million. The new owner was an unlikely railroader, Hiram W. Sibley of Rochester, New York, a philanthropist who had founded the Western Union Telegraph Company, but had no experience with railroads. Still, Sibley managed the Air Line well, trebling earnings and almost doubling revenues in three years. He also improved the road by replacing iron rails with steel and by altering tracks to standard gauge.

The Atlanta & Charlotte Air Line, as it was officially known, was flourishing when it was leased to the Richmond & Danville Railroad during the latter's expansion of the early 1880s, and was operated by that line until 1894, when it went into the Southern's fold. The Air Line became the main line of the Southern between Charlotte and Atlanta.

Another major route developed in Georgia in the postwar years is a monument to the Confederate general John B. Gordon, who had emerged from the war with seven wounds, including one that had cost him an arm. "Too tough to kill," he said, when asked how he had survived. Gordon was elected to three terms in the U.S. Senate, but resigned to promote a 600-mile railroad from Atlanta to Texarkana, Texas, where it would connect with a line to the Pacific. His dream, partially realized, resulted in the Georgia Pacific, from Atlanta westward through Birmingham to Columbus, Mississippi.

Gordon began by building on two earlier roads, the Georgia Western, from Atlanta to Austell, Georgia, and the narrow-gauge Greenville, Columbus & Birmingham, then building from the Mississippi toward the coal mines near Birmingham. Gordon made an agreement with the East Tennessee, Virginia & Georgia, exchanging half interest in the Georgia Western's projected extension in return for a cash loan. He then revealed his plans to offi-

Out of the Ashes

cials of the Richmond & Danville in Virginia, so convincingly that he received millions of dollars in pledges. Henceforth, however, Richmond & Danville controlled the Georgia Pacific, and constructed its westward line through a subsidiary.

The first Georgia Pacific train entered Birmingham, population 4,000, in November 1883, and six years later the entire 459-mile line from Atlanta to the Mississippi was complete. Although General Gordon resigned as president that year, he was not at the end of his career. He served as Georgia's governor and returned to the Senate in 1890. His successor as head of the Georgia Pacific was his friend John W. Johnston, who served for six years.

Johnston, in turn, yielded to Joseph Bryan of Richmond, the editor-publisher of the Richmond *Times*, who thus began a long family association with the Southern Railway System. Bryan served as president until the line's acquisition by Southern in 1894, and as director of Southern until his death in 1908. His son Jonathan was a member of the Board during the twenties, and his grandson, John Stewart Bryan, publisher of the Richmond Newspapers, served from 1933 to 1944. In 1953 Joseph Bryan's great grandson, D. Tennant Bryan, president and publisher of the Richmond Newspapers, became a member of the Board, a position he held until 1983. This record of four generations from one family serving on the board of directors of a railroad company is believed to be unique.

Other progressive leaders were opening regions of eastern and southern Georgia to rail service in the postwar years. The old Macon & Brunswick line, which had survived the war, began to prosper under the presidency of George H. Hazelhurst, who had advanced from chief engineer. Hazelhurst contracted with Morris Jesup, a New York merchant banker, to exchange railroad bonds in payment for locomotives, cars, and rail. It was a fortunate alliance, for Jesup's associates in the transactions were Henry B. Plant of Augusta, Georgia, then building a chain of railroads, steamship lines, and hotels, and Jeremiah Milbank, a New York investor who later became a large holder of Southern Railway securities—and whose grandson and namesake became a Southern director in 1923.

Capital from Jesup and his friends launched the Macon & Brunswick on a period of rapid expansion and the 185-mile line between the two cities opened in 1869, bringing new life to an isolated section of rural Georgia. The Macon & Brunswick also thus became a link in the most direct mail route between New

Out of the Ashes

York and Jacksonville. But this line, too, was vulnerable to the panic of 1872 and went into receivership. The state of Georgia, after trying to operate the line for two years, put it up for auction, but was forced to buy the line from itself. By 1880 the Macon & Brunswick was in the East Tennessee, Virginia & Georgia network, where it remained until the collapse of the early 1890s, and both parent and subsidiary joined the Southern.

In the region to the south, the Georgia Southern & Florida, chartered in 1881, was built by a group of northern investors who held large pinelands in southern Georgia and wished to take their timber to market. A line was planned from Macon to Palatka, Florida, on the St. Johns River, to connect with rapidly expanding Florida railroads. The line reached Palatka in 1890, reaching the southernmost point in the Southern System of the future. In 1895 the Georgia Southern & Florida entered receivership and became part of the Southern in that year. With the benefit of an extension from Valdosta and Jacksonville and other improvements, the line's revenues and net income more than doubled in the next ten years.

It was in the upper reaches of the Southern's future territory that some of the most vigorous—and reckless—developments took place after the war. The Virginia railroad companies whose excesses were to lead to financial disaster and the rise of the Southern became active in the very shadow of Appomattox.

The Richmond & Danville, one of the few Southern roads to weather Reconstruction with a sound reputation, began the new era under seasoned managers whose goals were fiscal integrity and efficient service, but political realities forced immediate changes. President Lewis Harvie, though he took a loyalty oath and offered cooperation, was ousted by the federal authorities and Col. Algernon Sidney Buford, a Danville lawyer and publisher, was named to succeed him (stockholders had voted overwhelmingly for Gen. Joseph E. Johnston as president, but were overruled). Buford, though utterly without railroad experience, was among the pleasant surprises of southern railroading in these difficult times. He was to remain in office for twenty-one years, transforming a broken-down 200-mile road into a regional system of 2,287 miles.

Buford began by rebuilding tracks and bridges and renewing rolling stock, spending almost $1 million during 1866–67 for this purpose. By 1870 he reported that all financial obligations had been met, the company's credit was restored, and the price of its stock had doubled. Buford then began making acquisitions that took his line into several southern states and eventually led to involvement with the Richmond Terminal Company.

The chain of events that led to the upheaval of the 1890s and a new day in southern railroading had begun with the distress of the little Richmond & York River Railroad, which entered receivership in 1872 and was taken over by Thomas Clyde of Philadelphia and R. S. Burrowes of New York. Clyde's coming was to prove fateful for railroads in Virginia and elsewhere in the South.

He was "the greatest ship owner in America," whose steamship lines connected New York with southern ports. When he reorganized the York River Railroad, Clyde also created the Baltimore, Chesapeake & Richmond Steamship Company, whose vessels connected with the railroad at the head of the York River. Soon afterward, the York River entered an agreement with the Richmond & Danville to build a connecting track in Richmond, and the Richmond & Danville leased both the York River road and Clyde's steamship line in 1881. It was still operating them in 1894 when they were acquired by Southern. The steamship line, which was celebrated for its service and lavish accommodations, was reorganized in 1896 as the Chesapeake Steamship Company, affectionately known as "the Old Bay Line." It was to operate for many years under the joint ownership of the Southern, Seaboard & Atlantic Coast Line, with its southern terminus in Norfolk.

Three other Virginia roads, all in northern Virginia, were destined to join the Southern after their postwar reorganization. The old Alexandria, Loudoun & Hampshire cherished dreams of reaching the Ohio River, but after two name changes and a time in receivership, it was leased by the Richmond & Danville, and so followed the well-traveled route through bankruptcy to the Southern's ownership.

A more important development was the merger of the pioneer roads, the Orange & Alexandria and Manassas Gap, in 1867—the latter still under leadership of its durable president, Edward Carrington Marshall, the son of Chief Justice John Marshall. The merged line, having consolidated with the Lynchburg & Danville in 1872, finally emerged as the Washington City, Virginia Midland & Great Southern, and under this grand designation entered receivership in 1876. Ten years later, having been reorganized by the Baltimore & Ohio as the Virginia Midland, the line was leased to the Richmond & Danville, which shepherded it into the great reconstruction of rail networks in 1894.

Out of the Ashes

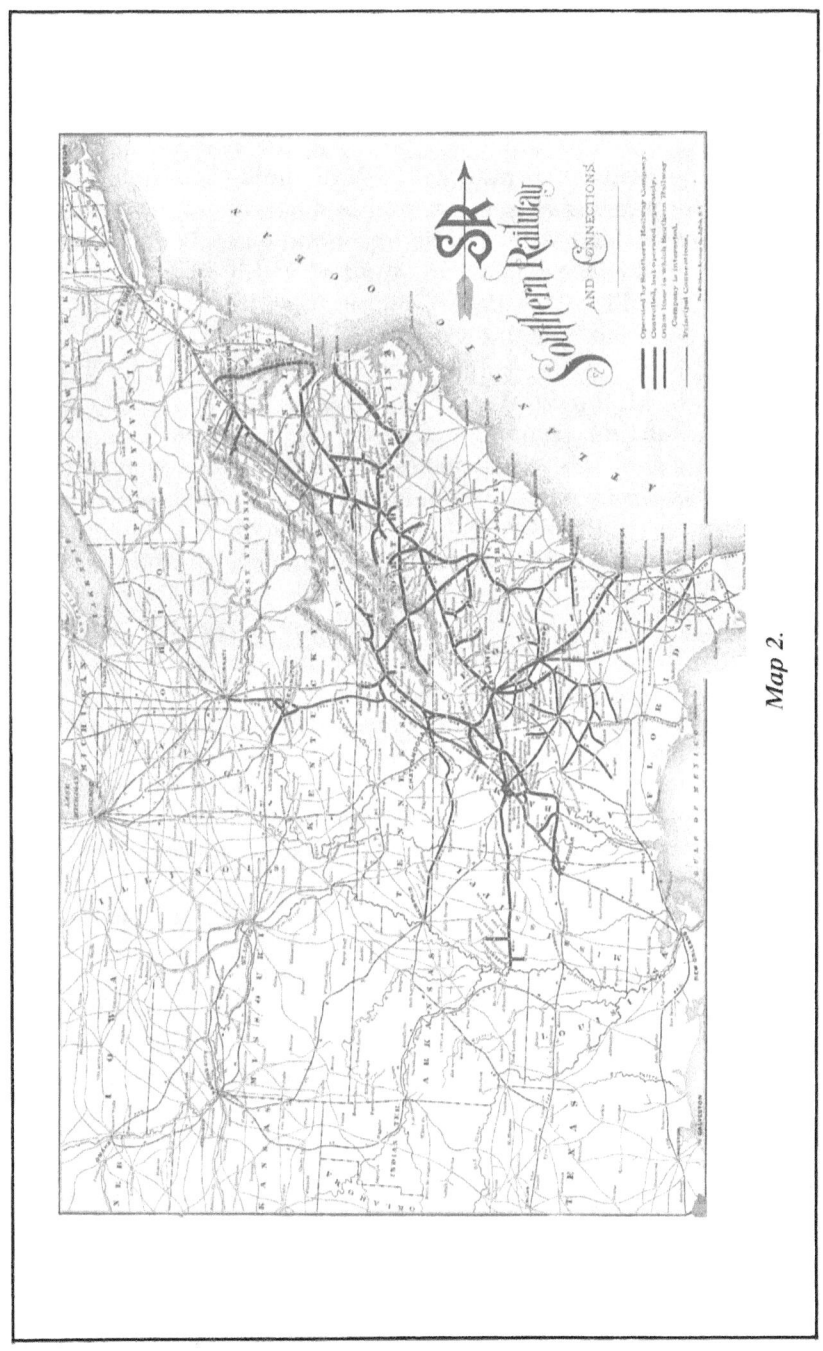

Map 2.

Out of the Ashes

North Carolina's contribution to the Southern System was to include some of the most painfully won railroad mileage in America. The 308-mile Western North Carolina line between Salisbury and Murphy, North Carolina, and between Asheville and Paint Rock, Tennessee, was completed in the postwar era in the face of apparently insurmountable difficulties. This line, first to traverse the Blue Ridge, penetrated the most mountainous region in the eastern United States, at one point passing through the highest tunnel east of Colorado, at an elevation of 2,516 feet. Its six tunnels, built within an area four miles long and two miles wide, were a unique engineering marvel.

The Western North Carolina began its new life after the war in the hands of Milton S. Littlefield of Maine, "the Prince of Carpet Baggers," and his accomplice George W. Swepson. The road's western division was first headed by Swepson, who resigned under criticism in favor of Littlefield, whose ascent provoked even louder protests. An investigation found that the two had stolen about $4 million in railroad funds, but though the thieves were caught after fleeing to New York, no more than a quarter of the loot was recovered. The scandal halted work for several years and the line went through receivership and into state ownership before ex-Governor Zebulon B. Vance was returned to the governorship in 1877. Vance improved matters by installing as "president, chief engineer and superintendent" Major James W. Wilson, one of the prewar contractors of the line.

Wilson and his chief assistant, Col. Thad Coleman, made quick work of the forbidding task. Coleman first conquered the stubborn Mud Cut, a formation that flowed, shifted, and "boiled" for weeks, until the crews managed to stabilize it. Workmen then moved to the most demanding task yet faced: carrying the road up an elevation of more than 1,000 feet in 3.4 miles, at the top of which they must blast out a long tunnel. Wilson negotiated this grade by laying more than 9 miles of track circuitously, with a total curvature of 2,776.4 degrees; in places the line nearly crossed itself. At one point a fill more than 300 feet deep supported two track levels. Veteran railroaders recalled for years how brakemen on eastbound trains often swung off their engines and slid 300 feet down the embankment to open a switch for their train several minutes before it reached the siding. In one place, travelers could see ten parts of the railroad beneath them.

Yet, in March 1879, after less than three months of construction, tunneling crews atop Swannanoa Gap, "holed through" and

Out of the Ashes

shouted in triumph. Wilson telegraphed Governor Vance: "Daylight entered Buncombe County, today through the Swannanoa Tunnel. Grade and centers met exactly." Crews then began the approach to Asheville and reached the village of 2,600 in October 1880.

About this time the state sold its interest to New York investors headed by William J. Best. Without means but with wealthy friends, Best borrowed money from William T. Clyde, Thomas M. Logan, and Algernon Buford, who were in control of the Richmond & West Point Terminal Railway & Warehouse Company. When Best was unable to repay his loan, he assigned his interest to the three Terminal executives, who promptly transferred it to their company. The Western North Carolina thus became involved in the tangled affairs of the Virginia speculators.

Still, the road retained its name and accomplished some of its most notable feats under the direction of Col. A. B. Andrews, who was sent down to become president. Andrews, known as one of the region's most able railroad men, had been serving the Richmond & Danville as vice-president, but he now turned his energies to completing the mountain railroad on which he had earned his reputation. His associates were Frank Coxe of Philadelphia, vice-president, builder of Asheville's Battery Park Hotel; Vardry E. (Bunch) McBee, superintendent; and Major Wilson, chief engineer.

With the labor of hundreds of convicts from the North Carolina state prison, Wilson made rapid progress and by January 1882 the rails reached Paint Rock and the Pigeon River. Tracks reached Waynesville in 1884, and Charleston (now Bryson City) in 1886. For the next six years progress was slow, as crews crept down the rugged Valley River region toward Murphy in Cherokee County— a route selected in order to avoid the boring of fourteen tunnels on higher ground. Completion of the road opened the isolated "Land of the Sky" to the outside world for the first time and brought immediate development to the area. Soon after the road reached Murphy, the Richmond & Danville, which had controlled the Western North Carolina for fourteen years, was forced into receivership.

In August 1894 the mountain road, valued at almost $17 million, was sold at auction at the courthouse door in Salisbury, North Carolina. The winning bidder was the Southern Railway, which bought it for $500,000.

Thus it was that these bankrupt rail properties, the residue of

Out of the Ashes

generations of sacrifice, struggle, and investment, came into the care of Samuel Spencer, who was quick to build on the accomplishments of the pioneers. Without the vision of Spencer and the financial strength of the house of Morgan, the twentieth-century achievements of Finley, Harrison, and Norris would have been impossible.

And on the first day of 1952, assuming control of the System from Ernest Norris, the new president, Harry A. DeButts, acknowledged the worth of the Southern's heritage and paid tribute to the thousands of men and women—most of them anonymous—who had created the rail system that was so soon to become known as the leader of its industry.

THIRTEEN

"We Were Happy, and It Showed"

Harry DeButts hastened to assure employees and stockholders that he had no intention of rocking the boat. As he declared in his first presidential message, "there will be no change in those sound, basic policies which have guided our railroad through the years." His goals, the new president said, were to expand efforts for development of the South, to "treat fairly" the thousands of men and women who kept the System running, and to pay stockholders an adequate return.

"We have a fine railway, an organization second to none and a wealth of public good will built up over the years ... we can face the future with confidence."

His audience might have assumed that Southern was to continue on its course without a change in rhythm. No one, including DeButts, could foresee that the System was on the verge of revolutionary change which would alter all American railroad operations and make Southern a leading force in the industry.

This upheaval in Southern's affairs was to be presided over by DeButts, but achieved in partnership with Bill Brosnan, who had become vice-president, Operations, with the presidential change. One of the most successful collaborations in the industry's history was to be conducted by these two leaders, whose styles and personalities were in such striking contrast. DeButts would have been an effective leader on his own. With Brosnan at his side, he was to create a new identity for Southern.

DeButts was to promote industrial growth in the territory and expand the System through the addition of thousands of miles of new track. Though he was a gifted salesman, DeButts was not merely "a front man." His knowledge of operations was thorough, his devotion to the railroad was complete, and despite his affable manner, he could be a firm, resolute executive.

Brosnan's contribution to the era was to be more spectacular, directing operations with a flourish, imposing an iron will upon problems that had plagued railroad men since the days of the first steam engine. Like DeButts, he was utterly loyal to the Southern.

The two were to work together closely, and though an air of

tension underlay their relationship, the welfare of the System seemed to be paramount throughout their eleven-year "partnership."

"Bill Brosnan did things on the railroad that nobody else could ever have done," DeButts later said. "He had more than ability—he had the vision and the nerve and the drive. Once he decided on a course, nothing or nobody could stop him. He didn't care what got in the way, he eliminated it. In some respects he was a little abrasive, because he had little patience with those who couldn't do the job he could do. There were times when I had to rein him in a little. But by and large, he was superb—no one ever like him on an American railroad, and we usually got along just fine."

DeButts was almost born into the Southern Railway. His father and one grandfather had worked for the railroad, the latter as station master at Delaplane, Virginia, where Harry was born, just a few yards from the railroad tracks. His paternal grandfather, Richard E. DeButts, had been an original stockholder in the Manassas Gap Railroad, which had been absorbed by the Southern System.

Before he was ten years old, Harry was spending most of his spare time at his grandfather's station, where he helped to carry cargo across the tracks on his back. In return, he was given a free ride in the locomotive cab or caboose to the next station, Rectortown, some five or six miles distant. "I never minded the walk back," he said.

He was also unquestionably an heir to strong southern and Virginia traditions. Both grandfathers had ridden with the legendary Confederate cavalryman Gen. Turner Ashby during the Civil War. DeButts was related by blood and marriage to the families of Ashby and of Robert E. Lee.

Harry attended a one-room country school of fewer than twenty students, whose ages ranged from eight to eighteen, and here he came under the autocratic control of Miss Lizzie Johnson, who gave him a basic education. While living with a kinsman in Front Royal, he completed high school and then, with the aid of a state cadetship secured through a political friend of the family, Harry entered Virginia Military Institute.

"There I learned what discipline means," DeButts recalled. "The honor system and physical training were superb. I wasn't a brilliant student by any means, but thank God I got along with people. All the DeButtses who've been there before me had trouble, too. In fact, it wasn't until about 1936, when John DeButts

"We Were Happy, and It Showed"

went there, that old General Olly Anderson, the head of the math department, declared, 'Thank God, I've finally got a DeButts with some sense.'"

Harry had no thoughts of a career other than with Southern. His application had gone in several months before his graduation in 1916, and he soon found himself in Fairfax Harrison's new apprentice training program, working on a track gang out of Culpeper, Virginia. Here, in company with five veteran black laborers, he came under the eye of section foreman John Gilbert, a stern taskmaster. "It took me two weeks to learn which was the heavy end of a crosstie," DeButts remembered. "Those old hand-hewn things weren't straight. I noticed that those black fellows always chose one end and gave me the other, and I had a hard time of it until I learned. But I was in good physical condition from VMI training and I lived through it."

He was moved to the nearby flagstop of Buena as section foreman, where he spent four months, "until my superior found out I didn't know enough about tracks to stay there." In fact, he was promoted to the Alexandria yard, where he served as assistant general foreman. When the United States entered World War I in 1917, DeButts volunteered as a marine private. He returned after the war to become a track supervisor in Virginia, first at Strasburg and then at Harrisonburg. Then, progressing from the division at Mobile and Selma, Alabama, he moved "about sixteen times in fifteen years" to posts throughout the System as assistant trainmaster, trainmaster, division and general superintendent, and became a general manager in 1934. Three years later, when Ernest Norris became president, DeButts had succeeded him as vice-president, Operations.

DeButts was the first graduate of the apprentice training program to become president, and he remained grateful for that early experience throughout his life. He attributed much of Southern's success in fostering high morale among its officers to this program and the attitudes it inspired.

"Through that training we built up a very strong, friendly type of organization—a kind of family affair. Most of our promotion has been from the ranks, and almost all of us came up step by step, beginning by doing the very hardest work on the railroad. And above and below, we had engineering graduates from southern colleges all along the line. I think it's one of the best posssible ways to build up spirit in a company. We knew each other, and all felt at home. We were happy, and it showed.

"We Were Happy, and It Showed"

"As a result, other railroads that failed to establish such a program often called on us to provide presidents for them. There have been quite a lot—at one time six Southern-trained men served as presidents of other railroads. I credit Fairfax Harrison for that."

When he became president on 1 January 1952, Harry DeButts was fifty-three, with thirty-five years of intensive training behind him, and a lively appreciation of Southern's traditions. He was also aware of the unique opportunities inherent in the System's strategic location.

His first concern was the basic vulnerability of the System in an era of rising costs. Largely through the vision of Brosnan and his insistence that the situation could be changed, DeButts came to realize that escalating costs of labor made inevitable by the demands of increasingly militant unions could throw Southern into an insolvent condition.

Though Norris had reduced the old Development and General Mortgage to a level of about $65.5 million by 1952—the date of maturity was now only four years away—there was no capital reserve to meet such a debt, and it seemed to be out of the question to increase revenues sufficiently within the period. DeButts turned to Brosnan for aid in increasing net income to generate the needed funds. The obvious need was to improve efficiency and reduce waste. Brosnan was not at a loss for ideas on how the goal should be accomplished. Brosnan's career, in fact, had been one long preparation for this assignment.

He began by calling a meeting in Atlanta barely two months after becoming vice-president. An atmosphere of an emergency war council pervaded the hotel ballroom where he faced a crowd of more than four hundred—general managers, superintendents, master mechanics, division engineers, and operating officers of all ranks. Brosnan's message was grim and his manner was firm, but he exuded confidence. He gave a dramatic view of the railroad's plight, delivered in the forceful manner that was his own: "The Southern is on the rocks. For all practical purposes, we're broke. Our credit is so bad that we can't discount our bills. We owe about $100 million, and within four years a large bond issue will mature. There's no way on earth the company can meet those payments—unless you and I do something about it."

He looked about belligerently. "The people who can do something about all this are in this room. You. Me. All of us together. If

"We Were Happy, and It Showed"

Southern goes to the wall, we'll all be harshly affected, so you have a real personal interest in this.

"I know how we can do it. I know the route we must take. It's the only way. I'll point it out and lead the way and give you all the support in my power—but it's you who must implement it. I can't do it alone. No one or two men can do it. It's going to take all of us. I want to know right now if I can count on you—if you're willing to go that way. If you are, stand up. But don't stand unless you mean it." Everyone stood. Brosnan smiled broadly.

"All right," he said. "We'll do it together. There's enough waste in this company to do what we want to do, if we can eliminate it. We've got to spend more carefully. We've got to replace people—I mean people by the thousands. Replace them with machinery and more efficient methods. There's no other way. We'll do it by using new equipment—equipment that we'll have to develop for ourselves. We need machines that don't exist today, and we'll use them all over the railroad. We'll have to change and improve transportation practices.

"It won't be easy. We may have trouble. We will have trouble, but when that comes, we'll just fight trouble.

"We must cut off thousands of people, as I said. Many of them will be people we all respect and admire. But we have no choice. If we want to work for a solvent company this is our hope, our only hope. But I'll assure you of one thing: you won't have to worry about being cut off yourselves. If anything, this program will need more, not fewer, supervisors. But we must be effective in what we're trying to do. If we don't do a good job, we'll all be casualties."

Brosnan talked well into the afternoon, but he could see that he had won his audience. Some thirty years afterward he said, "I can still feel the fire of determination in that room when the meeting ended."

Bob Fox, a Virginian who was supervisor of bridges, remembered more: "He told us that if we helped him, he'd help us, with raises and better working conditions and retirement and other benefits. The programs we had then were pretty poor. We took him at his word. We went back and went to work. And I mean work."

The campaign to modernize the Southern involved thousands of men, but it was begun by a handful of Brosnan's chosen specialists, working in a small shop building in Charlotte, North Caro-

"We Were Happy, and It Showed"

lina. It was there that Brosnan met regularly with the half-dozen men who were to revolutionize the industry. Among them were the brothers Herb and Bob Fox of Dry Fork, Virginia, sons of a Southern veteran who had trained them in construction trades from their childhood; R. E. (Dick) Franklin, at thirty-one the youngest master mechanic on an American road, his natural engineering skills polished by a correspondence school course; Joe Moore, "Doc" Cain, and Johnny Smith, who had been picked from various mechanical departments.

The pioneers had no time for the methods of orthodox engineers or designers. Franklin recalled: "Brosnan would come to our meetings with an idea for some kind of machine he wanted to develop. He would just draw a sketch of it on the concrete floor of the shop and we'd talk and figure out how it could be built. We'd have barrels put around the floor, with boards laid across them to protect the drawings. We made a sign reading, 'Don't move this.' And we'd work from the drawings."

The drawings were photographed by one of the crew, but were left intact until a machine model was ready. Bob Fox recalled: "We got drawings made by mechanical draftsmen—after we had the things built. All of us would come to those meetings with ideas. The only goal in each case was to substitute machines for men. Brosnan never quit reminding us that manpower was so expensive that it was killing us, that it could only become more expensive. He could foresee that labor would become the most expensive thing in any railroad budget."

One of Brosnan's early projects was a machine to remove old ties and insert new ones in their place, an idea he had been working on himself for some two years, but had been unable to perfect. As Fox said, "Brosnan wanted a machine that could be operated by one man—or two at most—so he could replace those big crews that worked the tracks, laboriously lifting the rails by hand, pulling out each defective tie, digging away the ballast, and fitting in the new tie. He drew the sketch of what he had in mind—a kind of ram to push out the old tie and drag in the new one behind it. It was a rig with a chain working over a wheel, with a number of blocks fixed to the chain. The tracks were to be raised by hydraulic jacks."

Within two months Franklin had made Brosnan's machine operable by minor changes in the design of the chain apparatus, and the replacement of Southern's large crews began. By 1962 all track was maintained by five gangs. For economy, replacement

"We Were Happy, and It Showed"

ties were stored centrally and taken to point of use as needed, rather than being kept in scattered warehouses manned by numerous watchmen—a saving of $.42 per tie. New machines came to Southern as if by magic. Brosnan bought labor-saving devices within an anemic budget. An early introduction was a power tamper developed on another road; Brosnan was resolved that the Southern should be first to utilize fully this replacement for large gangs of hand-tampers. He remembered the difficulties for many years: "Those tampers cost $50,000 apiece. So I cut my labor appropriation enough to buy one, and put it to work. It saved so much money that I could buy another one a month later, and kept that up, month after month, still managing to stay within my budget."

Brosnan worked his tampers sixteen hours a day, rather than the traditional eight hours, and in winter used lights over the tracks to keep men and machines at work. When unions complained that the shifts were sleeping in "hot beds" around the clock, Brosnan bought trailers to follow the crews about, adding to comfort and efficiency. On this and all other projects, Brosnan drove his men as if there were to be no tomorrow. Bob Fox once proposed that bridges be sprayed with protective grease, rather than by hand labor. Brosnan agreed—and demanded a working model within thirty-six hours. Fox recalled: "We worked without stopping for two days and a night, but we made it, and the machine was a success. He was like that—in a tearing hurry, and he wouldn't take no for an answer. He could be satisfied only by the ideal solution, and he wanted it day before yesterday. He was a hard man to work for, but a good one, and he never asked anyone to work harder than he did. I remember my brother Herbert said about Brosnan, 'He's the meanest, bestest, man I ever worked for.'"

Under Brosnan's leadership, Fox began reducing the section gangs in his department. He began with one section gang to every four miles of double track, or eight miles of single track; his first move was to cut off half these gangs, and this worked so well that he halved the remaining crews eighteen months later. Brosnan made the same cuts throughout the system.

Fox said, "By the time I retired, there wasn't a single regular section gang left. We had it worked down to the point that one man, an assistant supervisor, could inspect the track, tighten loose bolts, tend to switch repairs and the like. Then the extra gang did all the rest. What a change!"

"We Were Happy, and It Showed"

Machines then began to appear throughout the system, almost all of them developed and built by Brosnan and his hard-driven crew: an adzing machine to cut notches for fitting rails to ties, whose one operator replaced six men working with hand adzes; a multiple bolt-tightening machine capable of tightening a rail joint within forty seconds; a hydraulic bolt-cutting machine; a bridge jack; a pile driver that operated on both rails and highways; a mechanical bush hog to cut brush along the right of way; a machine for painting buildings; a spiker-nipper; machines for laying and lining up track; the bridge-spraying machine. Herbicide sprays replaced hand labor by men who had pulled weeds and grass from the ballast.

Such innovations had a dramatic effect. Brosnan recalled that the payroll was reduced from about 48,000 to some 16,000. His progress was impressive: "We made money, bought new equipment, and ran a taut ship. Officers and men were proud of their achievements." Bob Fox recalled details: "When we began this work, Southern had 81 bridge gangs. I reduced them to 26. We reduced the hands from 2,100 to 900 on the first cut we made, and by the time I retired the total had been reduced to 371 men." (By the mid-1970s Southern's ratio of labor costs to operating revenues was to be the lowest of any American railroad's.)

Such achievements meant single-minded sacrifice for Brosnan's team. As one old-timer said, "We worked 365 days a year, Christmas, New Year's, Saturdays, Sundays and all. The only way we ever knew it was Sunday was because of the thicker newspapers. And Bill Brosnan was apt to call us anytime, I mean any time, like 2 or 3 o'clock in the morning, when he had something he wanted done right away. It was tough but it was fun and exciting, because we knew we were getting somewhere. We were saving the railroad."

Brosnan also expected miracles of his suppliers. He once decided to have some of his new machines made on a rush basis—and this time Dick Franklin was prepared for the emergency. It was a Saturday, when most machine-manufacturing plants were closed. But Franklin had alerted presidents of several firms to stand by, awaiting the call, and he was able to have the orders accepted with dispatch—for thirty-six tie machines and eighteen spiker-nippers, the largest orders these firms had ever been given.

But Brosnan had only begun to overhaul the Southern. His next step in modernizing maintenance of way was the adoption of con-

"We Were Happy, and It Showed"

tinuous welded rail, which had been developed elsewhere. Characteristically, he set out to make Southern the first major beneficiary of the development; he realized that the elimination of thousands of troublesome open joints on the System's tracks would reduce costs immediately.

At Atlanta's Inman Yard he built a rail-welding and track-assembly plant, which produced welded lengths of rail 1,440 feet long—and he was then forced to design a family of new machinery and equipment to handle the heavy rails. Brosnan's original designs were so nearly complete that it was he who obtained patents on most of this machinery. Stanley Crane, a future president of Southern who joined the pioneering team about this time, played a major role in the design of this equipment. A special train carried almost seven and a half miles of rail to the site of installation, and other custom-made machinery was used to load and unload the rail, and to remove the old track and lay the new, meanwhile holding the rail to gauge. Year after year, Brosnan's men laid this new rail, until, by 1975, more than five thousand miles of the main line was welded rail, ending the familiar old clickety-clack known to generations of rail travelers—and effecting economies for Southern estimated at $1,000 per mile per year. In addition, the track-assembly plant turned out complete sections, with rails in place on crossties, for use in classification yards and on sidings.

Brosnan's intense focus on such problems led one economic historian to observe that the Southern "appeared to be obsessed with technological innovation and labor-saving automation. This ... was the manifestation of D. W. Brosnan's concern about the excessive labor content of railroading. He saw two trends that greatly disturbed him: (1) increasing labor rates, and (2) increasing militancy and constraints in freedom to operate to use labor in the most effective manner. His objective was to reduce manual effort and dependency on labor through the earliest possible introduction of automation."

During this offensive Brosnan's lieutenant, Crane, tackled one of railroading's oldest and most vexing problems—the hotbox. This universal affliction of railroads developed when bearings supporting freight car ends overheated and caused numerous breakdowns and derailments. Until Crane's work was complete, railroaders had been helpless to combat these costly failures.

Crane's solution was to place trackside sensors at scattered points around the system, connected to each rail with magnetic contacts. A few feet beyond these points he placed two metal housings at the level of the wheel hubs. Shutters flicked open in these housings at each passage of the wheels, and an electric eye measured the temperature from the infrared radiation emanating from the journal box.

The modest Crane gave credit for the development to Brosnan: "We were experimenting.... We installed a detector... the third in the country, I think—on the inbound side to Spencer, North Carolina. We had a little trouble with it, but finally got it to work." This detector caught a broken journal just before a train crossed a river bridge, and that sold Southern on the device. Brosnan called Crane and two others.

"I want those things all over the railroad," Brosnan said. "They can feed their data into a central location—Atlanta. The hot boxes can be spotted there, and the trains called and stopped."

Crane was dismayed: "Our hearts dropped down to our shoe tops. I had no more idea of how to accomplish that than I did of how I could fly out the window. I thought, 'Even if I could figure this out, Boss, you couldn't afford to pay for it, anyway.' But I kept my thoughts to myself, because I knew he would say, 'Whether we can afford it is my decision to make.' So we didn't say we didn't know what to do, and got busy instead. You see, it was Brosnan who made us do the things we couldn't accomplish."

Crane's system was soon flashing relative heat measurements to Atlanta, where readings were analyzed and an order was radioed to the proper train, if necessary, so that repairs could be made. By 1961, Southern had progressed so far with the system as to install 53 of these sensor stations throughout the System, and by 1982 had 187 in place. Protection against hotboxes grew more reliable as the work progressed and hotbox detection became commonplace on major railroads.

DeButts backed Brosnan to the limit in this sweeping campaign, though it was to be more far-reaching than he could have imagined in its early stages. Much of the progress made by Brosnan and his group was made possible by the advent of the diesel locomotive. Though it was Norris whose courage and foresight had enabled Southern to assume leadership in dieselization, DeButts was to complete the process, and it was his decision that made Southern the first completely dieselized American railroad.

Throughout the process, during the Norris regime, and particularly during the DeButts years, Brosnan bore major responsibility for the actual conversion of the System to accommodate the new power. Technical and mechanical reforms were formidable in-

"We Were Happy, and It Showed"

deed, requiring adjustments in virtually every practice on the operation side of the System.

Implementing Brosnan's reforms put demands on management and labor. Like other lines, Southern went through a time of learning by trial and error what maintenance the diesels would require, and what new machinery and equipment was needed. Each step was tentative, since the eventual scope of the diesel movement could not be forecast. Norris, DeButts, and Brosnan were all determined to push their efforts to the limit in the interest of efficiency and economy, but at first it appeared that steam engines would remain as the backbone of motive power for years to come. After a few years, when it became apparent that the diesel-electric locomotive was superior in every respect, and complete dieselization became Southern policy, Brosnan was given full authority to meet all problems involved.

Brosnan recalled, "We bought our diesel locomotives from the General Motors Electro-Motive Division mostly. We found that theirs were the best for us because of their minimum down-time; they were in service 92 percent of the time. With steam locomotives, we had to have two on hand to keep one running."

Brosnan realized that the modernization of Southern's shops and procedures should be directed by a plans engineer with talents and training not then to be found on Southern's staff. In a vigorous search covering several months, he interviewed potential prospects, advertised in the *Wall Street Journal*, and sought his man in other ways. At last, almost by accident, he found him in Robert W. Hamilton, a young industrial engineer who had worked in the Electro-Motive Division of General Motors. He offered Hamilton the job.

Hamilton hesitated. He felt that railroads were "too hidebound" to be interesting to him. "I know nothing about railroads," he said.

"No matter," Brosnan said. "You saw that elderly man in the outer office. He knows all there is to know about railroads, but he can't help me. I'm going to change the way railroads do things. I want to modernize our equipment and reorganize our shops on a production basis. I want you to come in as plans engineer—and I'll tell you now, you'll have plenty of authority to accomplish our goals."

Hamilton accepted, and within a few days he and Brosnan began a study of production methods of the automotive industry. Brosnan took Hamilton, Franklin, Joe Moore, the Fox brothers, and George Echols, chief engineer, to an automotive engineering

"We Were Happy, and It Showed"

show in Chicago, seeking new ideas. An official who learned their identity told Brosnan, "You fellows are in the wrong place. This is automotive, not railroading."

But Brosnan divided his group into teams of two or three each and sent them through the exhibit hall to study and talk with manufacturers' representatives and designers of tooling equipment. For two days the Southern's experts explored methods used in Detroit that might be adapted to improve procedures on the railroad. They left with an accumulation of knowledge that was soon put to use in the System's modernized shops.

Wheel-mounting in particular challenged Brosnan and his staff. Wheels were being mounted on Southern cars in fourteen shops scattered over the system, with a work force of about 125 men. As Brosnan said, "The work tended to be as good as our best workmen, or as poor as the worst. There was no uniformity. And some of our machinery was truly antique."

Hamilton recalled: "In each car repair shop, they thought they had to be able to do everything. We had force centralization and then we got some volume. I closed a lot of shops and cut hell out of the employees. I knew what needed to be done, and we reorganized the management of the shops. I could then justify getting good equipment, and set up production systems on freight car repairs—they said it couldn't be done with these cars, but we did it in short order."

When Brosnan and Hamilton and the gifted machinist Dick Franklin completed their work, Southern had one central wheel-mounting shop, at Knoxville, Tennessee, and the force of 125 men had been cut to 6. Lessons of Detroit's production lines had been assimilated, bringing significantly lower costs and greater efficiency to Southern.

Brosnan said of this effort: "When we set up this shop and closed all the rest, we got much better production and much more uniform quality. That was the first railroad shop of its kind, and even today—twenty years later—there are not more than three or four such shops anywhere."

During the program, which was conducted in detail by Hamilton and Dick Franklin, the fourteen diesel shops set up in prior years were reduced to three, and then to two. In the Chattanooga and Atlanta diesel shops Franklin installed a spot method of inspection, based upon Detroit production-line methods, so effective that each shop could handle eighteen locomotives daily. Franklin recalled: "We had to schedule this line so that no single

"We Were Happy, and It Showed"

locomotive would be tied up for long. It worked well then, and still works well today—better than ever, in fact. But it wasn't easy to do. I spent a year straightening out those old shops, rather than simply going out to buy new equipment."

Southern was ruthless in its shop reduction. Franklin once visited an old installation at Spencer, North Carolina, where he fell into a disagreement with state officials over a sewage-disposal system. Franklin simply began moving out men, equipment, and machines the next day. When he reported to Brosnan, the chief was elated. "I've been trying to get out of that place for years," he said.

The governor of North Carolina called Franklin about the move. "You can't do that," he warned.

"The hell I can't," Franklin replied, and he continued the move. This change of shop locations cut seventeen hundred men from the payroll. Southern left behind several sound, venerable buildings, which were developed into a historic site by the state. Southern later added a much larger installation nearby, with the opening of a $44 million yard at Linwood, a computer-operated facility that became the road's seventh modern yard for high-speed freight-car handling.

Bill Brosnan's influence was also felt in the more traditional aspects of railroading during this period, and tales of his resourcefulness and determination became part of a growing legend on Southern. One example of this was Brosnan's handling of a major derailment, when a locomotive and several cars had plunged off the track. His assignment to clear the wreckage brought a new attitude to Southern's operations.

When his men told Brosnan that he would need a 250-ton crane to do the job, and that the closest crane of the size was two days' distant, Brosnan said, "Use the 150-ton crane that we have here."

"It can't be done. It's too light for the job. You'd break the crane if you tried to lift that locomotive with it."

"All right," Brosnan said. "Pick up one end, and then the other. Lessen the capacity each time."

"We don't do it that way."

"We will this time. Let's do it. Now."

The crew went to work, and the track was soon cleared and the line put back into service.

FOURTEEN

"The Best Executive I Ever Saw"

Despite the dramatic improvements ushered in with the diesel era, many veteran railroad men sighed over the changes. Harry DeButts was not the only one who missed the old days. The public as well as railroaders saw the passing of the steam locomotives with pangs of regret.

To thousands of Americans, the most lamentable loss seemed to be the melodic wail of the old steam whistles that they had known for so long. The flat, piercing blast of the new air horns inspired such protests that the railroads tried to find a suitable substitute for the lost whistles. A Canadian researcher, Robert E. Swanson, chief inspector of railways in British Columbia, devised a set of horns, each with a distinctive tone.

DeButts, moved by his sentiment for the past—and by his sense of public relations—arranged for tests of the tuned horns in Potomac Yard at Alexandria, Virginia. The Big Blow went on for three days, as the new horns were blown in comparison and contrast with the old steam whistles. Lieutenant Charles Benter, a retired director of the U.S. Navy Band, was brought in as an expert in harmonics to preside over the tests and choose a new sound for Southern's trains.

After 204 tests, in which whistles and horns blew loudly and softly up and down the scale, while decibel meters and tape recorders monitored them, there emerged at last The Ultimate Sound. Benter ended the process when he heard the pleasing note that he liked. "That's music!" he cried—and Southern had its new air-chime whistle for the diesel era.

As the original air horns were replaced on the System's diesels, Lieutenant Benter's ear for music was applauded by thousands of people who lived within earshot of Southern's tracks. Letters poured in to Southern offices, expressing gratitude for bringing back the sound of the old-time steam locomotive's whistle—or something very like it. Inventive engineers often used their new tuned chimes to render songs or calls. One notable performer was "Dutch" Eiford of the Cincinnati, New Orleans & Texas Pacific

"The Best Executive I Ever Saw"

division, who liked to clear his tracks with renditions of "Oh, How I love Jesus."

The public's nostalgic interest in trains of the steam era also led Southern to donate one of its handsome old heavy Pacifics to the Smithsonian Institution, where it was to be preserved for generations of Americans who had never seen a steam locomotive at work. The project was inspired by Walter H. Thrall of Whittier, California, the son of a Southern employee. In 1952 Thrall wrote Harry DeButts to suggest that the Smithsonian might be interested in preserving one of the huge engines, many of which were already being cut up for scrap as new diesels replaced them.

DeButts passed the suggestion to Robert V. Fleming, a Washington banker who was also a Southern director, and chairman of the executive committee of Smithsonian's Board of Regents. The Smithsonian was definitely interested—but lacked a building in which to house such a huge exhibit. Plans for a new building had been made, but no one was sure when this major addition could be built. DeButts ordered an engine put in storage in Alexandria, until the Smithsonian was ready to accept it.

The engine chosen was the 1401, which had run the Washington-Atlanta line since 1926, one of sixty-four heavy Pacifics put into service by the Southern during the boom years of the 1920s. For most of her working life the 1401 had pulled the crack passenger trains—up to fourteen cars at a top speed of 80 miles per hour. She was among a breed of swift, powerful locomotives acclaimed by railfans as "thoroughbreds." The 1401 had run nearly 2 million miles before her retirement in 1951.

Perhaps the most memorable day in the career of the 1401 was in April 1945, when President Franklin D. Roosevelt's funeral train moved northward from Warm Springs, Georgia, up the Southern's main line to Washington. One of ten Pacifics sharing the work that day, the 1401 served as lead engine on the run from Greenville, South Carolina, to Salisbury, North Carolina, carrying an American flag from the Greenville enginehouse—the only special marking carried on the train.

The 1401 spent almost nine years in storage before the Smithsonian's new Museum of History and Technology began to rise on Constitution Avenue. In the summer of 1961 workmen began refurbishing the huge old locomotive. It was sandblasted and cleaned for a month. Crews then removed blemishes, scratches, and dents, and turned it over to painters, who used about 110 gallons of paint in restoring the 1401 to the green-and-gold elegance of her former years. Its trucks were jet black, and in the name of authenticity the front end was painted gray to resemble the mixture of oil and graphite used during the 1920s to treat areas subjected to intense heat. The main and side rods and valve-gear parts, all freshly chrome-plated, were then installed, and the 1401 was ready for her final journey, which proved to be the slowest and most laborious of her career.

The 59-ton tender was first moved to the new museum site, a relatively easy task. But after the 1401 had been towed from Potomac Yard to the Naval Weapons Station in the District of Columbia, and had been lifted by crane onto an enormous trailer, she was forced to sit for several weeks until experts could devise the safest way to move the 1401 through the city streets. At last, the tractor-trailer rig set out through downtown Washington, riding on fifty wheels, moving inch by inch over street intersections beneath which lay a network of sewer lines and steam tunnels. Some crossings were covered with seven-inch layers of sand and double layers of two-by-twelve-inch planks, to distribute the 132-ton weight of the locomotive.

Manhole covers were protected by steel plates. Police cars and motorcycles and a rescue squad ambulance led the slow-motion parade as railfans snapped pictures of the 1401's progress. The locomotive reached the construction site after a journey of a mile and a half that required twenty-two hours from start to finish. Ten days of patient labor saw the giant locomotive installed within the partially completed building—which was to be finished around the 1401. A plate-glass window, 110 feet long and 18 feet high, was installed to make the locomotive visible from the street.

When the Museum of Science and Technology finally opened in January 1964, the 1401, the largest item on display, was the star of the show, seen by a crowd of fifty thousand on the first Sunday of the opening—a new record for museums in Washington. A Smithsonian curator predicted that the 1401 would become the nation's best-known locomotive and that its chances of survival in the presence of humidity and temperature controls were better than those of any other steam locomotive. It was also destined to become the most often seen of the new museum's displays, gleaming behind its large lighted windows every night.

In this setting the 1401 loomed as a behemoth indeed, dwarfing the tiny Pioneer, a woodburner of 1851 from the Cumberland Valley Railroad. The 1401's stack towered almost fifteen feet above

"The Best Executive I Ever Saw"

the rails; her drive wheels were seventy-three inches in diameter, and with her tender the locomotive was almost ninety-two feet long.

Southern had made other gifts to museums. Three years earlier the 6100, lead unit of the four-unit first road-freight diesel-electric ever built, had been donated to the National Museum of Transportation in St. Louis. It was then twenty years old. In June 1982 this locomotive was designated as a national historic mechanical engineering landmark by the American Society of Mechanical Engineers.

Dieselization and Brosnan's modernization drive had dramatically reduced costs and improved Southern's financial health. While other roads were still struggling to adjust to the postwar era, Southern began a rapid climb to a new plateau of profitability. This was accomplished despite continuing woes with the passenger-traffic division. Fortunately for the System, its region was booming.

During the 1950s the South led the nation in rate of growth for virtually every category of business activity, a trend that was to continue. The Southern not only benefited from this growth but aggressively spread word of it in national advertisements as part of its continuing promotional campaign.

The U.S. Department of Commerce reported in 1962 on the dozen years between 1950 and 1961—a period during which forty-three new businesses were incorporated each day in the Southeast, in total almost 193,000 firms, representing an increase of 162 percent.

Unlike many railroads, Southern had not reduced services or the quality of its passenger trains during recent years of heavy losses, but was forced to terminate a number of trains. Many train-off requests went to the ICC during the early 1950s, but despite many terminations, passenger losses reached $13.4 million in 1952 and climbed to $14.7 million the following year. Trains that continued to operate, however, did so with full diner and sleeping-car service, on their familiar schedules, manned by the same crews as in the past. This drain was not serious enough to have a substantial effect upon profits.

By the end of 1955 DeButts had been able to reduce the Development and General Mortgage to less than $33 million, shrinking the debt by 50 percent. Additional bonds were redeemed in the first weeks of 1956, in the amount of $1.8 million. This set the stage for a red-letter day in Southern's history.

"The Best Executive I Ever Saw"

On 30 March 1956—two days before payment was due—DeButts strode into the Guaranty Trust Company offices in New York and handed the bank's vice-president a check for $31,589,521.12. This retired the mortgage and paid all interest due. DeButts recalled the day as one of the most rewarding of his life, and the financial community and the press made much of the affair. Not only was the size of the payment impressive in that era, but the entire mortgage of $111,333,000 had been paid out of income, without recourse to bond issues, a notable achievement in the history of American railroading.

Retirement of the mortgage was only a token of Southern's continuing fiscal progress. Three years earlier, both the preferred and common stock had been split 2 for 1, and in 1956 stock was split once more, on a basis of 2.5 for 1. In the decade 1952–61, Southern not only paid regular dividends on both classes of stock, but set a record for return to stockholders in a similar period. By 1962, dividends on preferred and common were to reach $1 and $2.80, respectively, a return of about 5 percent at the time.

DeButts had followed the policies of Ernest Norris, who had retired the RFC debt and used wartime profits partially to pay off publicly held bond issues and equipment trusts. Now, with the early fruits of Brosnan's cost-cutting campaign, DeButts not only retired the large overhanging debt of the System dating from 1906. He reinvested substantially in new equipment and still paid increased dividends.

By 1960, Southern stockholders were to number more than twenty-five thousand with an estimated six thousand more nominee holdings. These came from all states and fifty foreign countries, and 80 percent of them were individual owners—43 percent women and 37 percent men. Only 4 percent of the common was then held by institutions. In that year of 1960 Southern's stock was first in total value of all rail securities held by American investors.

During these years of rapidly expanding revenues and improving profits DeButts intensified Southern's campaign to attract new industries in an effort to build his traffic base—and of equal importance, he embarked on a major program of acquisitions. He added a number of strategically located railroads, with emphasis upon access to port terminals and to areas of potentially profitable industrial expansion.

His first purchase, in 1952 soon after he took office, was the Louisiana-Southern Railway which, though only twenty-one miles long, gave the Southern access to a rapidly developing industrial

"The Best Executive I Ever Saw"

area. This road extended from New Orleans to Braithwaite, Louisiana, along the east bank of the Mississippi. In 1955 Southern purchased the South Georgia Railway Company, which ran seventy-seven miles from Adel, Georgia, to Foley, Florida, and the next year acquired the fifty-eight-mile Live Oak, Perry & Gulf, a Florida line of considerable promise. In the same year, DeButts also acquired the previously leased Transylvania Railroad, which ran the thirty-two miles from Hendersonville to Rosman, North Carolina, a line destined to become a valuable feeder.

A more significant North Carolina acquisition came in 1957 after three years of negotiation, when the Atlantic & North Carolina Railroad—the Old Mullet Line—came into the Southern fold. This road ran for ninety-six miles from Goldsboro to Morehead City, North Carolina, an area which DeButts saw as rich in potential, largely because of the growing port of Morehead City, with its fine deep-water harbor and state-owned facilities. At this time the Southern organized the Camp LeJeune Railroad to operate a federally owned road thirty-six miles long, connecting with the Atlantic & North Carolina to serve nearby military installations.

Another vital acquisition came in 1961, when the Southern gained access to the rich new coal fields of southwest Virginia through purchase of the eighty-three-mile Interstate Railroad. This line, which served the small, scattered mines of the Wise County area, was acquired for 275,000 shares of Southern common stock. DeButts pointed out that the Interstate would enable the System to keep pace with the rapidly increasing demand for coal by electric power plants in Southern's territory. "Already there are forty-seven of these plants at points served by Southern," he said. "We are looking ahead to being able to meet the constantly expanding demand."

The planned program of acquisitions was one of the most successful of the many conducted by American railroads in the period, and was the result of careful study by DeButts and Brosnan and their staffs. DeButts had begun with a lean system.

Southern's investments in several lines had been lost over the years, when depressions forced small railroads into bankruptcy; the line from Columbus to Greenville, Mississippi, had been lost during the 1920s, and interests in the Mobile & Ohio, in the 1940s. In 1948 the System terminated its lease of the Atlantic & Danville, from Norfolk to Danville, Virginia, at a saving of $305,000 annually. Thus, though Southern abandoned lines only in cases of necessity, and few branches had been eliminated, DeButts presided

"The Best Executive I Ever Saw"

over a system with a minimum of "fat" when he began his expansion program in the 1950s.

The Southern's status was seriously challenged in 1960 when its regional competitors, Atlantic Coast Line and Seaboard Air Line railroads announced their proposed merger. Since the combination threatened an unprecedented concentration of railroad resources in the Southeast, DeButts made a vigorous protest. He pointed out to the ICC that the Atlantic Coast Line owned one-third of the stock of another Southern competitor, the Louisville & Nashville; the ICC eventually approved the merger despite Southern's long and spirited opposition. DeButts warned of the consequences of the end of competition in several areas, especially in Florida. He demanded that the Atlantic Coast Line be forced to divest itself of its holdings in the Louisville & Nashville and asked that Southern be allowed to purchase a Savannah-Jacksonville-Tampa line. The ICC refused, but did permit Southern to cancel its lease of Seaboard Coast Line lines from Hardeeville, South Carolina, to Jacksonville, and from Selma, North Carolina, to Pinner's Point in Norfolk, Virginia, moves that saved Southern $500,000 annually.

The Southern was now surrounded by the newly merged Family Lines, with their large holdings in both the Louisville & Nashville and the Clinchfield railroads. There was resulting damage to Southern's traffic structure, but this was short-lived. By contrast, the merger devastated the Central of Georgia, which lay entirely within the territory of the new network, and as a consequence, lost numerous traffic connections. Since it had not been in robust health in modern times, the Central of Georgia faced a return to bankruptcy.

DeButts made a proposal that Southern strengthen itself and save the Central of Georgia by acquiring Central. That plan would involve purchasing control of Central of Georgia from the St. Louis–San Francisco Railway—the Frisco—which held 71 percent of the stock in the wake of a complex series of events and negotiations. The Frisco, whose major lines were in the Southwest, had acquired Central of Georgia stock during the 1950s as a means of reaching Atlanta and Savannah from its lines that extended to Memphis, Mobile, Birmingham, and Pensacola, Florida. This Central stock that DeButts sought had been placed in the hands of a trustee under an order of divestiture by the ICC, and the fate of the Central of Georgia was still in limbo. Southern's proposal now

"The Best Executive I Ever Saw"

promised a new era of stability and profitable operation for the regional line, but acquisition was to be delayed.

Meanwhile, DeButts intensified his campaign to develop new traffic. He traveled frequently to the North and Midwest and occasionally to the West Coast, promoting the South as the land of the future and proclaiming the Southern's motto, "Look Ahead—Look South." DeButts visited Southern's offices in the West and called on many shippers, some of whom greeted him with surprise.

When he entered the offices of the Weyerhaeuser Company, the firm's young president took DeButts by the hand and said, "You mean you've come all the way out here from Washington to get a carload of freight?"

"That's exactly what I'm here for," DeButts said. "I want a car of your lumber."

The two went to lunch and conducted a lively business discussion from which important new traffic resulted. "I don't know *how* much traffic came from that call," DeButts said many years later, "but it was a lot, an awful lot. I did all that I could, covering the country and telling big shippers and their friends the Southern story."

There was more to this pattern of salesmanship than was apparent. Charles M. Davison, Jr., who served as vice-president, Finance, said admiringly, "Harry DeButts was the best executive I ever saw or had to do with. He could do more work than anyone I knew—and he also played, and hunted, hard. He was magnificent in dealing with people. All kinds of people."

The Southern's sales teams were also constantly on the road, seeking the "right" industries for location within their territory. E. R. Oliver and Mason King, traffic vice-presidents, successively made major additions to a diversified traffic base, by convincing industrialists of the benefits awaiting them in the South. King pioneered a new trend by buying land, laying track, and locating distributors to occupy one of the nation's first industrial parks, in Charlotte, North Carolina. Many other such projects followed. To add to textile and furniture industries already located there, Southern's experts helped to usher the paper-pulp industry into the Southeast. The first important paper plants in the region had come long before—to Canton, North Carolina, in 1906 and West Point, Virginia, in 1930. But until the late 1940s the industry was still concentrated in New England, New York State, and the Great Lakes region, and was, in fact, beginning a migration to Canada.

"The Best Executive I Ever Saw"

Postwar advances in the technology of paper manufacturing made possible the production of newsprint from the pulp of the plentiful southern yellow pine, and this, coupled with Southern's persistent sales effort, brought a wave of migration. After 1950, when the first southeastern mill successfully turned out newsprint from the native pines at Childersburg, Alabama, there was a rush to capitalize on the new resource, and the Southern System benefited. Mason King, who followed Oliver as vice-president, Traffic, in 1953, found major firms in Europe willing to move, including Bowater Paper in England, which built the first large American newsprint plant in Tennessee. King recalled: "We helped them out with a scale of low wood-hauling rates within a 350-mile radius. When times were good they could bring in wood pulp from great distances, and in hard times they could pull back to the 350-mile limit and still prosper."

Satellite industries followed, including an envelope plant in High Point, North Carolina. "The secret of this paper development was the southern growing season," King said. "A southern pine grows into pulp-wood size in fifteen years—in Maine it takes forty years. And the companies have improved yields by genetic selection and use of fertilizer."

The results of the System's efforts at industrial development were reflected in annual reports of the period. In 1959, a typical year, 112 new plant sites along Southern's lines had been occupied, 36 distribution centers had opened, and 121 plants had expanded facilties. From this activity, more than 21,000 new jobs had been created. Capital investment totaled $368 million for the projects—and Southern could attribute to this growth about $3.5 million in added revenues.

In the decade ending in 1961, more than 1,100 new plants had located on the System, 774 distribution warehouses had come in, and about 1,500 existing plants had expanded. The total new capital investment involved was $5 billion, and jobs had been furnished for 175,000 workers.

Mason King summarized Southern's policy of this era, "If you can't put people to work in an area, it'll never develop." King, a business college graduate from Charlotte, North Carolina, who had been reared on a cotton farm, had risen rapidly as a salesman. Soon after reaching the Washington headquarters, he revamped Southern's sales effort. "I decided we needed a new type of railroad salesman—people who were capable of fully understanding customer needs, so that they could serve them. So, with others, I formed the National Freight Traffic Officers Association, to interest clerks, who then comprised most of the traffic department forces. We set up a system of examinations, and many young people on all the railroads passed them. We sent tutors around the Southern and the idea caught on like wildfire. I recall one association meeting in Cleveland where we had 147 Southern graduates of the program—as many as all the other railroads put together. This effort improved the sales level on all railroads, but I believe Southern benefited more than any."

As his campaign gained momentum, DeButts had opened industrial offices in Charlotte, Atlanta, Birmingham, and Louisville, each staffed by full-time industrial representatives. An experienced geologist and an engineer worked from the Washington headquarters, serving industrial clients who had come to locate in the territory.

Both DeButts and Brosnan realized that these efforts must be supplemented by specialized campaigns if they were to meet demands of a changing America and push their traffic volume to significantly higher levels.

It gradually became clear to both men that the times demanded new concepts in design of cars and equipment. In the twenty-five years since World War II Southern had acquired what was virtually a new fleet of freight cars by an investment of $170 million. Fifty percent of its fleet was of the most recent design and in excellent condition. Still, as Brosnan complained, these cars were not helping shippers. They had need of special cars tailored to their unique traffic problems; and Southern had need of providing them, in order to cut costs and build volume.

Like all other railroads, Southern had lost much traffic to newer forms of transportation, including trucks, and barges, whose operations were subsidized by government, directly or indirectly. But unlike other railroads, Southern proposed to meet that competition by lower, rather than higher, rates. DeButts and Brosnan felt that the hope of long-time prosperity for railroads, as well as the prospects for equality of opportunity in the competitive field of transportation, lay in rate reduction and in the improvement of service. Thus, in 1957, when American railroads in general sought a broad increase in freight rates to counteract the decline of revenues, the Southern refused to join the petition, on the ground that higher rates would merely divert more traffic to nonrail competition and surrender the most profitable cargoes to trucks, pipelines, and barges. The press applauded Southern's po-

"The Best Executive I Ever Saw"

sition, and the System plunged into a battle that was to drag on for years.

Southern had fully adjusted to dieselization, modernized track maintenance, new terminals, equipment, and communications, and DeButts and Brosnan were confident of their ability to compete. They sought only the freedom to do so, at the lowest possible rates.

Brosnan's revolutionary developments with special cars led Southern into the struggle. It began with the solution of problems in the coal fields of south Alabama, where Alabama Power was building a generating plant at Wilsonville, which was to be supplied with coal from company mines near Jasper, 135 miles to the north. Southern's rate for hauling coal in its seventy-ton hopper cars of the day was $3.30 per ton—too costly for the new power plant, whose consumption was to be ten thousand tons daily. The power company said it must have a price reduction, or build a slurry pipeline.

Brosnan sent his group of experts to a resort hotel, under orders to remain until they found a solution to the problem. An outside consultant reported that a pipeline could deliver coal from Jasper to Wilsonville for $1.65 per ton. Stanley Crane and Bob Hamilton and others of the group realized that Southern could not meet that price by using its small cars. The solution lay in building larger cars. The group drew preliminary designs for one-hundred-ton cars, to be made of aluminum—Silversides, as they were to be called—capable of loading and unloading in four hours. Most important of all was the concept of operating unit trains, composed only of Silversides cars, dedicated to year-round, round-trip delivery of coal for this customer, shuttling back and forth from mine to plant on overnight runs.

These were to become the world's first unit trains, a pioneer development that was to create new standards of efficiency in the industry. Brosnan accepted the idea with such enthusiasm that an immediate order was placed for $33 million worth of new cars. Years later, Brosnan recalled that the inspiration for the huge hoppers and unit trains came from Crane—but Crane credited Brosnan himself.

The 200 cars ordered by Brosnan did the work of 740 smaller hopper cars, and Southern's coal rate on the run dropped from $3.30 to $1.35 per ton. Since these trains were kept intact, except for repairs, the equipment was used six or seven times the normal rate, further increasing profits. Brosnan ordered 132-pound rail to

"The Best Executive I Ever Saw"

be laid on the line for the heavy traffic, and the problem was solved. As Stanley Crane said of Brosnan's accomplishment, "This was an outstanding example of marketing technology."

A kindred problem arose in the coal fields of southwest Virginia, along the newly acquired Interstate Railroad, which served numerous small, scattered mines. Crane and his group devised a gathering system, with locomotives picking up three to five cars daily from the small mines and taking them to a central loading facility, which was invented for the purpose. The new facility at Appalachia, Virginia, was essentially a huge silo in which coal could be stored and then loaded swiftly into unit trains capable of carrying ten thousand tons over long daily hauls. Obsolete fifty-ton cars were used in the gathering service, and the one-hundred-ton Silverside giants in the unit trains.

The Silversides first purchased in 1960 were not merely effective; they were so durable that 80 percent of them were still in active service more than twenty years later. Unit trains were still running endlessly in the 1980s, some of them over long distances—mines in Indiana, for example, were furnishing coal to power plants in Georgia.

Brosnan was now at the peak of his powers, and despite his concern for developing huge new cars, he also gave attention to traditional aspects of railroading, as he did in impressive fashion during 1961, with a $35 million reconstruction of the troublesome "Rat Hole" between Cincinnati and Chattanooga. This was a vital line, but to railroaders it was a nightmare of long, narrow tunnels through mountains and ridges, twisting curves, deep cuts, and sharp grades. Brosnan proposed a formidable task—to rebuild the Rat Hole by elimination of ten tunnels through "daylighting" or bypasses, to end clearance problems with deeper and wider cuts, and to reduce grades and curves.

Charles Davison conceived the project's financial structure: the city of Cincinnati issued $33 million in tax-exempt bonds, and Southern would pay increased rentals for use of the line. The city was to enjoy a bonanza in its income, and Southern gained speedy, economical, and profitable service on the route. Davison and DeButts persuaded the city to agree, and with Davison's guidance Southern bought the B&O's share of the line at a favorable price. As President W. Graham Claytor, Jr., of Southern said later, "This was one of the most successful financial arrangements ever made by Southern."

Stanley Crane, who had spent years under Brosnan's eye, had a

"The Best Executive I Ever Saw"

vivid recollection of a prelude to this project: "The Rat Hole was so bad that men had to wrap wet towels around their heads in the steam days, because of the smoke. They went so far as to build a trough over the cab so they wouldn't have to eat so much smoke. As a result, the brotherhoods had won a concession that we would operate no more than seventy cars on a train—this was under steam."

This "roller coaster" line had been the first to get diesel power, and as Crane recalled, "That seventy-car limit drove Brosnan up the wall, it was so costly and unnecessary. He was determined to break it and served notice on the union that he was ready to take a strike on the issue." The unions then asserted that there was a danger of death by carbon monoxide to exposed crews.

Brosnan asked Crane if there could be such a danger, and was assured that the diesel engines produced no carbon monoxide. Brosnan then sent him to make secret tests in the tunnel to see whether the gas could be detected. He ordered Crane to tell no one what he was doing.

Crane recalled the experiment: "Oh, what a mess. We had bottles with aspirators to run the tests. We could mark the presence of CO by the color of sulphur in the aspirators. The engineer of the train, whose cigar was making more CO than the engine, became curious. He turned the throttle over to his fireman and came tiptoeing past so he could see what we were up to. Well, we found no CO."

When Brosnan completed his project, he broke the seventy-car limit and pressed on with his efforts to make the line a more useful link in the network. Since the Rat Hole carried the heaviest volume of traffic in the Southern System, with its connections with the Penn Central and the Chessie and the Louisville & Nashville, Brosnan foresaw that the two-year project would be a boon for the railroad. Once the tunnels, grades, and curves had been improved and 2 million yards of stone and shale removed, the line was opened to much longer trains with the most modern cars, and permitted the passage of more frequent trains. The taming of the Rat Hole meant a substantial increase in Southern's profits.

Harry DeButts had worked for a decade as president to expand the System and bolster the economy it served. Under his leadership the Southern had grown from fewer than 7,900 miles of track to almost 10,500 miles in 1962. The Southern was no longer a "granger road," but one of the nation's giants. Its strength in the growing and strategically important South was enormous. The

"The Best Executive I Ever Saw"

unprecedented regional boom was continuing, bringing new industries to the sites Southern had provided. During the DeButts regime, revenues and profits had set new records. Not since the days of Samuel Spencer had the railroad progressed under such a builder.

It was generally realized, and especially by DeButts, that much of the progress made during these years had been due to the vigorous leadership of Bill Brosnan. Few were aware of the skill and patience exercised by DeButts in his relationship with his aggressive lieutenant. Charles Davison, who worked with DeButts on an intimate basis, recalled: "DeButts was as smooth as silk himself, but he had the capacity to recognize and appreciate qualities of toughness in others. He had the vision to see what a good surgeon Brosnan was. I remember DeButts saying when Brosnan became vice-president of operations, 'We've got one this time. A mean one. He enjoys being mean, when he has to get things done.' And DeButts realized that only tough negotiations would solve railroad labor problems in those days, because he knew human nature so well—and knew railroad working conditions up and down. He realized that Brosnan was just the man to face up to all the problems of dealing with the Brotherhoods and protect the interests of Southern and its investors." DeButts also felt that Brosnan was the man to lead the System in the years ahead. He recommended the Georgian as his successor.

DeButts moved from the presidency to become chairman of the Board in January 1962. Brosnan was to assume the role of leadership he had been conducting in fact, if unofficially, under the administration of two of the Southern's most capable presidents.

FIFTEEN

Bill Brosnan: "It Can't Be Done"

Bill Brosnan was another of those leaders who seemed to appear just as Southern needed him. Brosnan had been a marked man—even a famous one—for almost twenty years when he opened his presidential career. More than once he had declined offers to become head of other railroads, largely because of his dedication to Southern and the South. He felt that there was yet much to be done to modernize the system he had come to know so well over thirty-six years of service. None of his predecessors had known the road more intimately.

Brosnan was resolved that his presidency would not be anticlimactic. He intended to press his unorthodox ideas until he had recast every facet of Southern's operations, to convince the nation that railroads were a growth industry, and that Southern was among its leaders. The industry came to know Southern's style in that era as "Railroading the Brosnan Way."

DeButts, in retiring after a brief term as chairman, praised Brosnan's contributions to the System's technological revolution. Brosnan, in turn, paid eloquent tribute to DeButts and the Board, and to the "magnificent teamwork of as competent a staff of officers as ever operated a railroad." Brosnan, like many predecessors, viewed Southern as a quasi-military organization in spirit, and it was clear to Southern's personnel, high and low, that Brosnan expected the utmost of every officer and every man and woman in the ranks—and that he would drive himself as hard as he drove others.

Like most American railroads, Southern has always been "run" by its presidents, and this was never more obvious than during Brosnan's administration. But, as he said of his accomplishments in creating a modern railroad: "To do things like that you must have highly motivated people. You do need a top man pushing, one who's cognizant of costs, and thinking ahead as to how the system can be improved. Planning is the key. Painting the outlines with a big brush and assigning the details to others, but continuing to look over their shoulders to be sure that they're carrying out the plan.

Bill Brosnan: "It Can't Be Done"

"My job has been to inspire our good people, to figure out where we ought to go, what we should do, and how to get there. They did it, not I. It does, however, take one man for decisions—and only one. You can have all the committees you like, but they can't make tough and timely decisions. They can develop information and alternative methods, but the top manager has the final decision. He fights the ship."

Some observers may have failed to appreciate the importance of Brosnan's training of junior officers throughout the organization, two of whom, Stanley Crane and Harold Hall, were to become presidents of the System. In two other remarkable cases, those of Dick Franklin and Robert Hamilton, he brought out the best in men of singular talents and was rewarded by seeing them contribute significantly to Southern's progress.

As a salesman, Brosnan could be as courtly as Norris or as persuasive as DeButts, but operations were his forte and he saw the world of railroading through the eyes of an operations man. It was not strange that many of his ways were rough and ready.

He was not always the most patient of executives, and his disdain for red tape and what he considered useless paperwork sometimes produced amusing results. He could devote weeks to the most detailed study, as he had in the process of revolutionizing Southern's technology, but had little patience with unnecessary complications.

Stanley Crane recalled that Brosnan's intolerance of long-winded subordinates, or prolix correspondents, was so pronounced that he refused to read a letter more than half a page in length. In fact, Crane felt that it was his ability to condense important messages that won Brosnan's favorable attention to him and marked Crane for future leadership.

The background of the aggressive new chief of Southern had been one in which hard work and independent thought had always played major roles. His family story was typically American; but Bill Brosnan himself was unique.

Of English-German-Irish extraction, Dennis William Brosnan was the great-great grandson of an Irish fugitive who settled in southern Georgia in about 1810. The young founder of the Brosnan clan in America had shot a stag illegally and fled Ireland to escape the inevitable punishment—the lopping off of a thumb. The immigrant Brosnan landed in New England and worked at manual labor until he had accumulated enough money to buy a tract on the Georgia frontier—a purchase that included passage

Bill Brosnan: "It Can't Be Done"

by sailboat down the coast to Appalachicola, Florida. Young Brosnan made his way inland to his land, near the present city of Albany, Georgia, where he began to farm.

The Brosnan farm was on the former site of a Creek Nation village, which had been a base for Indian warfare upon white settlements until Andrew Jackson subdued the Creeks and Seminoles. Even so, the Brosnan family lived within a stockade for a time and thus survived Indian raids in the area.

Bill Brosnan was born on this farm in 1903 and grew up there under conditions little less primitive than those known by his forebears. In his youth the house lacked plumbing; water came from a well in the yard, with a windlass-and-pitcher pump on the back porch. The installation of a windmill provided power for a water supply in the house when Bill was in his teens.

The Brosnan family raised cotton and endured the hardships of crop failures—and of low prices in good growing seasons, when overproduction devastated markets. The family virtually lived in work clothing, and Bill had only one suit, for Sunday wear; he passed it down to a younger brother when he had outgrown it. Their father, though he had only a seventh-grade education, was an omnivorous reader, and both parents were determined to educate their children.

Brosnan's father farmed for most of his life, but for some years clerked in a railway mail car to supplement his income. In his later life he became chief of the Albany Fire Department and won a reputation as a leader in his field. The elder Brosnan was a dynamic, driving man who demanded much of his children; they were expected to work as soon as they were able, and to save their money. Religion and discipline were important in the family's life.

Bill Brosnan attended public schools in Albany, where he was neither a leading scholar nor a star athlete, but he played football, at the weight of 135 pounds. By the time he graduated, Bill had saved about $2,000, enough to pay a large part of his costs at Georgia Tech, where he graduated in 1923 as a civil engineer. He finished in the upper 10 percent of his class. Brosnan joined the Georgia State Highway Department at once, but he found it ridden with politics and left after three disappointing years.

He took an engineering job with Southern and within a few months entered the student apprentice program. As other company executives-to-be had done before him, Brosnan worked as a track laborer. "That experience was invaluable," he recalled later. "I slept and ate with the men in camp cars out on the tracks, and

Bill Brosnan: "It Can't Be Done"

got to know working conditions and thus the basics of many union attitudes. That early student apprentice program produced good officers who knew what the Southern was all about—DeButts, Oglesby, Burwell, Echols, Hungerford, Moon, and many others."

After about a year and a half of this life, Brosnan was sent to Macon, Georgia, as an engineering assistant. By now he had grown to 170 pounds and, hardened by a life of farm labor and work on the tracks, was strong enough to swing a 200-pound crosstie over his shoulder. In Macon, he met and married Lou Geeslin, the daughter of the chief clerk to Southern's superintendent of transportation.

The Great Depression, which soon broke upon the country, caught the Brosnans as it did all others on the Southern System. For about two years the young engineer earned less than $50 per month. To eke out his income, Brosnan and his wife began operating a small dairy farm near Macon, starting with two or three cows. Bill milked long before dawn, then went to work, while Mrs. Brosnan delivered the milk from their Model T Ford touring car, whose back seat was removed for the purpose. This enterprise was sustained for only two years, but Brosnan never forgot it. "That was a Christianizing experience, I'll tell you," he recalled more than fifty years later.

It was in these grim years of the depression that Brosnan began his climb through Southern's ranks—a climb that began in quite literal fashion. Soon after he was assigned to a new post in Somerset, Kentucky, Brosnan was out on the busy line, inspecting the several towering steel bridges that bore traffic through the mountains. No one had climbed those bridges for years, but Brosnan clambered atop one of them to the dizzying height of 337 feet and found a serious, unsuspected problem: its steel members had corroded from the constant dripping of brine from refrigerated cars. He found similar damage on other bridges and his report prompted an immediate program of repairs. His general manager, L. F. DeRamus, a hardened Southern veteran, took note of Brosnan's initiative.

Brosnan was soon made a trainmaster and sent to Oakdale, Tennessee, then to Birmingham, and on to Selma, Alabama. The last post, where he was superintendent, was trying: "The railroads had lots of drinking in those days," he said, "men drinking on the job. I was firm on violations like that, and we just about cleaned it up. I felt a sense of obligation to do that—I'd pulled several dead men out of wrecks, and saw the great waste and loss caused by

Bill Brosnan: "It Can't Be Done"

drunkenness, and the hard, lasting effects on some railroad families. I became a stickler for enforcing operating rules. It was rough on me but worth it in lives saved and families preserved. I had some wonderful experiences, and in those days I learned to cope with many different kinds of men."

At the opening of World War II, when he had won the attention of DeButts and Norris, Brosnan was well on his way. By 1947 he was general manager of Central Lines, out of Knoxville, and was already advocating his radical methods of running a railroad. He became vice-president, Operations, in 1952, executive vice-president in 1960, and president two years later, at the age of sixty.

Looking back long afterward, Brosnan said of his early heresies: "There were some of us who recognized that if we were going to have a company that would be any kind of a force in the modern age, we had to make some substitutions. One substitution was mechanical power for human sinew—mechanical means, instead of just swinging a hammer. Railroads were still using coolie methods—human labor." By the time he reached the presidency in 1962, Southern's payroll was down to eighteen thousand, reduced from thirty-seven thousand a decade earlier.

One of Brosnan's first moves as president was to challenge a previously made decision to buy three hundred new diesel engines to add to the fleet. He doubted that these were actually needed and felt that Southern could get more out of diesels already on hand. By reshuffling train schedules and maintenance work to take advantage of the greater power and longer range of the diesels, he found that Southern could manage with only eighty-four new locomotives. "That meant that we didn't buy more than two hundred additional diesels that we'd planned to buy, because we put the ones we had to work," Brosnan said. The new diesel locomotives were then priced at $160,000 each.

Since he had heard at almost every step of his unconventional career a chorus of "It can't be done," Brosnan had the phrase printed on signs for display in offices throughout the System—with a slanted bar crossing out the "t" in "can't." Brosnan felt that these signs became "a kind of prod" to the people of Southern and played a role in bolstering the traditionally high company morale.

Visiting reporters found the new president as vigorous and active as ever. *Fortune* magazine wrote: "Bill Brosnan is a hard-driving boss; his subordinates often feel the sharp edge of his impatience at any carelessness, indifference, or imprecision. He watches every crosstie of his road ... he spends 20 or more days a

Bill Brosnan: "It Can't Be Done"

month traveling over the 10,400 miles of his 'plant' in two office cars. Wherever he is, he stays in touch by telephone and radio, and if an important train ... is delayed, he is almost certain to inquire into it. 'We hear from him right much,' Operating Vice-President John A. Rust wryly admits."

Fortune, which headed its report on Brosnan, "A Hell of a Different Way to Run a Railroad," found the new chief refreshingly outspoken. When asked if his reform movement had been resisted by DeButts, Brosnan replied, "I couldn't have done what we did do if I'd had any interference from outside—the Presidency."

Brosnan's chief concern as he opened the new phase of his career was the threat of overregulation by the ICC as Southern and other roads sought to meet competition. "The railways ... are going to live and die by how well they meet private unregulated competition," he told *Forbes* magazine. "Unregulated competition is the music we must dance to, if we are going to dance at all. And we choose to dance."

Brosnan's style of "dancing" was to become a triumph of his presidency, perhaps equal in importance to his contributions toward railroad efficiency through improved and modernized maintenance of way. After his earlier success in developing new ways of hauling coal, cement, and alumina in oversized hopper cars, Brosnan had sought ways to move other bulk cargoes in major categories. One day he told Stanley Crane to build "the biggest car you can to haul grain." With the aid of Reynolds Aluminum engineers, Crane and his group designed a giant car of 5,000-cubic-foot capacity, with four compartments, capable of carrying 4,000 bushels of grain. Brosnan called his new car Big John, after an Indiana newspaperman's suggestion based on a popular song of the era. In the wake of Big John came one of the most celebrated controversies of Brosnan's tempestuous career.

The grain-hauling business in the South was more involved than Brosnan, or anyone else, had realized. Southern's study group soon discovered why its own service was not popular with shippers in the region: the old boxcars then in use were leaky and weevil-infested, resulting in losses en route, and subject to government inspection of cargoes. Rates were artificially high, since shipments were being made in two stages—from the Midwest to terminals in the South, and thence to the point of use. Shippers also complained that the cost of loading and unloading the boxcars was too high.

Brosnan's group, led by Crane and Hamilton and John Ingram,

Bill Brosnan: "It Can't Be Done"

proposed new all-metal cars, much like bathtubs within, with no crevices, offering protection from insect and weather damage. The Big Johns were to be loaded with spouts and unloaded from the bottom through hoppers, onto conveyors, reducing labor costs to a minimum. Hamilton and Ingram worked out lower rates based on these efficient cars and Brosnan took another gamble—this one for $26 million—by ordering Big Johns in hope of reclaiming Southern's lost grain-hauling business. He then published new rates, offering dramatic savings to customers in the Southeast. Southern would now haul, under a single waybill, as much grain in five Big Johns as it had formerly hauled in twenty-five boxcars. Improved payload revenues and reduction in switching and paper work made the new rates profitable.

Brosnan created a sensation with the new rates, which cut the standard schedule in half. The old 50-ton minimum rate for grain from St. Louis to Gainesville, Georgia, for example, dropped from $10.50 to $4.17 per ton in five-car lots.

The reduced rates were greeted by furious complaints from barge companies that hauled grain along the Mississippi waterway system; from the Tennessee Valley Authority (TVA), which faced loss of barge traffic on its lakes; and from midwestern grain companies, which feared the ruination of the trade. Brosnan accepted the challenge eagerly. "We're going to win," he said firmly. "We'll win because we're right."

He denied that the barge lines were the targets of his rate-reduction campaign in the grain-hauling case. "Hell," he said, "they don't have enough business to bother about." Southern was after the large volume of business it had lost to gypsy truckers.

To another reporter Brosnan declared, "We need to go to work and run our business like a business rather than as a railroad." But he realized the obstacles that lay ahead, since he was not to be allowed to trim rates as he pleased, or to cut off unprofitable trains or make dozens of other decisions that the law left to the ICC.

His defiant statement to *Forbes* reflected confidence in the outcome of the grain case, which was still oozing its way through the courts. "They can build all the six- or seven- or eight-lane highways they want to, make all the river and harbor improvements they choose, but they can't tell me how to run my business. We can't compete on flexibility of service with the truckers, but we can on cost. . . . You can't legislate illegal carriage out of existence, but you can price it out, and that's what we're going to do."

Bill Brosnan: "It Can't Be Done"

Brosnan left no one in doubt as to his fighting mood. When TVA Counsel Charles J. McCarthy declared that Southern had set its rates below cost, prepared to raise them once the barge traffic had been eliminated, Brosnan replied sharply, saying that McCarthy's statements were made "with a complete lack of knowledge or were deliberate fabrications designed to obscure the fact that ... new low freight rates on grain will save the people of the South millions of dollars they are now being forced to pay out in unnecessarily high freight rates."

Brosnan added: "Neither Mr. McCarthy nor anyone else at TVA has any real knowledge of Southern's cost of furnishing this service. TVA has apparently been suckered into playing a puppet role for a few big private interests who use its $200 million taxpayer-built waterway system as a means of ringing up exorbitant profits."

He prepared for the case as if Southern's survival were at stake. He began by directing Hamilton to lead research into all phases of the problem—he must know every detail of the rate structures involved, and the basic facts underlying them. Hamilton and Ingram produced what he asked; Hamilton was to become the star witness of the lengthy hearings ahead—for he had to justify his slashed rates before the ICC.

Hamilton soon identified the road's true competition: the unregulated truckers, who were exempt from laws governing other carriers. "We added shipments by barge and rail and found them only half the total. The rest was going by unregulated truck. Citrus trucks from Florida, for instance, carried fruit into the Midwest, bought grain there, and hauled it back home. Since they were selling under the delivered price by rail, it was Southern they were hurting. We got proof of that."

With an eye to the political climate during the Kennedy administration, Brosnan determined to choose an influential lawyer to direct the case. "I asked our people for a list of five liberal lawyers who might present our case to the Supreme Court. One of them was Dean Acheson."

Brosnan called on Acheson and offered a rudimentary summary of his case. He was, he said, trying to help the southern people. "If we birth a calf and send it to the Midwest to be raised, we must buy it back at an unreasonably high price because of all the unnecessary transportation. We need to raise them ourselves. Barge rates on grain are too high to effectively control costs of animal feed production. We need sensible grain rates, and we're being

Bill Brosnan: "It Can't Be Done"

stymied by artificially high rates imposed by our competition. We can save most of this wasteful cost and improve our existing poultry industry and develop a cattle industry—and Southern could make money in the process."

Brosnan made it clear to Acheson that he would be content with nothing less than victory: "Are you interested in helping us? I mean really interested. I don't want a paper presentation. I want a real one, a fight to the finish."

"I'll take it," Acheson said, and they agreed that the case was to be fought with all possible vigor.

Meanwhile, Brosnan had won other allies. An aggressive publicity campaign had set up a clamor from farm and cattlemen's groups, schools, civic clubs, and chambers of commerce. These were joined by the U.S. Department of Agriculture, the National Grange, the American Farm Bureau Federation, the Farmers' Union, and the Southern Governors' Conference. Congress and the ICC were deluged by protests and demands for explanations of opposition to cheaper rates for shipping grain, when the unnecessary costs came from the pockets of consumers. No convincing response was forthcoming, even when the ICC began its hearings in the case.

Brosnan's new rates, slashing old tariffs in half, were to take effect 10 August 1961, a few months before he became president. The ICC suspended these rates 9 August and set hearings for January 1962. Brosnan was the first witness as the ICC opened the longest case in its history, a case in which witnesses were to leave almost 16,000 pages of testimony and 765 exhibits on the record over a period of thirty weeks—and in the end was to drag on for four years, to be heard thirteen times in Federal appellate courts, and twice by the Supreme Court.

Hamilton, the chief witness for Southern, followed Brosnan, and before he was through was subjected to eight days of cross-examination. "He did a wonderful job," Brosnan recalled. "Day after day they shot their computer tapes at him—all baloney based on faulty computer studies—and Hamilton batted them right back at the lawyers."

In the end, with the aid of a favorable ruling from Justice Stewart Potter in a Missouri court, the Southern prevailed and the new schedule of lower rates went into effect on a permanent basis. The road's case had stood on Hamilton's virtually uncontestable market analysis.

It was estimated that Southern's new rate structure saved grain

Bill Brosnan: "It Can't Be Done"

consumers of the Southeast about $40 million annually. More important, the poultry industry was now expected to expand to a production value of $2 billion annually. And, since the Southeast was then consuming two and a third billion pounds more meat than it was producing, southern agriculture could add about $1 billion per year to its income to satisfy that need. Brosnan declared that southern poultrymen, livestock growers, and millers between them would save about $100,000 daily under the new structure. The cost of beef production fell by $1 per hundred pounds; pork fell by $.60; and milk by $.04 per hundred weight.

Another impressive dividend of the Big John victory was the 1970 opening in Culpeper, Virginia, of the first new American flour mill in five years. Seaboard Allied Milling Corporation of Kansas City, responding to the cheaper grain transportation provided by Brosnan and Hamilton, began shipping in wheat from Minnesota and Kansas. The route was by barge to Chattanooga, thence by Big Johns to Culpeper. Soon after opening, this plant had a capacity of 700,000 pounds daily production, making it the largest in a six-state area. It was then served by from twenty-four to thirty Big Johns weekly.

For its part, Southern gained more than $3 million in grain revenues. Though this was a small fraction of the System's $230 million freight business of the time, grain was only one of a range of bulk commodities on which Southern was to offer lower rates—cargoes ranging from coal and cement to alumina and powdered lime.

The Big John case, as it happened, coincided with the phasing out of Southern's agricultural policy, which had been formed by Samuel Spencer in 1895. In 1961 the last of the System's farm agents retired, leaving the field to farm bureaus and county farm agents, who had come in the wake of Southern's pioneers. It was also in 1961, just as Big John brought an era of more favorable commodity rates, that Southern established its Agri-business Services, a symbol of a new day in southern agriculture.

Of the final decision in this landmark case Brosnan said: "The ICC deserves the highest praise and thanks of the American people. This is regulation in the public interest, benefiting all consumers and particularly the grain-deficient South and farmers in the grain-surplus Midwest." But, he added, "... it cost the people of the South $70 million or more in the delivered prices of grain they used during the 22 months of waiting before the reduction could lawfully be made. This is just one example of the cost to the

Bill Brosnan: "It Can't Be Done"

public of outmoded and unnecessary regulation." He pointed out that the ICC had been created to curtail the freedom of railroads to compete with other modes of transportation then in their infancy. "Those infants are now full-grown and more than able to fend for themselves."

The Big John case changed the course of Southern's operations as Brosnan applied the concept to the entire System; the industry was to follow his example in later years.

The business that Brosnan was determined to run for the benefit of employees, shippers, and stockholders was now the nation's ninth largest railroad in revenue volume, and was the most profitable line in the South. *Forbes* declared that its "net operating margin" of 19.4 percent in 1960 was second highest among American railroads, exceeded only by the Norfolk & Western's 38 percent. These records had been accomplished, as *Forbes* said, through managerial skill in "wringing economies out of an antiquated plant" on a scale "probably unequalled in U.S. industrial history." Even though deprived of revenue growth in the period, Southern had managed to offset a steady rise in operating costs. Southern was one of the few roads that earned more on the average in the last half of the decade of the fifties than it had in the first half. Brosnan could claim a lion's share of the credit for that achievement.

One crucial Brosnan accomplishment was completing the acquisition of the Central of Georgia, which had been initiated by DeButts, a purchase that enabled Southern to maintain its competitive position in the region.

The Central occupied a key territory in the developing South, covering the state of Georgia. Its 1,950 miles of line ran from Savannah to Atlanta via Macon, with branches to Augusta, Athens, and Chattanooga; another line ran through Columbus, Georgia, to Birmingham and Montgomery. The road's credit was such that it could borrow no money for improvements or equipment, or to launch a program of industrial development. Its operating ratio had soared to 86.54, and its long-term debt to $45 million. Fixed charges in 1962 reached about $1.5 million annually.

The road had a long, if largely unprofitable, history dating from 1833, when the Georgia legislature had issued a charter for a line from Savannah to the interior, hoping to meet the challenge of South Carolina's new railroad. Construction had begun two years later, but inadequate funding and periodic recessions had plagued the company. Irish track gangs imported from New York rioted

Bill Brosnan: "It Can't Be Done"

when they went unpaid, and contractors using other white labor withdrew from the project. Black track gangs took over and the Central completed 26 miles of track in 1838, but did not reach the Ocmulgee River until 1843, at a point just across the river from Macon. It was not until fourteen years later that a bridge had given access to the town.

The Civil War, and especially Sherman's march to the sea, wreaked havoc with the troubled Central, and the road remained an insignificant short line until near the end of the Reconstruction era, when it opened a period of vigorous expansion. A large tract in Savannah was purchased for wharf construction, and six Central steamships were soon plying between the city and New York. The Southwest Railroad, from Macon to Columbus, was leased, and Central acquired a number of short lines throughout the state. By 1893 the Nancy Hanks, which was to operate on the fastest passenger schedule in the world, had begun operating from Savannah to Atlanta. By 1901, Central had gained access to Chattanooga.

The strategic location of the expanded system drew the attention of the acquisitive E. H. Harriman, who gained control in 1907 for a purchase price of $20 million. Harriman's Illinois Central was to hold this control for more than forty years. The Central flourished during the 1920s, but the collapse of the Florida boom in 1927 doomed it to failure. It went into receivership in 1932 and operated under court supervision for the next 15 years. It was 1941 before the line again met its fixed charges, and despite heavy wartime traffic that permitted substantial payments on its debt, the Central was still deeply troubled when, in 1948, it was reorganized and obtained its independence. The Illinois Central holdings disappeared at that point. The Central of Georgia was still struggling in the 1950s when the Frisco began its purchases, and the stage was set for acquisition by the Southern.

Brosnan looked beyond the undernourished small system to the potential it might have with an infusion of funds and the technological advantages the Southern could offer. Savings to be generated by the merger were estimated at $6.3 million annually, and DeButts realized that prospects for industrial development were great. With new equipment and aggressive management, the Central could become a major addition to the Southern System.

Southern paid $22,655,000 for the Frisco's stock in the Central and offered to buy the remaining shares at the same price—a total of $32,700,000 for complete control. In return, in addition to 1,950

Bill Brosnan: "It Can't Be Done"

miles of track, Southern received 146 diesel units, 9,439 freight cars, and 98 passenger cars. Southern was to benefit from the 20 percent of the traffic volume which Central had generated on its own. The property was valued at $126 million, and the Central had been grossing $42 million at the time of purchase.

With ICC approval the acquisition became final in June 1963, completing Southern's most important addition in the twentieth century. Substantial improvements were made immediately and the line's financial condition was stabilized. Dick Franklin was sent to Savannah in 1967 as assistant to William E. Dillard, president of the Central of Georgia, and succeeded him as president the following year. After four years of losses, Franklin's system made a small profit in 1968 and was soon to confirm the predictions of DeButts that the line would become highly profitable.

Southern floated a $50 million bond issue to pay for the Central and for the Georgia & Florida Railroad, the latter an unprosperous line running from Greenwood, South Carolina, to Valdosta, Georgia, with a branch line to Moultrie, Georgia. DeButts paid the Georgia & Florida's receiver $7.5 million for the road, which had been in receivership for forty-four of its forty-seven years. Southern quickly improved the track and supplied diesel power to develop traffic from the growing industries of the region.

As president, Brosnan also accelerated the program of rail and tie replacement he had begun in 1946, to such an extent that the Southern replaced 25,000 tons of rail and 966,000 ties annually between 1962 and 1970. To critics in the industry who argued that Southern's maintenance ratio of 34.7 percent was too high, Brosnan responded that the operating ratio of 72.6 was one of America's lowest. This ratio had fallen steadily in the ten years after 1946 when Brosnan had begun—from 81 percent to only 68.6 percent. The heavy expenditures on track and equipment that he had sponsored proved to be a sound investment for the system. But much remained to be done.

In 1962, at the age of sixty-six, the Southern was what one commentator described as "a corporate nightmare, even by railroad standards." Despite all the work done by Fairfax Harrison, the parent company owned, controlled, or leased five other unconsolidated Class 1 railroads, including the three lines comprising the Queen & Crescent Route between New Orleans and Cincinnati—not to mention twenty-nine short lines. But these were complexities that Brosnan found of secondary importance. Though numerous lines remained legally separate, he fully intended to

Bill Brosnan: "It Can't Be Done"

continue managing them as "a smoothly functioning operating entity."

As Brosnan took stock in the winter of 1962, he realized that though Southern had cut its costs of wages and materials by more than $125 million annually, it had barely been able to hold earnings on an even plane because of rising costs and leveling revenues. Brosnan had seen Southern's average work force cut in half in a decade of his mechanization program—he had also seen productivity rise rapidly: The average track worker now put down about $9,750 worth of materials each year, in contrast to the $2,100 worth of 1952. In repair shops, the average workman's performance had risen from the use of $880 worth of materials annually to a total of $6,800 worth. It was clear that little further progress could be expected in that field. Now, a fresh effort had to be made to improve revenues.

Southern was a good deal better off than most railroads in the period, since its earnings of $4.03 per share in the recession year of 1961 were only 27 percent below its peak earnings of $5.53 per share in 1955. By contrast, other Class 1 railroads had fallen 45 percent behind. Brosnan intended to improve Southern's revenue flow at once by winning back some of the traffic lost to other carriers, through his schedule of lower rates. "Southern's largely defensive emphasis on cost control," he told *Forbes*, must be broadened into "a more positive and aggressive attempt to build traffic through carefully calculated reductions in volume rates."

There was one promising field of technological change in which Brosnan saw hope for improving profits—through the addition of new and more efficient automated yards. This development had begun in the late 1940s with the first applications of automation in yards. Other railroads were also investing heavily in similar yards, but Brosnan went beyond any of them in his drive for greater efficiency and lower costs.

First, he insisted that the number of yards in which a car was handled be minimized, since congestion and possible errors would be reduced if cars could avoid a yard. Second, cars were to be classified and blocked internally, within the system, rather than at major terminals or connections. This would relieve pressure on the most congested points. Third, all cars were to be blocked as early as was possible. These benefits were soon to be reaped, as new, ever more efficient yards appeared in the System.

The modernization of Southern's yards over the years was at the heart of Brosnan's program. Using the latest technology available,

Bill Brosnan: "It Can't Be Done"

he attacked the bottlenecks in classification yards, and embarked on an $82 million program to speed traffic through the System. The first of these yards, the renovated John Sevier at Knoxville, opened in 1951, featuring a hump and retarders and special techniques developed on Southern. The daily capacity of the yard jumped from 2,900 to 4,500 cars.

The Ernest Norris Yard, then the South's largest, opened as a new facility in Birmingham in 1952. An "ultra-modern, push-button, electronic car-retarder facility," it could handle 5,400 cars daily on its fifty-six tracks, partly as the result of experience gained in rebuilding the Knoxville Yard. Freight cars passed through the Norris Yard without interruption, guided by men with radios and telephones and talk-back loudspeakers in communication with yard towers.

The Oliver Yard in New Orleans opened the same year, bearing the name of vice-president, Traffic, E. R. Oliver. This modernization increased the yard's daily capacity from 963 to 1,310 cars.

Citico (now called DeButts Yard) in Chattanooga and Inman in Atlanta were the next yards to be renovated, in 1956 and 1958, respectively—at a combined cost of $34 million. By 1961, Citico's daily car capacity had reached 6,300, and Inman's was 7,800.

These improvements had a telling effect upon the transit time of freight cars moving between New York and New Orleans, which fell from seventy-two hours to thirty-two hours after completion of the Atlanta and Birmingham yards. Other yards still to be renovated or completely built were Brosnan, to open in Macon in 1965; Sheffield, in Alabama, in 1973; and Linwood, in North Carolina, in 1980. Modern technology was to be added rapidly, until in the end seven large, efficient yards used closed-circuit television, radio communication, and radar speed meters to help take apart incoming trains and reassemble them rapidly into outgoing trains.

The outcome of the protracted Big John case, which ended in 1965, affected the Southern and Brosnan's staff more significantly in some ways than did the efficient Big John cars themselves. The most obvious effect was a shift from domination by operations to a genuine concern for marketing. This shift was remarkable in light of Southern's managerial history, and of Brosnan's role as an operating genius. As Daryl Wycoff pointed out in his study of modern American railroads, "Marketing in the early periods of the Brosnan era was essentially nonexistent.... Selling might be characterized as being undirected. While the operations were definitely

Bill Brosnan: "It Can't Be Done"

improving, the growth in traffic and revenues was nominal. It was as if Brosnan believed that the excellence of the Southern operations would be sufficient to attract traffic. The failure of this approach greatly frustrated Brosnan when he became executive vice-president in 1960."

Now, though Brosnan approached marketing with all the forcefulness he had applied to operations in his early career, his first attempt, in Wyckoff's view, "could hardly be dignified as a marketing effort since he merely assembled a group of Southern managers to attempt a solution to a problem these men did not fully comprehend. It was only after Brosnan had studied marketing in other industries, and had discovered Bob Hamilton, that progress began to be made. In the wake of the grain-case victory, he was on the threshold of unanticipated gains."

During that case, Southern had brought together a team of market research experts—who were now ready to undertake a new function for Southern. While the ICC had placed one frustrating barrier after another in the path of Hamilton's group, it had actually been stimulating Southern's study of the possibilities in marketing. Hamilton's group, in its study of the poultry and livestock industries, had created a new pattern for the System. Southern's interest henceforth was to broaden from merely retaining a share of a market to assuming an active role in the agribusiness of its area. The principle was to be applied in numerous other fields.

This shift to developing the regional economy aggressively gave the marketing role a prominence that Wyckoff depicted as the first step toward a true marketing function. It was to be the first such on an American railroad.

The stage was set for the return of Bob Hamilton, who had left Southern briefly for service on the New York Central, then left New York with the idea of abandoning the railroad business and returning to manufacturing. Brosnan changed his mind.

"I want you for an entirely new job," Brosnan told Hamilton. "I'm in trouble. We don't really know what our costs are and we surely can't do much selling that way. We're floundering. I want you to develop what our costs are and then do research into what we ought to do to get more business."

"But I know nothing about that."

"Well, you told me once you knew nothing about railroads—and besides, nobody knows anything about this problem, either. We've got to find out."

Hamilton was intrigued by the challenge, though it was far removed from his field, and he took the job. "The first trouble we got into was in cement," he recalled. "Southern had been hauling most of it in the Southeast, but there was a trucking threat. The traffic department had handled it badly. I worked out new rates—and a new system of transport. These cement companies sold all over the South, and made their own deliveries to customers. We persuaded them to set up bulk terminals from which they made sales—and we could then give them multiple car rates to make it all feasible. So we kept the business." Hamilton was the principal witness for Southern in the ensuing ICC hearing on the case, and his successful performance impressed Brosnan.

There was also trouble with rates for hauling fertilizer from new plants in the South, and Brosnan complained to Hamilton, "We aren't doing this right. Let's find a better way."

"What you want is marketing," Hamilton said. "Marketing is really tailoring your service for the market, and making a place for it. Wherever we can get an edge, we must take advantage of it. We're now just selling what we have, without really knowing whether our customers need what we're giving them."

Hamilton consulted experts in other industries, including men from Allied Chemical, General Electric, and Du Pont. He found them helpful, and was soon devising a new strategy for Southern. He discovered that simple rate reduction was not enough: "It wasn't merely a question of cutting rates. We had to be better off than we were before in each case. In fact, we had to have a separate strategy for each case."

He established a customer service department to handle special cars and equipment, and he partially staffed it with design engineers. Southern now went so far as to help customers revise their loading patterns to determine what material handling equipment was needed. Hamilton also set up a markets management staff, with most of its personnel drawn from sales, and this group became the heart of Southern's unique new system.

To handle fuel transportation, Hamilton brought in a man who had directed a coal firm, as well as several mines; chemicals were supervised by an engineer who had been designing chemical plants, and was intimately familiar with the transportation needs of the industry. "He could tell precisely what a chemical company could and could not do economically," Hamilton recalled. Southern's new steel-hauling expert was brought in from a major steelmaking firm. Other specialists were assembled to direct the program in major fields: furniture, lumber, tobacco, and so on.

Bill Brosnan: "It Can't Be Done"

But these men, under Southern's system, had no real authority. They developed marketing programs in their fields and were then required to convince the sales people of the soundness of their approach. They could neither set rates nor assign people to the work. They were given full cooperation, "but no blank checks," as Hamilton said. Rate setting was left to those with intimate knowledge of the Southern's cost structure. Hamilton recalled much later: "Other railroads sought to copy this program, and failed. They used the same titles we used but made errors in carrying out the system. Some of them gave the marketing managers authority to set rates on their own, with disastrous results."

Eventually, about 1971, sales and industrial development were also placed under Hamilton, and the entire process of studying customer needs, rate setting, marketing, and sales was consolidated. Brosnan said of Hamilton's work in this field, "He made a tremendous contribution, not only to Southern, but also to the whole industry."

Hamilton remembered: "Our program was a success because, for one thing, Brosnan supported me tremendously. He gave me real authority, and I was almost unique in the industry. I could speak for Southern and the trade knew it. I could say what we would do about rates, when they would be lower or higher—and I could tell customers when we didn't want them at all. That was hard to convince people of, Brosnan as well as customers. Brosnan just couldn't see that, and I had to convince him each time I wanted to raise rates—or when I wanted to turn away some customers."

A key factor in Hamilton's success was the fleet of special cars developed under Brosnan's direction in the wake of Big John's birth. With numerous oversized cars already in service to haul grain, cement, and alumina, Stanley Crane and his crew were assigned to develop new types for use in every major traffic category.

Brosnan himself discovered a solution to one of Southern's vexing technical problems and thereby helped to create a new type of more efficient freight cars. Like other railroads, Southern had too much breakage of expensive cargoes in its yards. Small electric transformers were a special concern, since the railroad had damaged so many that it had lost that business. When questioned, the transformer manufacturers replied, "If we ship with you, we'll have to spend as much in crating as in shipping, so we've had to move elsewhere."

Bill Brosnan: "It Can't Be Done"

Brosnan called in his "bunch" and asked how the underframes of freight cars could be cushioned to minimize damage to fragile cargo. He pointed out that the device then in use absorbed little of the energy from the shock of coupling cars. His experts were working on the problem when an inspiration was forced upon Brosnan.

"I was on a commercial airline flight which came in for a landing in Washington—and dropped suddenly to the runway, a fall of about thirty-five to forty feet. And yet we landed without much of a bump. As soon as I left the plane I crawled up beneath it and found that the shock of the landing had been absorbed by a hydraulic strut. It was not very large, but obviously it had done the job. Of course I thought of the jolting our freight cars took during humping in the yards."

Brosnan told Stanley Crane of his discovery. "If they can cushion a plane," he said, "we can cushion a car. Why don't you find out who makes those things?"

Crane conferred with Bendix engineers, and together they designed, and patented, a sliding sill so effective that it was still in general use twenty years later. Brosnan followed the work in detail. He and Crane and several others saw the device tested in Southern's Alexandria Yard: "We humped our car loaded with uncrated lamp chimneys and bottles without any protection whatsoever—the most fragile things we could think of."

Though the car was humped without braking, and crashed heavily into loaded coal cars, the new sill "worked like a charm," as Brosnan said. The device was so effective that when Brosnan unintentionally left a soft-drink bottle in the doorway of a car, it remained in the same spot through the car's humping and crash coupling and return. "We got lots of the transformer business back," Brosnan recalled.

Southern had a number of new cushioned cars built by Pullman Standard and sent them to Westinghouse and General Electric plants, where they were loaded with uncrated transformers. Brosnan invited plant officials to watch the tests and offered to pay for any damage incurred. "They were astonished at the performance of those cars," he said. The road later decked the interiors to double capacity, reducing shipping costs so dramatically that transformers were soon being shipped on transcontinental runs in these cars.

Other types of cars joining the fleet were equally effective. One of Brosnan's friends once asked him, "If truckers can use forklifts,

Bill Brosnan: "It Can't Be Done"

why can't you use them with lumber and other cargo?" As a result, Crane and his crew developed an open "chain car" with steel bulkheads at each end, which could be loaded and unloaded with forklifts in a matter of moments—eliminating 80 percent of the labor costs previously involved in manual loading. The expensive steel bands and wooden side stakes formerly in use were also eliminated, since the car's chains were fitted with ratchet-type load binders to prevent shifting of the lumber. Shipping costs per thousand feet of lumber fell below those by truck, and Southern's business in the field improved at once.

There were to be fourteen types of new cars in all, designed to carry such varied cargo as furniture, coiled steel, pleasure boats, pipe, and metal alloys. One type of the new Super-Cushioned cars that resulted from Brosnan's precipitous plane landing was a tobacco car that carried ninety-eight hogsheads in its approximately ten-thousand-cubic-foot interior—a huge car eighty-four feet long inside, almost eleven feet tall, and nine and a half feet wide. Southern also purchased trilevel automobile cars to reduce freight charges on new motor vehicles. Usefulness became the basic consideration in new car design, with the result that later emphasis was placed on cars for general, rather than specific, purposes.

The Big John victory not only spawned new car types and ushered in a new day of marketing. It also gave Southern officials such confidence in dealing with the ICC that their attitude afterward developed an independent spirit. The System had discovered that it could "take on the regulators and win."

Southern's new car designs may have influenced the development of a new technique for railroads and truckers—containers carried on flat cars. The road's role was typically Brosnanian. Once he decided to join other railroads who were carrying highway truck trailers on flat cars to distant destinations, Brosnan moved aggressively. Since he wished to carry containers without wheels, he needed overhead cranes to move them on and off flat cars. He called in a salesman, who reported that he could deliver six overhead cranes to load and unload the trailers for $250,000 each.

"When could we get delivery?"

"About six months."

"Six months! Why so long?"

"Well, first we'll have to develop engineering drawings..."

Brosnan shook the salesman's hand. "Thank you for your trou-

Bill Brosnan: "It Can't Be Done"

ble," he said. "I'm sorry to have bothered you. We'll do it ourselves."

He summoned the Fox brothers, Franklin, Crane, Moore, and a couple of others to a conference around his dining-room table. They worked with drawing paper for a few hours, and by the next day had a final design for the machine shop. Within two weeks the huge loader was at work—without an engineering drawing having been made.

Thus, in 1960, the Southern entered the new business by joining the pool of the Trailer Train Company. Brosnan leased a fleet of long flat cars, and bought a fleet of aluminum trailers of 40-, 20-, 10-, and 5-foot lengths, the smaller units designed to regain less-than-carload-lot business that had been lost to truckers. To expedite piggyback movements, the Southern also bought a nationwide freight-forwarding business. These moves cut shipping costs and brought the system a new source of revenue. In the year Brosnan became president, Southern invested $3.5 million in new piggyback equipment, doubling the number of 40-foot containers and truck chassis in service.

There were not only fleets of special cars in this era. There were also special trains, developed for specific marketing purposes, to serve unique needs of Southern's customers. The "Spark Plug," billed as the longest automobile assembly line in the world, was devised in the late 1940s to serve the busy car assembly plants in the Atlanta area. The special train, then the only one of its kind serving the South, ran the 490 miles from Cincinnati to Atlanta in seventeen hours, carrying almost 2,700 tons of parts—chassis, motors, valves, wheels, bodies—on a schedule devised to supply the plants at a steady pace.

Brosnan presided over the opening of another vital new field in Southern's affairs in 1964 when he called for overhauling Southern's system of finding, training, and dealing with its employees. This marked the end of old patterns of hiring and firing by individual offices and departments. Southern soon opened its first centralized personnel program of recruiting, selecting, training, and appraising the performance of railroad employees.

In 1963 Brosnan changed Southern's approach to the computer. Though he was a layman in the computer field, Brosnan sensed that this revolutionary new tool might be used to solve the most troublesome railroading problems—not the least of which was the control of the thousands of freight cars on their passage through the system. He hoped to end the wasteful searches for "lost" cars

Bill Brosnan: "It Can't Be Done"

with no waybills, and to supplant the hundreds of clerks in the Atlanta offices who spent their working lives poring over mounds of records in an effort to account for car movements.

Actually, DeButts and President L. H. LaMotte of IBM had opened Southern's computer effort in Atlanta in December 1956, by pushing buttons to start an IBM 705 Model 2 in operation, another first for American railroads. But Brosnan had in mind improvements that would expand computer functions at Southern beyond the traditional use in accounting applications.

To consolidate computer activities and to avoid giving control of the data-processing function to any of the departments that used it, Brosnan brought in a new vice-president from outside. The newcomer was Jack Jones, a tall, lean Iowan who had spent fifteen years with the air force as a computer expert, and was chairman of the prestigious Conference on Data System Language. Jones was widely known as a computer scientist, but he lacked managerial experience. Brosnan assigned Hamilton to the computer effort and to the training of Jones as an administrator. He proved to be an apt pupil.

Jones realized that Brosnan intended to break new ground by using computers to improve Southern's operations procedures. It was a radical departure for the day, but Jones said philosophically, "The earliest Christians get the hungriest lions," and set out on his pioneering effort.

Brosnan and Hamilton appointed Jones to design a system that would monitor the movements of all trains and cars. This meant that Jones must use computers to create a "phantom railroad," one that existed on a "real-time" basis, a mirror reflection of the Southern system in which each movement of rolling stock could be recorded on an up-to-the-minute basis. No one knew whether this could be accomplished. Though Jones was unaware of it, another line, the Southern Pacific, had begun feasibility studies with IBM on the problem, but these were yet tentative, and were to continue for years before bearing fruit. The Southern was on its own.

As Jones described the problem, "My knowledge of railroading was zero. The Southern's operating people had zero knowledge of the capabilities of computers. We began there." Jones met with a small committee of officers and began to study the System's operating problems, learning from the veterans whose working lives had been spent in coping with the practical problems of railroading. In turn, he described the capabilities of computers, at

Bill Brosnan: "It Can't Be Done"

first with limited success. The group worked together for months to plan toward the first and most important goal: the passage of current information from the field to a central computer in Atlanta. This continual flood of information, received around the clock, daily, would then be stored—and from that moment would be almost instantaneously available to Southern, its shippers, and their customers, and to other railroads. This information would include car identification, contents, movements, and destination. For the first time, a major railroad system could become aware of conditions at any point on a truly current basis. Potential savings were great, and the promised improvement in efficiency was a railroad man's dream.

Southern's basic computer system was in operation within less than twenty months of the first committee meeting. In June 1965 it became the first railroad to conduct any phase of its operations with computers. The program had been hastened by the completion of the first phases of Southern's new microwave communications system. The first leg of this, Washington to Atlanta, had gone into service just as Jones began his work, and a second leg, Cincinnati to Atlanta, was completed six months later. Brosnan then advanced his plans to extend the microwave system to all main lines, giving the railroad the most extensive private modern communications system in the world at that time. Within a decade this system was to cover more than forty-five hundred path-miles (more than 1.5 million circuit miles), a vast expansion from the first major step, which was the Washington-Atlanta link in 1963. The scope of the system had brought Southern into a dispute with American Telephone & Telegraph, later amicably settled.

Jones and his staff then began expanding their computer operation and, after four years of experience, found that transportation officials not only grasped its potential but "began a flood of ideas on how we could use computers."

By 1966, the last full year of the Brosnan era, Southern had been able to reduce compensation costs (excluding taxes and benefits) to 33 percent of operating revenues, compared with nearly 49 percent for all Class 1 railroads. The transportation ratio on Southern had fallen to 32.5 percent, compared with the Class 1 average of 38.9. Only 32.3 percent of Southern's maintenance of way and structures cost went for labor, while 55.8 percent went for materials—proportions more commonly reversed on other railroads.

The labor costs of maintaining locomotives and cars were nota-

Bill Brosnan: "It Can't Be Done"

bly lower on Southern than on other roads, making it obvious that Brosnan's innovations were effective. As one historian noted, Brosnan's timing had been crucial: "Major capital investments were made before the railroad had been weakened by financial drain and the cost of the investments had inflated. The costs of similar investments in the next decade were considerably higher. Also, by innovating early, the Southern was able to eliminate redundant labor before the unions were fully organized to maintain jobs. In most cases, the Southern was able to maximize the benefit of automation and technology, which other railroads were unable to do a few years later."

Brosnan appeared to be as active as ever, but as he reached retirement age he felt that it was time to step aside. He said, "I do think sixty-five is a good retirement age—for the company and for the young men who need more opportunity to advance and to put their ideas into effect." He had served Southern for forty-one years.

His role in the transformation of the American railroad industry had been widely recognized. He had been named Man of the Year in 1963 by both *Modern Railroads* and *Modern Metals* magazines. Sales and Marketing Executives International had honored him as National Salesman of the Year, an award covering all United States industry. His special cars program had won for Southern the Golden Freight Car Award two years in succession. Freedoms Foundation awarded Brosnan the George Washington Medal of Honor in 1965 for his "outstanding achievement in bringing about a better understanding of the American way of life."

He served on advisory committees for several colleges, and established scholarships for dependents of Southern Railway employees at three universities of the region. Clemson, Mercer University, and the University of Chattanooga awarded him honorary degrees.

In November 1967 the former Georgia country boy retired, having left his mark upon Southern and upon virtually every other railroad. He passed the helm to a leader of his choice, Graham Claytor, a brilliant Virginia-born lawyer who was to conduct Southern into a new era, building upon Brosnan's accomplishments but introducing a style of management new to American railroads.

SIXTEEN

Graham Claytor and His Team

Graham Claytor, Jr., a tall, raw-boned Virginian, was regarded as one of the most able young lawyers of his time, with an exceptional career already behind him. A graduate of the University of Virginia and Harvard Law School, he had been president of the *Harvard Law Review* and had served as clerk to the federal appellate judge Learned Hand and to Supreme Court Justice Louis D. Brandeis, before joining the Washington law firm of Covington & Burling, in which he became a senior partner. Claytor entered World War II as an ensign in the Navy and ended as a lieutenant commander, after having commanded a sub chaser and two destroyer escorts. Soon after the war he married the former Frances Hammond, who had also reached her husband's rank in the Navy.

The son of an electric utility executive, Claytor was born in Roanoke, Virginia, in 1912. In Claytor's youth, his father had been superintendent of the local electric light and streetcar company. Since Roanoke was a railroad town, and many people had passes on the Norfolk & Western, young Claytor's "saving social grace," as he recalled it, was that he had streetcar passes.

Claytor's interest in railroads, and the Southern in particular, came about naturally. In 1826 his great-great-grandfather, James S. Boatwright, had been an original incorporator of the South Carolina Canal & Railroad Company, Southern's earliest predecessor. In addition, his grandfather, James S. Boatwright III, had worked in his youth as a train dispatcher for the Savannah, Florida & Western Railroad (later of the Atlantic Coast Line).

Not surprisingly, young Claytor had been a railroad buff since boyhood, and still spent much of his leisure time with model trains and their equipment. He was a member of the National Railway Historical Society. It was perhaps his lifelong fascination with trains and railroads, as well as his family associations, that led Claytor to accept Bill Brosnan's offer of a job in 1963.

Charlie Davison, who had been a contemporary of Claytor's at the University of Virginia, said of the young newcomer, "He was the best-prepared young lawyer in America, coming out of law school." Davison had left Southern to return to Charlottesville and

Graham Claytor and His Team

a teaching career, despite Brosnan's pleas that he remain. On seeing that Davison was adamant, Brosnan said, "Get me a lawyer. The best. I want brains."

Davison took Brosnan to Claytor's office in Washington, where the two talked for about five minutes. "Then," Davison recalled, "they shook hands and Brosnan hired Claytor. And that was the best day's work I ever did for Southern Railway—getting Claytor to come over there."

Claytor joined Southern as vice-president, Law, but only after Brosnan had agreed that he might continue part-time with his practice at Covington & Burling. Since he had worked closely with Dean Acheson on the Big John case for Southern, Claytor was familiar with many company activities and problems, and had been strongly impressed by Brosnan's abilities. Claytor felt that though Big John was important in itself, the trend it set was much more so, and he viewed Brosnan as the most effective railroader of his day. "The whole concept of creating cars that could be loaded and unloaded and put back into service within twenty-four hours, rather than being tied up for a week at each end of the haul—that changed railroading forever," Claytor said.

Claytor also evaluated Brosnan's leadership in the Big John case as an inspired assault upon too-rigid government regulations of rates: "He was a pioneer in this, too, and though frequently criticized by others in the industry, we got relief at last, thanks to Brosnan." For these and other reasons, he said, Claytor regarded Brosnan as the greatest innovator in railroad history.

Yet, as the Claytor era opened on Southern, there was a clear break with the past. As a historian of the industry wrote, this was "the pivotal period in the change of strategy, management style, and organization at Southern Railway." The challenge to Claytor was to "capitalize on the efficient operations" developed under Brosnan. As a lawyer without railroad experience, Claytor took over a company with highly motivated, competent officers who were confident and determined to lead the industry. But, as Claytor realized, the operations group was still dominant.

Stanley Crane, who observed Claytor closely from his post in the top echelon, was impressed by the new president: "Graham Claytor's intellectual ability was unsurpassed. He knew more about operating rules and their origins than anyone in our industry—and he brought unimpeachable integrity to the management of Southern, and this was most important. When he took over the half-billion-dollar corporation, we had nothing resembling a bud-

Graham Claytor and His Team

get, but he soon had the concept of long-term planning in place, with all its implications for our future." Like other insiders, Crane seemed to agree that the choice of Claytor as his successor had been one of Brosnan's most prescient decisions.

Claytor began by streamlining top management. He found that from twenty to twenty-five people were reporting to him directly, and he began a reorganization that reduced this number to four some three years later. These four, who were raised to the new rank of executive vice-president, served with Claytor as the management team, though the efforts of scores of other officers were channeled to aid and support the five leaders. Claytor called his group a "management committee," but did not view its function as "management by committee." In the end, he pointed out, only a single vote could be cast on a disputed issue.

Claytor exhibited rare managerial skill in directing the efforts of his top managers, including such able leaders as Stanley Crane, Bob Hamilton, and George S. Paul, any one of whom "could have run the company." Claytor conceded that it was not always easy to keep all working as a team, but with the aid of Paul, a gifted peacemaker and wise counselor, the system worked well from the start, though it required time to reach full effectiveness. Daryl Wycoff, who studied Claytor's regime in detail for his book *Railroad Management*, found a remarkable lack of departmental jealousy on the committee, and concluded that its members prided themselves on recognizing needs of departments other than their own, in their effort to improve Southern's overall performance.

When Claytor began, Southern lacked an orthodox budgetary system; like other American railroads, it had used an "appropriation" system for many years. Each department was given operating funds by the president's office (sometimes rather belatedly), a one-man system of control that went back as least as far as Fairfax Harrison's day. Claytor and his team gradually worked out a budgetary system and a five-year plan for the System. "It was hard going," Claytor recalled, "since momentum in an old company was so strong. There was resistance all along the line. We first put together a plan and then held System-wide talks to educate our people. Most of the old-line men thought this would never work, that it was just another thing to be talked about—lip-service reform."

The key, Claytor discovered, was to force supervisors on lower levels to develop their own budgets, with the full realization that they must compete with all others in the System for the limited

Graham Claytor and His Team

number of dollars available. Claytor and his team began with division superintendents and shop foremen, telling them, "Here's next year's plan. Say you'll repair X number of cars. You must prepare a budget, assuming no change in costs of materials or labor. Each supervisor must defend his budget before his superior, who will have to carry a number of budgets to higher levels, and defend those, as well."

As Claytor said: "At first all the lower-level people were puzzled and uncertain. Like other changes, this one had to be gradual. The first year of the new budget was rather unsuccessful. I had to call in one general manager who had done nothing about it and give him a going-over. He had simply stapled together all the papers on budgeting that came to him, and had never read them. But once he understood that we meant business, he became the best budgeter of all. He simply hadn't realized that we meant what we said about all this."

Claytor set up a budget committee consisting of the four executive vice-presidents and the comptroller, which expedited the process of budget building from the bottom up—this committee, more than any other factor, forced the resolution of departmental conflicts at relatively low levels. This promoted companywide harmony, aiding training at all levels, and reinforced "integrative behavior"—which simply meant working for the goals of the company, rather than specific departmental goals.

It was the developing budget that drew most of Claytor's attention, and its progress was typical of his initial difficulties. The budget involved more than dollars. Claytor recalled, "For instance, I'd talk to the transportation department people, and then ask for questions and comments, and I'd get none at all. When I asked why, I was told, 'When the president comes, you listen and ask no questions.' I put a stop to that. I warned supervisors that I was going to get questions and comments from lower levels or I'd hold them responsible. I let it be known that I would have free communication from bottom to top. We finally broke it open, and got a good, free exchange of ideas."

Claytor got ideas and observations from his rank and file in other ways, as well, for he satisfied his old railroad buff's longing for the road by riding the rails on many weekends. He frequently packed his bag, flew to a distant point on the network, and rode the cab with an engine crew over some particular stretch of line, familiarizing himself with the right of way as well as his men and their problems.

Graham Claytor and His Team

By the third year, Claytor found, "The budget was working." Second-level department heads were defending their budgets in detail, and this brought about "a candid, useful, educational look at all railroad costs and helped us to accomplish the very important purpose of educating all our people to what every division was supposed to be doing. It helped us to pull together." The effect on the System's general efficiency was soon evident. Revenues rose steadily, from less than $470 million in 1967, to $724 million by 1972—and were to go over the $1 billion mark for the first time in 1976, shortly before Claytor left Southern.

Personnel and labor problems that had accumulated also drew Claytor's attention. Brosnan, as Claytor pointed out, had handled labor negotiations personally, "and was very tough—rightfully so, in his earlier career. His being tough at the right time had saved Southern. Other railroads had followed a policy of never taking strikes, negotiating as best they could, but always giving in to the unions in the end, and then simply raising rates to pay for the settlement. Brosnan saw that this would lead to the ruin of railroads in the end, and he broke that pattern. The low labor ratio Southern still enjoys was accomplished by him."

The trend thus set in motion, however, had outlived its day. Claytor set about healing the breach between management and labor, and was able to conduct his broad program of reform in a period of relative calm.

Some of the new president's most impressive achievements were in reaping benefits in the field of marketing, in which Southern had been a pioneer. Since he was unaligned with any particular Southern group, Claytor determined to establish a balance of power between the operations department, long dominant, and the commercial functions, whose future was so promising. To an observer's comment that Claytor was forced by his lack of experience to delegate authority in this and other matters, Claytor responded that "The only sensible way to operate in this situation was to give authority to good people and then, if they didn't perform, to move them out. This was time-saving for the president, and gave us the benefit of competent experts in many fields. These experts guided me to many important decisions."

Under these principles, "a novel form of management" evolved on Southern, based on its management committee. Claytor's organizational chart, which bore a deceptively traditional aspect, revealed the president as leader of the management team, with the four executive vice-presidents reporting to him. Backing up the committee were nine vice-presidents in fields ranging from information services and real estate to sales and engineering. One important change in the hierarchy saw the elevation of Harold Hall to vice-president, Transportation, to strengthen leadership of the operations department under L. S. Crane, executive vice-president, Operations (Crane's experience was chiefly in engineering and research). From this period, Hall became the transportation expert at headquarters, highly regarded by Claytor and his successors.

Though daily operations of the railroad were now guided by committee, the staff noted no relaxation of discipline. Claytor's style was more subtle than Brosnan's, but as Claytor himself conceded, he was not easy to please: "I tried to impress all hands with the necessity for making the new system work and made my wishes plain—to let them realize that we meant business with the changes we were making." And discipline, he felt, was essential, "especially in the field of safety—and that went for officers, as well as for union people." Claytor's chief goal, throughout, was to give all managers and all divisions "a clearer understanding of what the company actually did." His success in this effort made his accomplishments in various fields much easier.

The installation of a merit system was one example. Claytor saw that "it was very difficult to review the performance of managers," but that the potential rewards of the system were great. Southern had previously given flat cost-of-living raises annually, across the board. It was decided, instead, that supervisors would be allocated 5 percent of the total salaries of their departments and required to determine what raises should be given. Guidelines mandated only that raises might range from none to 20 percent. Each supervisor was to rate his staff in several categories, then make a division of available funds for raises.

"This," Claytor said, "was the hardest thing for the system to digest. At first supervisors simply gave all hands 5 percent raises, but the committee rejected that, and they tried again. They had to justify and defend their raises before superiors, and to their own personnel, as well. Supervisors, of course, had to call in employees to whom they gave minimal or no raises, and explain why. This nearly killed the supervisors accustomed to the old easy-going ways." In the process of forcing the system into operation, Claytor said, "we uncovered a significant number of managers who couldn't manage. They said they wouldn't do this thing—they couldn't choose between their people. Half a dozen or so actually

Graham Claytor and His Team

took early retirement rather than comply. They were entirely incapable of making these decisions. The older men said it would destroy morale to reward one or two people in each division above all others. We told them they were in trouble if they couldn't do that, and then handle their other people.

"This system separated the sheep from the goats. We found some people who had retired on the job. The system forced managers to start weeding out dead wood." There were more significant results: "Supervisors were forced to understand that their people were human beings. They had to identify loafers and punish them, and the exceptionally efficient workers and reward them. They also had to deal with customers on failures of service—and they had to learn that they could not waste their time in squabbling with people from other departments with whom they had to work on a daily basis."

Claytor felt that the merit system was more difficult to install on a railroad than on most businesses, since people there "were so set in their ways." All told, Claytor conceded, "it was a traumatic experience for Southern management—but for the System, a most beneficial one." After two or three years of effort the merit system became effective, and once it became clear that superior performance would be rewarded, employee morale improved considerably. Though some managers did well and others rather poorly for a time, "our progress was upward," Claytor recalled.

Another major change in this period was the creation of a computer-usage committee, to assure equitable access to this new management tool. Claytor prepared himself for this phase by taking a short course at IBM, "just so that I could cope with my own people and with salesmen."

The need for the new committee grew out of allegations that the marketing department had first call on the computers, since they were managed by Hamilton, the marketing chief. Though Hamilton was not abusing his position, the situation invited criticism, and since Hamilton was already overburdened, the computers were assigned to the administration division. The usage committee thereafter presided over the division of time between all Southern departments. A valuable byproduct of this committee's work, in a pattern now becoming familiar, was that each functional group was forced to convince others of the value of its own programs to the common objectives of Southern, creating a spirit of give and take between divisions.

Numerous decisions rendered by the management committee

Graham Claytor and His Team

broke with both Southern and industry tradition. The Claytor era, it was already clear, was to feature creativity in management parallel to the more dramatic gains in operations during the Brosnan era. Some key factors:

1. It was made clear that division superintendents would run the railroad, and that top management respected their authority. This helped to retain the efficiency possible only through local autonomy, local automony that gave Southern the advantages of prompt, accurate decisions in operations.

2. Brosnan's yard program was not only continued (in 1974 a major new automated yard opened in Sheffield, Alabama), evergreater investments were made in equipment and plant—with the result that Southern was to invest $1 billion in these fields during the decade of Claytor's tenure. This trend was reflected in net capital expenditures in the years 1968 to 1977—when this figure soared from $78.7 million to $197 million.

3. A salary review for all officers and managers was established, together with a bonus system, which was based upon company-wide profitability, rather than upon departmental performance. The latter lessened competition between departments and stimulated efforts toward achieving common goals. The bonus system applied not only to officers, but was designed to reach down through the ranks to include nonscheduled employees.

4. Southern mounted a major effort to monitor train performance and develop a broad data base, so that alternate train operations might be evaluated. The road was soon capable of simulating numerous such changes, and of predicting resulting improvements in speed, fuel consumption and reliability. Profitability improved. The new effort was undertaken by people drawn from many departments, and decisions in the field were no longer left to single departments.

5. While other railroads were making substantial, across-the-board rate increases, Southern was selectively reducing and increasing rates, with special attention given to the most profitable traffic. Despite growing intermodal competition, Southern was able to retain profit margins with lowered rates, because of growing efficiency.

6. Managers at all levels were reviewed annually, their performance judged, and recommendations for improvement were made. A key concept in these judgments was whether the manager might be handicapped by "narrow parochial attitudes" that dimmed his "broad perspectives of the goals of the railroad." This

Graham Claytor and His Team

concern was unknown on most railroads, and was one of the secrets of Southern's robust progress under Claytor.

7. Finance officers were asked to simplify the Southern's fiscal operations where possible, and one detail that drew attention was the filing of some fifteen hundred separate tax returns annually for federal, state, and local governments. Claytor also launched his own major effort to simplify the corporate structure by tightening and streamlining fiscal relations with component and associated lines.

For all of Claytor's insistence upon the team approach, he realized that final decisions were his alone, once he had heard the opinions of his officers and weighed the ensuing discussions. In one important case, as Southern debated the wisdom of joining the government's Amtrak program for salvaging passenger service, in 1972–73, Claytor took the unusual step of overruling his committee. All of the executive vice-presidents had voted to join Amtrak, but Claytor reversed their decision and Southern became one of only four railroads to reject the system—and the only major road to do so. "We had gone over all the pros and cons of the question," Claytor recalled, "and it was up to me to decide."

In most cases Claytor followed the consensus and "tried to make a decision in such a way as to command the support of all. These were usually very close questions, when I had to make the decision myself." In an effort to make the process less rigid, Claytor did not await regularly scheduled meetings to discuss issues, but took them up with his four committeemen as they arose. They also frequently discussed general Southern concerns on which no immediate decision was called for. Claytor saw to it that information from these sessions went down to lower levels, on the theory that "communication, vertical as well as horizontal, is the most important thing in any company." His goal was always to develop a highly coordinated organization to lead Southern.

Though he sought to avoid rigidity, Claytor regarded the operating rules of the System as "articles of war," and also continued to insist that many (even most) decisions be made by those on lower levels, where detailed information was available. He was fond of telling his executives, "We don't want a system designed by 'headquarters geniuses' to be run by 'fools in the field.'"

The lawyer-president found the Southern adaptable under the new system, though the process of maturing its budget and other tools continued for years. Claytor later gained a fuller appreciation of Southern's achievements in the budgetary field. "In four

Graham Claytor and His Team

years at the Pentagon" (as secretary of the navy and later deputy secretary of defense in the Carter administration), he said, "I found that costing was an art, and not a science, and that estimates are estimates and sometimes you're away off the mark."

Despite all that could be done with new techniques of management, the vital factor influencing railroad revenues was the state of the national economy, so that Southern's estimates had to be frequently adjusted in order to survive. Under Claytor, the road's management developed this agility to a notable degree. "In the recession of 1974," Claytor recalled, "business went to hell in January. At the end of the first week things were bad. At the end of the third week it looked as if they'd be bad for a long time. We closed the shops right then, at once, since we knew that cars that went without repairs would not be a burden to us in the short-term."

As a result of prompt retrenchment ordered by Claytor and his committee, Southern showed a first-quarter profit very near the record high of the previous year. Many other roads showed losses for the quarter. Thus it was not by accident that *Dun's Review* chose Southern for special honors during this year.

Though his predecessors in the presidency deserved a share of the honor, it was largely Claytor's leadership and management style that placed Southern among the five "Best-Managed Companies" of 1974, as selected by *Dun's*.

The magazine declared that its five corporate champions of the year had excelled in a hostile economic climate in which many large and traditionally strong companies—such as General Motors and Sears Roebuck—had floundered. The year 1974, as *Dun's* commented, was a time when "a company had to know not only the skills of management but the skills of survival" as well.

As Claytor pointed out at the time, the chosen firms had to have been "strong and solid to begin with," but the magazine added, "the five best-managed companies had something else, some ability that enabled them to move faster than inflation, to outpace recession and to weather a crashing stock market ... [they] outran adversity because their own goals, their targets, were set beyond normal corporate reach."

Of the five select corporations Southern was the surprise—a *railroad* among the nation's elite managements. But, as *Dun's* said, Southern's service to the South had been accomplished by "one of the nation's most efficient railroads," whose "boxcars were laden with freight in a flat year because of long-term modernization and market goals." Though Claytor was quick to point out that he was the beneficiary of tough, sagacious management of the past, *Dun's* made it clear that Claytor's own role had been one of incisive leadership. He was now in his seventh year of the presidency. Southern's earnings in the period had grown more rapidly than those of any other major railroad.

As *Dun's* reported, Southern was "highballing towards its most successful year ever" and was likely to end the year with a net of $6 per share on revenues of $850 million. "The Southern," it was said, in words that were to become familiar in the industry, "has the strongest management of any railroad."

The magazine paid tribute to the Southern policy of modernization, which had opened with dieselization and continued with mechanization of track maintenance, computerized classification yards, repair operations, improved car usage, and microwave communications.

Though *Dun's* cited the drop in Southern's labor force from thirty-one thousand to fewer than twenty-two thousand in the two decades after 1954, Claytor said, "This is still too many. Railroading is a labor-intensive as well as a capital-intensive, industry. Bill Brosnan, my predecessor, saw that wages were going to continue rising very fast, and so we substituted things for people." Because Southern "pays a smaller portion of its operating revenues for labor than any other major railroad in the country," the magazine observed, "it has been able to put more of its revenues into maintaining track and equipment. So while other roads are now faced with the staggering ... task of repairing and replacing long-neglected equipment, the Southern can speed along with reasonable comfort on a rail network that is in enviably sound condition."

Claytor pointed out that another factor in Southern's success was the absence of nonessential track to maintain: "Growing up in the poverty-stricken South in our early days, we did not have the railway boom that they had in the Northeast, where rail was laid down all over the place so that it looked like spaghetti dumped from a bowl. And so these days we are not dragged down by a lot of unnecessary rail. Here and there we have an oddball line, but abandonment is not a big problem for us."

The award to Southern, *Dun's* said, was also based on the company's aggressive marketing techniques, developed by Brosnan and Bob Hamilton, and enthusiastically supported and expanded by Claytor.

Graham Claytor and His Team

But Claytor declared that Southern was confident of increasing its share of the market—even above the doubling of traffic during the 1980s forecast by the Department of Transportation. Claytor said Southern hoped to expand into other forms of surface transportation, including the barge business, to take advantage of the large number of navigable rivers in the South. Claytor said, "I think everybody ought to be in the transportation business—not just the railroad or the truck or barge business. The customer doesn't care how you ship his goods. He just wants to get them there, and sometimes speed is most important, and sometimes, price."

But Claytor was also careful to point out that Southern had no ambitions to follow some of its competitors who had expanded into unrelated fields of business. "I don't ever want to make the company a conglomerate," he said. "We don't know anything about the ladies' panty hose business. But we do have a management that knows something about the transportation business." *Dun's* added: "In view of the record, a modest observation."

This award may have been indirectly inspired by Claytor's effort to strengthen Southern's ties with the financial community, an effort that stressed regular meetings of top officials with securities analysts. "Meetings in the past had been rather catch-as-catch-can," Claytor recalled. "We had good financial results, especially our operating ratio, but not too many friends in the financial community. A large percentage of Southern stock was held by institutional investors, and there was a need to keep them informed."

When Claytor asked analysts how they would prefer to communicate, "they ruled out dinners, and even lunches, and asked for informational meetings." The slide presentations developed by Southern to meet this need packed later meetings in New York, Chicago, Boston, Philadelphia, and other cities and established a pattern followed by many other railroads. Southern and Norfolk & Western became the only two lines to hold regular meetings with New York financial analysts each quarter.

But excitement on Southern during Claytor's regime was not confined to committee rooms and meetings with analysts. Business began to boom, and profits increased steadily. Freight revenues alone jumped from $478 million in 1968 to $620 million in 1971—and to $871 million in 1974. Total operating revenues in the same period moved from $517 million to $909 million. Meanwhile, labor productivity moved up spectacularly.

Graham Claytor and His Team

Investments of the Brosnan era had begun to pay dividends, as high-speed, automated yards and internal blocking made feasible the use of shorter trains. Increased speed improved the ton-miles per train-hour ratio and the Southern's new large-capacity cars increased revenue tons per loaded car. Coupled with other benefits of Brosnan's career and internal reforms by Claytor, these factors brought gratifying increases in earnings. On an adjusted basis, the per-share net soared from $2.76 in 1967 to $7.04 in 1977.

Southern's stock, split only twice in the company's seventy-eight-year history, was split two for one in 1972—both common and preferred. (Previous splits: two for one in 1953; two and a half for one in 1956, both in the DeButts era, when the first fruits of Brosnan's labor-saving techniques were being harvested.)

In Claytor's program of consolidating many of Southern's-one hundred-odd subsidiaries, the most important moves were toward acquiring 100 percent control. The Cincinnati, New Orleans & Texas Pacific, for example, was only 80 percent Southern-owned, a "sticky situation" that had given Brosnan some anxious moments. The Alabama Great Southern posed the same problem because of minority stockholders. Claytor and his team acquired 100 percent of these vital lines in the System to prevent stock pirates from attempting raids.

Another of Claytor's major moves was the acquisition of the Norfolk Southern Railway, which entered the busy port of Norfolk by lines running from both Charlotte and Greensboro, North Carolina, through Raleigh, North Carolina. This ended the era of Southern's limited service to the Hampton Roads port area over tracks of a competitor, which had restricted Southern to handling through-traffic only. The acquisition, which became final on 1 January 1974, added 622 miles to the Southern system in southeastern Virginia and coastal and Piedmont North Carolina, where Southern's economists foresaw active growth.

Claytor recalled, "Bob Hamilton and I negotiated the final agreement on the Norfolk Southern with Henry Bruns, its chairman—in a three-hour session in the Waldorf-Astoria Hotel in New York." Claytor was determined to absorb the Norfolk Southern in leisurely, orderly fashion. The team had allowed eighteen months for integration of the line into the System, but things went so smoothly that the process was complete within seven months.

A few months later, Claytor added a smaller line, the bankrupt Tennessee Railroad, which served a number of coal mines and

Graham Claytor and His Team

coal reserve sites over a fifty-six-mile line that connected with Southern at Oneida, Tennessee.

During this period Claytor made significant improvements in employee benefits, so that all shared in Southern's growing prosperity. He also insisted on improving technical training on Southern, which, like other railroads, had been training a few of its workmen, but in separate programs. Based on a proposal by Richard (Dick) Melious, who was experienced in training in other industries, and had a background in behavioral psychology, Southern built the nation's first modern railroad technical training center, an extensive facility at McDonough, Georgia, where an expert faculty taught skills to newer employees from throughout the company, using the latest teaching devices in classrooms—and offering actual experience on a rail line adjoining the property.

This technical training center conducts programs for managers as well as for craft employees, and its teaching aids are so complete that its capability for making training films rivals that of many television stations. George Paul said, "It's hard to quantify the success of something like the training center, but we know it works, and works well. To take just one example, we are able to produce qualified electricians in just thirteen weeks, whereas under the old apprentice system it used to take four years."

Southern Railway's corporate advertising, which had made the slogan "Look Ahead—Look South" a byword among industrial planners in the 1940s and 1950s, took a new tack in the late 1960s. Sales, marketing, and advertising people, and the company's advertising agency, put their heads together and came up with a new theme—"Southern Gives a Green Light to Innovations that Squeeze the Waste out of Distribution."

The highlight of the campaign was the green light itself—the solid circle of green that filled the center of the "O" in "Southern." It blossomed in hundreds of magazine advertisements, on the lapels of railroaders and the sides of thousands of boxcars, and eventually on the necktie of the road's chief executive.

To be caught without a green-light lapel pin, especially by the boss, was every Southern salesman's nightmare. One salesman who was caught clapped a hand to the offending lapel and moaned: "Good grief, I must have forgotten to take it off my pajamas!"

Southern's green light, and the accompanying slogan, eventually shortened to "Southern—the Railroad that Gives the Green Light to Innovation," became one of the industry's most famous symbols. It continued to be the focus of Southern's advertising until consolidation with Norfolk & Western Railway in 1982 shifted the advertising function to the holding company.

It was under Claytor's administration that Southern inaugurated an outstanding railroad promotion, the steam excursion program, which carried railfans from all over America on nostalgic rides behind restored steam locomotives each weekend from April through October. Claytor, the grown-up railroad buff, had never lost his affection for the steam days. With his brother Bob (who was to become president of Norfolk & Western, and later chairman and chief executive officer of the merged Norfolk Southern Corporation), he owned a small steamboat that operated on Virginia's Claytor Lake, named for their father. President Claytor also cherished a superb collection of antique toy trains, and kept an elaborate model railroad setup at his Washington, D.C., home.

Thus, when the opportunity arose to return the Southern to the steam era for the enjoyment of railfans, Claytor acted at once. Members of the Tennessee Valley Railroad Museum or, more accurately, railfan Paul Merriman—a DuPont engineer from Chattanooga—had bought an old Southern Mikado, Number 4501. Merriman, who had paid $5,000 for the antique, wanted to run the engine over the Cincinnati, New Orleans & Texas Pacific's welded rails from Stearns, Kentucky, to Chattanooga. Southern's operating divisions resisted this, for fear of damage to rails, but Claytor saw it as a potential boon to the railroad. "I thought it was senseless to oppose running steam over the road and took the matter to Brosnan, who decided it would be a good move. It turned out to be great public relations."

Claytor went out for the trip with other Southern dignitaries and rode the train into Chattanooga—Southern's first railfan trip. It was quite an affair. As the Chattanooga *Times* said, "it would be impossible even to estimate how many thousands saw No. 4501 during her journey south." As *Trains* magazine described it, the Mike's trip of 6 June 1964 was a spectacle

> of furious whistle blasts and cinder fallout.... In the wake of 4501 rolled the sleeper *Shenandoah Valley*, gondola-with-roof-and-seats 117852, and office car No. 6, all filled with guests of

Graham Claytor and His Team

the system.... It was grand, dirty, loud, sometimes fast, once frustrating, predictably memorable, ultimately successful.

No. 4501, restored to SR decor by Merriman (silvered smokebox, white running board and tires, graphite firebox, yellow numerals, red cab window sashes) and flapping white flags, proved a willing if somewhat lame iron horse. Her valve timing was badly off ... but she was wonderfully audible and given to bursts of up to 50 mph-plus ... the engine consumed only 8 of the 18 tons of coal aboard. "Consumed" is not quite the word either, for at least a quarter of the fuel barely grazed the fire, rifled through the tubes and up the stack, then reminded all the riders why there was so much excitement about the introduction of air-conditioning years ago....

Extra 4501 South impressed people, not to mention horses, cows, dogs and one mule. The animals stared, then bolted. The people, riders or onlookers, were entranced. There was Paul Merriman in coveralls, riding the cab, anxious and proud. And SR Vice President Frank Worthington all over the place, feeling journals, helping lay hose to the tank, taking a turn on the scoop. And best of all there was big, bluff Road Foreman of Engines Walter Dove at the throttle.... thundering past Citico Yard with the whistle cord tied down, putting on the dog for all the admiring engine crews and yard clerks and switchmen that we swept past, giving the Mike her head. He hadn't lost his touch.

It was a call from the Southern's past, heard clearly by many modern Americans. Two years later, with substantial investments by Paul Merriman and Southern itself, a restored 4501, sparkling in green and gold, chuffed from Chattanooga to Richmond to attend the convention of the National Railway Historical Society. This time, at Claytor's insistence, the engine carried the old Southern passenger colors and drew a baggage car, five coaches, and a heavyweight ten-section, three-bedroom Pullman as its permanent train.

Claytor had tried in vain to persuade Southern to preserve a huge old Pacific for its excursion train program, long before he joined the System. He contained his enthusiasm for the performance of 4501 by commenting, "It's a good thing to let another generation know what a steam locomotive is," but he meant it, and his subsequent support of the steam program was evidence of

Graham Claytor and His Team

his lifelong enthusiasm. For the runs of the 4501 were followed by similar outings throughout the System, during which crews made an elaborate show of watering, coaling, opening petcocks, puffing black smoke and cinders, and setting off passengers, and the New Steam movement was begun. By 1972, eight years after Claytor's first trip, steam trains carried thirty-five thousand railfans over the System, distances of more than eight thousand miles.

Claytor neared the end of his service in March 1976, when he was promoted to chairman of the board and chief executive officer, succeeded as president by Stan Crane. A year later Claytor was named secretary of the navy by President Carter and Crane was in command of Southern.

Historian Daryl Wycoff, summarizing the Claytor years, declared that Claytor was "the" president to devise and carry out building the Southern on operating foundations laid by Brosnan. He praised Claytor for having advanced the company's marketing programs. Claytor's innovations, the historian said, provided "vigorous initiative" and "innovation became the ... successful surrogate for the more conventional ... decentralized profit-center methods." Claytor's achievements, Wycoff added, had been won "the hard way," for he had demonstrated that his lofty goals for Southern could be accomplished "with diligence and energy." Claytor's leadership had proved what was probably the only approach to "restored vigor and integration on railroads."

Southern's directors, in bidding him farewell, praised Claytor's "incisive grasp of the needs of this Company and our industry," and his "talent for inspiring teamwork among Southern's people." The Board's resolution on Claytor's retirement added: "His enlightened approach to management included both an openness to the ideas and suggestions of others and a personal decisiveness when the facts were in. The combination helped keep Southern strong, growing, profitable, and readily responsive to the changing needs of the territory it serves."

Evidence that both industry and government observers agreed with this estimate of Claytor's talents was demonstrated as late as 1982, when, at the age of seventy, he was chosen to head Amtrak, the government's effort to save passenger rail service in America.

SEVENTEEN

Stanley Crane: "If We Are Smart Enough"

Stanley Crane began his term as chief executive officer as a Southern veteran of forty years, experience that included some of the most exacting service under Brosnan. Once more, the System was in the hands of a seasoned railroader with a unique blend of talents. Though primarily a research engineer and inventor, Crane had become familiar with every phase of operations, particularly during his years as a member of Claytor's management committee. He was soon to make himself well known throughout the industry.

Crane, a native of Cincinnati, had joined Southern in 1937 as an assistant in its materials testing laboratory in Washington, at $100 per month. "I was a glorified bottle washer," he recalled. "I washed beakers and test tubes." Crane was only nominally a railroader, working his vacations and spare time while a student at George Washington University. His lab work was a decided improvement over his previous summer job as a track laborer, earning $.25 an hour. Though he was soon classed as a chemist—after graduating in chemical engineering—he was laid off in the depression year of 1938. He returned after a brief period and began his singular rise to the top.

Crane's father, Leo V. Crane, was a Southern veteran who was to retire as an assistant vice-president of traffic, but young Stanley had won his job on his own. In fact, his superior knew nothing of Stanley's father when the son was hired. "About six months later," Crane said, "someone happened to come through the lab one day who knew me, and that was the first my boss knew of my Southern connections. My father believed in letting me row my own boat. He didn't hinder me, but he didn't help me, either. He had a kind of sore feeling against nepotism, and felt that I should make my own way."

The lab in which young Crane began work served as the quality control center for Southern, testing materials and equipment used

Stanley Crane: "If We Are Smart Enough"

in daily operations, and its reports gave management insight into technical problems of crucial importance—failures of equipment, breaks in track, tie treatment, efficiency of ballast and lubricating oils, and the like. Fortunately for Crane, the lab staff assumed a more important role about this time, with the coming of Charlie Bryant as lab chief. Bryant's aggressive leadership improved lab functions so that its staff was soon counseling management on problems of design and evaluating major equipment that Southern should be buying—so that lab testing was to become a key factor in the process of modernizing Southern's equipment and procedures.

Crane was able, bright, and well-prepared, and he applied himself to this work. By 1941 he had become chief material inspector of the lab, which was then manned by an expanded staff of sixty-five. By 1945 Crane was assistant engineer of tests, and in 1949, as the new engineer of tests, assumed full direction of the lab (his duties included evaluating virtually all goods and equipment bought or operated by Southern). He was accumulating a body of knowledge with a direct bearing on profitability. An important phase of his work was the sampling of lubricating oil used in diesel locomotives, which was done every five thousand miles. The tests checked viscosity, flash point, and ash, in addition to contamination from dirt or water. As a result, lubricants were drained and replaced when needed and the danger of overheating was minimized; since broken crankshafts entailed a cost of $10,000, the work attracted favorable attention from management. Crane's staff tested twelve thousand lubricant samples in 1948, and the incidence of broken crankshafts was reduced to five. Since the operating department was turning to the lab more frequently for support, Crane's status as "one of the more knowledgeable oil chemists in the U.S." impressed his superiors.

The testing of track ballast was another priority for Crane's men. The lab simulated conditions of weather and wear in track usage by battering the gravel with steel balls in the drum of a testing machine, after sizing the ballast through screens. The effectiveness of such controls in the laboratory drew numerous visitors from other railroads to Chattanooga, where this work was done. Max Brockmann, Dick Franklin, and Bruce Gunnell, successive heads of the mechanical department, established working relations with the lab that increased Southern's profitability, since maintenance practices were improved by Crane's experimental

Stanley Crane: "If We Are Smart Enough"

work. Because about half of the railroad's costs were incurred in maintenance, there was an urgency about lab support.

Crane's superiors took note of his versatility during these years. Because Southern had no metallurgist at the time, Crane took a course in the field and became the company's expert—so effectively that he designed modern rails which were to come into general use in the industry. Crane was to serve as chairman of the rail committee of the Association of American Railroads for thirty years.

By 1955, as mechanical research engineer, reporting directly to the chief mechanical officer, who reported in turn to Bill Brosnan, Crane began his close association with the leader who was to transform the industry. Once Brosnan had detected Crane's abilities, he shifted him, and the laboratory as well, to the mechanical department. Crane recalled, "I had taken a good deal of mechanical engineering in college, and wasn't a stranger to the field. I could figure stresses, and knew cars and locomotives intimately from my lab work."

Crane became a leading figure in the small band which worked so closely with Brosnan to implement his broad-scale program of modern technology and locomotive maintenance and car design that made Southern an industry leader. As Brosnan remembered it: "I appointed a group of bright people to work on our problems, a mixed group. One of them was Stanley Crane. I discovered his talent just as I did that of other men, just from talking with him. The Lord puts the push and go in a man, and that's what you look for. Stan Crane had it."

Crane's work in the long series of mechanical improvements on Southern was so vital that he obtained several patents for his inventions, including some in France and Great Britain. He was one of four patentees of Southern's device for cushioning freight cars against the shock of coupling, but he did not profit from that patent. He designed the cars for hauling and laying the great lengths of welded rail; he made the hot box detector a major asset in Southern's effort to reduce waste and improve efficiency. Crane also contributed the design of the winch used to move cars in repair shops, equipment featuring the unusual device of double gears.

Crane retained a vivid memory of the moment that Brosnan resolved to modernize Southern's car repair shops: "One day we were inspecting a shop, and Brosnan looked out over a crowd of

Stanley Crane: "If We Are Smart Enough"

men wearing hard hats—we had ninety working there in three shifts in those days—and he suddenly roared, 'Who in hell are all those blankety-blank hats out there?' From that time on, we began streamlining our shop." Once a production line was set up, under the direction of Bob Hamilton and Dick Franklin, with Crane's considerable assistance, this crew was reduced to a total of twelve men, four for each shift. Production improved dramatically as the work force dwindled. Shop improvement throughout the system was so spectacular that Crane recalled years later: "The power shop at Chattanooga is still second to none. The air-brake shop is of the same quality. These developments led the industry, and are still in the forefront in the 1980s."

But Crane felt that his own major contribution was in the car development programs, the phase of his career which he seemed to enjoy most. He played a leading role in the design of Silversides coal cars for the unit trains, Big John, and numerous specialized cars that followed. Crane felt that Brosnan's uncompromising leadership produced other things of value than cars and new techniques to aid railroad progress. The hard-driving Georgian also developed his lieutenants in remarkable ways. He said of Brosnan, "The man is a genius. He threatened me. He cajoled me, he led me, he drove me in any way to achieve the things that needed to be achieved. If I ever achieved anything, it's all because of Bill Brosnan."

Brosnan advanced Crane rapidly, but had reservations about his protege: "Bill thought I wasn't mean enough," Crane remembered, "so when Dick Franklin left Southern for the Pennsylvania, Brosnan wouldn't give me his job, but brought in Bill Moore to handle it. I was half afraid he'd give me that job, and half afraid he wouldn't."

In 1963, Crane followed Franklin to the Pennsy, where he served for two years as director of industrial engineering, a period about which Crane sometimes joked, "I like to brag that when I joined Pennsy its stock was selling for about 18, and earnings were barely covering the $.25 dividend—but when I left in '65, the stock was up to 65 and they were paying a $2 dividend." Brosnan, at any rate, had a lively appreciation for Crane's capabilities and lured him back to Southern to become vice-president, Engineering, with responsibility for a combined engineering and research department. Bob Hamilton returned to Southern at about the same time to begin his work in marketing and other fields, including a

Stanley Crane: "If We Are Smart Enough"

difficult assignment of controlling movements of empty freight cars, which resulted in development of the system now used throughout the United States.

In 1970, President Claytor chose Crane from a number of eligible veterans to become executive vice-president, Operations. Crane was moonlighting in Canada when he was called to the high post that placed him in line for the presidency. While directing track inspection work for the North Shore & Labrador Railroad as a part-time consultant, he had a call from Claytor, who said, "We want to make you the executive vice-president, Operations, but before we release the news to the press we want to be sure you'll accept."

Crane accepted at once. Recalling that promotion, he said with a grin, "You know, I thought that was very nice of him to give me a choice."

Crane's work as a member of Claytor's management team brought him recognition in industry and professional circles. He won the Research Recognition Award from *Progressive Railroading* magazine in 1967, and was named Man of the Year by *Modern Railroads* in 1974. In the following year the American Institute of Industrial Engineers presented Crane its Outstanding Achievement in Management Award. He was honored as a fellow in the American Society of Mechanical Engineers and was a fellow and president of the American Society for Testing and Materials.

As he entered his new job as executive vice-president, Operations, Crane told a *New York Times* reporter that the basic problems facing railroads in America were political, economic, and sociological, rather than technical. "The constraints on pricing, operations and labor," he said, "are far more severe than the technological problems."

Nevertheless, he insisted that the special field in which he had made his career was still of significance to railroads: "Much technological research and development work that is badly needed is not getting done," he said. "We can survive and prosper only if we have physical facilities—track, yards, locomotive-control systems—adequate to maintain and hopefully to increase our market share."

In his new post Crane threw himself into Claytor's "participative management" with enthusiasm: "Claytor developed lots of interpersonal relationship programs, and called in outside people to hold seminars. I remember one of these held in Williamsburg,

Stanley Crane: "If We Are Smart Enough"

Virginia, where each man in turn—all of our vice-presidents—stood up to tell all about the detailed relationships between their departments and others, and we had a real rhubarb, because everyone really got into the spirit of the thing.

"We acted out scenarios before cameras, playing the role of adversaries—as the vice-president of engineering versus the vice-president of management information services (MIS), for example. I remember Bob Hamilton lost his temper and made a spectacle of himself. When he saw himself on the tape, he couldn't believe it, that he had behaved in that way. Anyway, these programs were very beneficial. They helped us to understand ourselves and each other and finally created a spirit of teamwork in the whole organization."

When Crane became president as Claytor rose to the chairmanship in March 1976, it was with the blessings of Brosnan and many others who had known him well—especially the former Sales Department head, Mason King, who helped to persuade directors that Crane's air of quiet reserve masked a brilliant and resourceful executive who would become an exceptionally capable chief. Crane's forty years of experience included some seven years of testing as director of Southern's day-to-day operations, and the concurrent experience of working at Claytor's side during the remarkable overhaul of the System's management practices.

Not unexpectedly, the Southern under Crane's presidency continued as one of the best-maintained roads in the nation, but his recent broad experience also had prepared him to meet challenges in marketing, legal and regulatory matters, and finance. In his first year in office, in fact, Southern revenues topped $1 billion for the first time. It had required seventy-four years for the System to reach a record of a half-billion dollars in revenue in 1968—and only eight years more to top one billion.

Southern's fiscal progress was sound as well as spectacular. On revenues of $1,028,000,000 in 1976, there was a net of $89,000,000 ($5.85 per share). Return on equity was 9.7 percent; more than $52,000,000 was reinvested in the business. Growth in the next two full years of Crane's regime, 1977 and 1978, was even more impressive.

Revenues climbed to $1,141,400,000—and then to $1,467,300,000. Net income rose to $107,000,000, and then to $127,300,000 in 1978. Per-share earnings were $7.04 in 1977 and $8.35 the next year. Return on equity rose to 10.9, and then to 12 percent. The $66,100,000 reinvested in the business in 1977 rose to $83,000,000

Stanley Crane: "If We Are Smart Enough"

in 1978. Capital expenditures from 1976 to 1978 rose more impressively, from $152,300,000 to $196,900,000—and then to $251,700,000. Revenue ton-miles also advanced: from 45.7 billion to 49.3 billion, and to 51.3 billion. Shareholders remained constant at around 30,000; common shares issued were about 14 million, and employees numbered around 21,000.

In February 1977, when Crane had been in office less than a year, he succeeded Claytor as chief executive officer; the chairmanship was vacated.

Like several of his predecessors, Crane began his term as chief executive officer with an assurance that he planned no major changes in the management approach that had made Southern a leader. To reporters seeking a hint as to the course Crane might follow in Claytor's absence, Crane pointed out that he had been part of Claytor's team under which recent advances had been made and that he was a firm believer in Claytor-style management with its involvement of many individuals from bottom to top.

Crane also entered his new role optimistically. Southern, he said, was in a fortunate strategic position. "If we are smart enough, we can maintain or increase our share of the freight-hauling in competition, especially with trucks." He cited forecasts of continued industrial development in the Southeast as positive signs of Southern's opportunities for further growth. Among other encouraging trends, he noted, were strong gains in traffic on the newly acquired Norfolk Southern line, and an expansion in coal traffic. The Norfolk Southern investment now included $16 million in track improvements during 1975 and 1976.

Crane also identified some challenges facing Southern:

1. It was losing much of its highly profitable business hauling furniture from southeastern manufacturers to the West Coast, as unregulated truckers competed with their sharply lower rates. This had occurred when railroads ended their former practice of using refrigerated cars for hauling California fruits and vegetables eastward, and for hauling furniture west on the return trip. Truckers had seen the opportunity and moved in. Crane planned to meet this competition by expanding piggyback service, but the basic problem, he said, was the lack of a national transportation policy. "These truckers," he pointed out, "may choose just which goods they haul for which customers"—whereas Southern, as a common carrier, must carry all classes of goods offered.

Barge lines were also unfair competitors, Crane declared, since they made free use of waterways maintained by the government,

Stanley Crane: "If We Are Smart Enough"

in contrast to railroads, which maintained their own tracks. "They don't pay a damn dime to go through the locks," Crane said. "The taxpayer is subsidizing the guy who uses that mode of transportation."

Crane was already attacking these problems by "beating the tom-toms" to persuade Congress and the Carter administration to devise a national energy policy that would recognize the fuel efficiency of the railroads. "They are four times as efficient as trucks in hauling freight," he said. Once a national energy policy was adopted, Crane told congressmen, a national transportation policy should also be developed, to provide "more even-handed regulation" of the industry.

2. Crane hoped for a further reduction in train crews. He was negotiating with the unions in hopes of reducing crews from four men to three. "This is one area in which we haven't gotten the productivity increases we would like to achieve," he said.

3. Passenger service, though now provided only by the Southern Crescent, was running up losses of $5 million per year for the System. The Crescent still ran a daily schedule from Washington to Atlanta, and went on to New Orleans three days weekly. "If the train ran at 100 percent seat capacity we'd still lose money on it," Crane said, "and that means only above-the-rail costs—fuel, crew wages, and maintenance of cars and locomotives. Still, we feel an obligation to operate the Crescent so long as there is demand for it—and it is a good public relations service. But sometime down the road, in two or three years, perhaps, we're going to have to make a decision on equipment replacement for the Crescent, and that means we'll have to buy new equipment or turn over our passenger service to Amtrak. That equipment would cost several million dollars—and what we're using is already over twenty years old."

As to the future of passenger service in general, Crane was as pessimistic as his recent predecessors had been. "With the possible exception of the northeastern corridor, from Washington to Boston, I can see no prospects for revived passenger service in the country. I don't see a revival coming unless there are serious constraints on the use of automobiles—gasoline at $3 or $4 per gallon or severe government rationing of fuel. I don't think these things will happen."

Crane emphasized that one service Southern was determined to maintain was the program of steam excursions so popular with the nation's railroad buffs. "A whole lot of people have nostalgia

Stanley Crane: "If We Are Smart Enough"

for the old railroad steam operation," he said. "They are friends of ours and we are friends of theirs. We want to continue it indefinitely. Those trips don't cost us too much, either. We almost break even on them."

To Crane's gratification, the long process of modernizing Southern's tracks, with which he had been involved, reached a stage of maturity during his regime. In November 1977 the last link of welded rail on the Washington-Atlanta line went into place at Duluth, Georgia. Southern's crews had laid 419 miles of the new rail during the year; a few months later, the Atlanta–New Orleans link of the main line was also to be completed with welded rail.

Soon afterward, in 1978, Crane had the satisfaction of seeing the Southern's unit coal trains and cars he had helped to design play leading roles in a unique transportation advance. An enormous coal transloader built by Southern at Pride, Alabama, opened as a link between barge traffic on the Mississippi, Ohio, and Tennessee rivers, and Southern's tracks leading to plants of the Georgia Power Company, owner of the facility. The ingenious system was fed by fifteen-hundred-ton coal barges, in tows of two to fifteen barges; these docked at one side of the transloader, whose bucket elevator unloaders emptied a barge within forty-five minutes, dumping the coal in any of six separate piles, according to sulphur content and other factors. From storage piles, Southern's unit trains were then loaded with special coal blends designed for a specific power plant. The ninety-seven cars of each train circled slowly around a loop until, after four hours, they were fully loaded and ready to depart. Some seven million tons were moved in 1980, and the total reached about 8 million tons a year later. No one appreciated the success of this striking blend of Southern's engineering and marketing skills more than Stanley Crane.

He was also gratified by Southern's achievement in winning another Golden Freight Car Award from *Modern Railroads*, this time for its imaginative handling of a lagging business in agricultural limestone, which had become marginally profitable. This marketing success story involved basic changes in traditional methods of shipping and storing limestone, which was needed by consumers only in spring and fall—chiefly in spring—which caused a rush in shipping. Southern's marketing experts reasoned that limestone could be moved at any time, and distributed more economically from strategically located stockpiles. Once receivers saw the possibilities of profits, the system began to work. Once more Southern found the handling of the commodity worthwhile. Volume had

Stanley Crane: "If We Are Smart Enough"

increased fifteen percent between 1974 and 1978—with a seventy percent increase in revenue. This transformed a marginal operation into a dependable contribution to Southern profits. *Modern Railroads* commented that the turnaround was most impressive: "Certainly, Southern Railway has won, and seems likely to retain, an impressive booty of new traffic."

On 1 October 1979, after three years as president, Crane was promoted to chairman and chief executive officer, Harold Hall advanced from executive vice-president, Operations, to succeed him as president. At the same time three other senior officers advanced: Edward B. Burwell to senior vice-president (later executive vice-president), Operations; Paul R. Rudder to vice-president, Transportation; and Thomas E. Gurley to general manager, Western Lines.

Chairman Crane, reflecting on the state of the rail industry, expressed dissatisfaction and a certain unease. The technological field, he said more than once, was now being neglected by railroaders. "The role of technology today is crucial," he said. Since the industry was dependent upon hardware it could survive only if it had adequate equipment. "In recent years, the pace of technological improvements and innovations on American railroads has not been adequate. We have simply not applied innovative technology fast enough or widely enough.... There is a technology lag."

He pointed out examples which, if not simple, were obvious. Track structure needed improvement: "For the future we will probably need a much more massive track structure." He added, "We should start with a hard look at how we fasten our track together. If the purpose of the track spike is to hold the rail in gauge and at the same time hold it to the tie, we ought to be able to develop a better attachment than the nail to hold it with."

Such deficiencies, he said, meant that Southern and other progressive roads had gone as far as they could in developing cars of large capacity—they were already outgrowing their track support. As to new car design, he urged the American industry to use dynamic freight car simulators, such as those in use in England, France, and Japan, so that actual track conditions could be measured—for the first time.

As to evidence that all was not well on the rails, Crane cited recent derailments due to "high lateral forces"—when locomotives rounding curves under heavy dynamic braking tended to spread the rails. Rails had also been pulled over. "These prob-

Stanley Crane: "If We Are Smart Enough"

lems indicate to me that our track structure simply is not good enough." He suggested a study of European methods, and predicted government intervention if American roads did not emulate Europeans and improve standards for track, especially control of gauge, surface, and alignment of track for high-speed trains bearing enormous weights.

In partnership with Harold Hall, Crane reported on 1979 results in the first days of 1980. He took satisfaction in Southern's continuing fiscal progress. Once more, there had been records in revenues, earnings, and traffic volume. Carloadings were up 3.1 percent and revenue ton-miles 6.5 percent—but more striking were the 16.4 percent jump in revenues and the 26.2 percent increase in net income. Southern had earned $160.6 million on revenues of $1.47 billion, or $10.39 per share. Dividends were increased by 15 percent, the ninth boost in the past ten years.

Southern's top management team warned that deregulation of railroads, while promising, should be done "with the utmost skill and care" in order to preserve the vitality of the industry. One example of their concern was through traffic: "Since 70 percent of all freight business moves on more than one railroad, this is vital to railroads and their customers."

In reviewing the 1970s, Crane and Hall reminded readers of the stormy economic climate that had been so difficult for some railroads, and had sent the Pennsylvania Railroad, "once the standard of the world," into bankruptcy. Conrail had been devised as a federally supported system to save some northeastern and midwestern railroads. On the brighter side, Southern and other roads had made extensive improvements in plant and quality of service. "Southern, like the railroad industry as a whole, enters this decade of the 1980s much stronger than we began the last. The challenges of energy and inflation are still with us, but so are the opportunities to make the railroads' energy efficiency serve us and the country as well."

Later in 1980 Crane retired from Southern but shortly afterward accepted the challenging post as chief of Conrail. Though most railroaders regarded the attempt to save the troubled railroads as hopeless, more than one Southern official remarked, "If anyone in the world can make Conrail work, Stan Crane is that man." He did make it work. By 1982, to the industry's amazement, Crane had Conrail "in the black."

EIGHTEEN

Harold Hall: "One of the Very Best"

Harold Hall was a mountain boy, born in Nantahala in the rugged high country of southwestern North Carolina. Though his father, Odell C. Hall, was a Southern Railway telegrapher, Harold had limited interest in railroading as a youth. He planned to study electrical engineering at the University of Tennessee. But World War II caught him just after graduation from high school in Andrews, North Carolina, and while Harold waited for the navy to accept him, his father taught him the Morse code so that he could hold a temporary job until he was accepted as a gunner in a dive-bomber squadron.

Hall had reason to remember his early days with the railroad. He "hung around" the small station, loading cars by day, and at nights and in odd hours practiced the Morse code with his father. Within two months he had mastered the key. Southern then gave him a job at Wesser Creek, a nearby outpost where the railroad was making a change in its line during construction of the huge Fontana Dam of the TVA system. Hall's job at the temporary post, he recalled, "was to prop up a telegraph line on the north wire and tell all the construction crews when the trains would be coming through." To permit passage of trains, workers were to remove debris from their operations upon receiving word from Hall.

Though the work was usually routine, the seventeen-year-old Hall had one memorable experience after a rainstorm flooded the river, which washed away some of the railroad track: "I didn't know who knew it, and who didn't," Hall recalled, but he was resolved to do his duty.

He made his way into the tiny trackside shack that served as his office, struggling through deep water. "I walked in to be the hero, to save the railroad, to tell the dispatcher that he couldn't send through any trains. I opened that telegraph key and damn near got electrocuted. I was standing knee-deep in water and the shock knocked me halfway across the room. It wasn't that there was so much juice in the key—but it doesn't take much if you're standing in water." Hall was not to be denied. He climbed atop the table and

Harold Hall: "One of the Very Best"

used a pencil tipped with a rubber eraser to operate his key and warn the dispatcher of the washout.

He spent only three months of 1944 in that post before the navy accepted him and he was off to his bomber squadron. "I thought that was the last I'd see of the Southern Railway," he said. But when he returned early in 1946, with plans to enter college, an insistent Southern dispatcher called with the offer of an agent-telegrapher's job at Bryson City, North Carolina. Hall declined at first, but relented after several calls and took the job—temporarily, he thought. "I really wasn't interested in Southern as a career." Electrical engineering was still on his mind.

However, he was married in September of that year to Mary Abernathy of Durham, North Carolina, and a few weeks later his division superintendent, impressed by Hall's industriousness, promoted him to train dispatcher, based in Asheville. Now twenty-one years old, Hall was responsible for all trains on a segment of line near Asheville. He found his first day trying, and was anxious lest a careless dispatcher send two trains crashing into each other. "I was somewhat nervous," he conceded. "The responsibility to a very young lad was somewhat awesome." But Hall's performance continued to win the attention of his superiors.

He remained in Asheville for eight years, until it was clear that he would not be going to college. "I realized that I would be staying. Looking back, I really can't attach much significance to my first job. It was almost an accident, and in my view, temporary. And I certainly never, back in those days, saw myself sitting in the chair I'm in today—never thought about it, never even considered it."

Hall began a steady, if unspectacular, rise in those years, moving first to Danville, Kentucky, as trainmaster on the New Orleans & Northeastern, and in 1961 became superintendent of the Birmingham, Alabama, division. By now Hall had drawn the eye of Bill Brosnan who, as vice-president, Operations, was on the threshold of the presidency. Hall was shifted to Macon, Georgia, as superintendent later in 1961 and had been there but a short while when Brosnan summoned him to yet another post.

"Brosnan called me one Friday and told me I'd be superintendent at Asheville on Monday," Hall recalled. "I was shocked, and protested that I knew all the people there too well, including my former superiors, to take over."

Brosnan insisted: "You'll be superintendent anyway. I'm having

Harold Hall: "One of the Very Best"

trouble there and want you to straighten it out." Local problems soon disappeared under Hall's quiet, firm management, and within two years he moved once more. The rate of his climb to the top accelerated. After his several posts as division superintendent, he became general manager of eastern lines in 1966, and took over the western lines two years later.

His rise to a vice-presidency under Claytor in 1970 confirmed the status he had won under Brosnan: Harold Hall was Southern's expert on operations and transportation. He had worked closely with Claytor as expert witness in a number of hearings and labor cases over the years, and was now in frequent contact with the president, who found his knowledge of day-to-day railroading encyclopedic. Claytor thought Hall "one of the very best transportation men in the U.S. He had enormous experience, and was very bright." In addition to the broad range of knowledge his working experience had given him, Hall had profited greatly from management training courses he had taken at Harvard. He had found his lack of a college degree no handicap.

When Graham Claytor formed his five-man management committee to head Southern, and Hall became vice-president, Transportation, he served as a vital source of information on operations matters to top management, and won increasing attention and respect from his superiors.

By 1976, when Claytor became chairman and Stanley Crane stepped into the presidency, Hall was named executive vice-president, Operations. It was clear that Hall had now moved into the line of succession to the presidency. In his new job, as Hall observed, "I handled 85 percent of the people employed by Southern, and 89 percent of the money." This experience was his final training for leadership of the System, during the challenging years of deregulation and preparation for the merger with Norfolk & Western.

Hall's rise through the ranks was not that of a plodding, conventional operations man. He had made substantial, and creative, contributions to Southern's progress that had added to the System's profitability and efficiency. During his time as general manager of western lines Hall had developed the concept of run-through trains, which were to prove of great benefit to the industry and provide shippers with much faster long-haul service. In the spirit with which Brosnan and other strong leaders approached problems, Hall grasped the possibilities of run-through

Harold Hall: "One of the Very Best"

train service. Despite his grounding in conventional railroad operations, he responded to the challenge and did not hesitate to commit Southern to the revolutionary service without consulting superiors.

The nation's first run-through train, passing from one railroad to another toward a long-haul destination without being delayed by the usual switching and reshuffling at connection points, was organized in 1968 by Harold Hall, then general manager, Western Lines, and Richard Spence, who was vice-president, Operations, for Southern Pacific. The two railroads had been working together from their terminals in the busy port of New Orleans for many years, under all the handicaps of breaking up trains and switching equipment as freight cars moved from the tracks of one railroad to the other.

Hall and Spence met in New Orleans to discuss the long-haul problem, in light of growing competition by other carriers. Hall recalled, "We talked of all the time we'd save if I could put an engine and a caboose on pre-sorted cars—say, at Birmingham—and run them through without even entering our New Orleans yard, bypassing everything and delivering the whole train to the Southern Pacific yard on the west bank of the Mississippi.

"The Southern Pacific would take the train intact directly to Houston and classify it for local delivery or for movement to points beyond Houston. No switching would be needed until the train reached Houston, and we'd get the same kinds of benefits in the operations division. We could save about twenty-four hours on the run to Houston, and even more to the West Coast.

"We weren't sure either one of us had the authority. Dick Spence asked me if I had authority to do it on my own and I said, 'Hell, I don't know. Let's start it and find out.'"

Two days later, Hall had begun the operation in Birmingham by presorting a group of cars, most of them bound for Houston and the West Coast. These were humped in Birmingham and sent to New Orleans, where they bypassed the Southern yard and crossed the Mississippi to be delivered to the Southern Pacific.

The scheme worked so well from the start that many in the industry wondered why run-through service had been so long in coming. Shippers were so pleased with the improved service that other firms became anxious to get their own shipments aboard the swift trains, and within a month the train was solidly booked. New ones then went into operation. The first addition was made

Harold Hall: "One of the Very Best"

by the Southern and the Cotton Belt in Memphis, and somewhat later Southern and Missouri Pacific established another in New Orleans. Others were developed with the Pennsy and Chessie systems and the Burlington Northern. In 1970, Southern and the Missouri Pacific and Union Pacific participated in a run-through train from Jacksonville, Florida, to North Platte, Nebraska, that made its run in sixty hours, providing a striking example of the ability of railroads to compete over long hauls. By 1977 Southern was participating in nine such runs.

These developments were resisted by labor, which opposed the waiving of a routine brake test at the points of interchange, in the interest of safety. Hall and Southern had prepared for the controversy by making an unusually thorough inspection of the trains in Birmingham, and when the case was heard by the ICC, Southern prevailed. As Hall recalled the case, "The regional inspector was so impressed by our plan and the way we were operating that he testified for us at the hearings and helped us to win."

Hall had also made notable contributions in his pioneering work with Southern's safety program, an aspect that railroaders often took too casually. Though he had worked in the program since early in his career, Hall found it rather ineffectual and was determined to see that Southern placed more emphasis upon this vital matter. He formed the first, experimental, safety committee on Southern in 1967 at Asheville while he was general manager of eastern lines. The meetings of this group prompted numerous complaints of conditions from labor. Hall recalled, "We tried to guide them towards improved safety, and handled all the complaints we possibly could, even those that seemed most insignificant. But we let them know that we would handle legitimate complaints only. We considered such matters as poor walkways, bad footings, obstructions to signals and the like, and always tried to respond fully."

Though he was resolved that the new program should not be used by labor merely as a vehicle for negotiations, Hall realized that the involvement of employees at every level would be essential to success. This, in fact, was "the most important factor in improving safety," Hall said. "These people on the committees then also became interested and involved in other areas. They became better employees as their interest and information increased."

After Claytor became president, Hall and others pressed for

Harold Hall: "One of the Very Best"

more funds and personnel to advance the safety program. Claytor brought in Harvey Bradley to head a revitalized safety program and supported Hall's contention that safety should be given top priority in railroad operations. (The program was later to be handled by Frank Kaylor, who by 1977 had a staff of twenty-five directing the System's efforts in this field.) Hall, by then a general manager based in Atlanta, held monthly dinner meetings of the safety committee and welcomed the presence of union members, who were in the majority. When a study revealed that almost 90 percent of accidents on Southern were due to human error rather than to mechanical failures, Hall's enthusiasm for the program increased: "We're trying to make the Southern the safest place to work among railroads—the safest of any industry in the U.S. We have an obligation to do that."

Hall pushed safety in a realistic fashion by publicizing accidents and their causes in detail, to help educate both employees and the public. There was also prompt, full disclosure to official agencies: "We were always very strict in reporting accidents and injuries to the FRA," Hall said.

Hall staged in-house safety contests pitting employees against their peers in other locations. Interest increased and the program's resulting effectiveness was reflected in the steady, sometimes dramatic, improvement in accident statistics as Southern forged one of the nation's outstanding safety records for its hazardous industry. In 1976 Southern won the Harriman Gold Medal for employee safety, after having won silver and bronze medals in 1971 and 1973. U.S. Secretary of Transportation Brock Adams, in awarding the medal, pointed out that the System's fatal accidents had fallen from 158 in 1973 to 98 in 1976, an improvement of 38 percent—and the first time in the modern era that the System's fatalities had fallen below 100. Southern repeated as a gold-medal winner in 1978, and took a silver medal the following year. In 1980, for the fifth consecutive year, Southern won a medal (another bronze) in the Harriman competition, and also became the first repeat winner of the Dow Safety Award. In 1981, Southern garnered its third Harriman gold.

The expanding program included several special projects, as Southern sought to solve difficult problems. After a serious explosion on the western lines, Frank Kaylor and his staff created a go-team of trained experts to respond to emergencies involving hazardous materials. The team investigated all accidents of this kind and made recommendations for future policy. These often included requests for improvement of track and addition of new ties and the like.

After years of intensive work had reduced employee accidents, Southern discovered that more deaths and injuries were occurring at grade crossings than elsewhere on the railroad. The System then launched a campaign to reduce these accidents which involved people who were beyond railroad control.

A program called Operation Lifesaver had been used with limited success on a short-term basis in western states. Southern studied the program's three-pronged approach—engineering, enforcement, and education—and decided to launch a long-term effort with the commitment of the railroad's full resources.

Georgia had more Southern Railway mileage than any state in the System—and the worst grade-crossing accident problem. Gwinnett County, outside Atlanta, had a local program under way that was producing encouraging results. So Georgia became the testing ground for the entire program.

It was a success by any standard. Crossing fatalities in the first full year of Operation Lifesaver were reduced from sixty-nine in 1974 to twenty-five in 1975, and were held at that level the following year. By 1981 the number of crossing deaths annually was down to ten.

After the first successful year, Southern recognized the value of Operation Lifesaver not only as a means of saving lives but as a source of community goodwill. It gave communities and railroads an important project for collaboration. The program was expanded into other states.

With the help of other railroads and numerous community organizations, Southern coordinated the spread of Operation Lifesaver to Alabama, then to North Carolina, South Carolina, and Tennessee. Southern also became heavily involved in the program in several other states, where railroads with more tracks were prevailed upon to assume leadership.

Unlike some earlier Operation Lifesaver experiments, the programs involving Southern have been strikingly successful because of strong and continuing commitments by the railroad and the communities. Sustained programs produced results in accident reduction and lives saved.

Hall felt that the key to such progress was strong leadership. "A good chairman's influence in a given area was amazing. I could glance at the statistics and tell whether a good, energetic chair-

Harold Hall: "One of the Very Best"

man was at work, motivating his people. The strong ones really accomplished wonders." It was Hall's own leadership that had given the program much of its vigor and made it a continuing success in the face of formidable handicaps.

By 1979, when Hall was chosen to succeed Crane as president and chief administrative officer, he was known throughout the system as a capable, resourceful, tough, resilient manager whose habitually quiet manner and soft voice were somewhat deceiving. Though not so well-known outside the industry, he was considered by his peers as an excellent choice for a leader. It was clear that he must deal with problems as difficult as any of those which had faced his predecessors—persistent inflation, deregulation of the railroads, and the looming merger with the Norfolk & Western. Hall's training and personality, as well as his exposure to a demanding work ethic in his youth, were to become corporate assets for Southern.

Hall said that he was motivated throughout his career by the increasing demands at each new administrative level, rather than by the mystique of railroading. "I like the challenges of the jobs. I've enjoyed that type of challenge. I'm not a railroad buff by any means."

The *Wall Street Journal* saw Hall as "a genial, graying man," but added, "He may look genial, says a staff member, but he can be tough. He recalls Mr. Hall threatening to fire a yard manager for wasting fuel by moving cars unnecessarily."

The Southern's last president before the merger with Norfolk & Western was keenly aware that all divisions of the System must share in its efficient operation and success. "I came up through the operations department, of course, but I've worked very closely with marketing and sales during my entire career. So I'm very familiar with what they do and what their objectives are. The same is true of accounting. We get involved in all facets of that."

He was proud of his operations background and expected it to stand him in good stead: "I'm inheriting an absolutely first-class railroad system, but I must be a little immodest and point out that I've contributed to it for thirty-seven years."

In 1981, when Hall was awarded a medal for excellence of management by the *Wall Street Transcript*, the newspaper cited him for maintaining the high traditions of his predecessors, particularly in "capitalizing on the growth of the Southeast, motivating the railroad's employees so that labor productivity is the highest in the industry and developing depth of management at all levels."

Harold Hall: "One of the Very Best"

The *Transcript* praised Southern's achievement in posting record earnings for the fifth consecutive year and quoted an unidentified securities analyst as saying, "In each of the past few quarters while he was president, Southern Railway has surprised all of us.... Hall has taken over the stewardship extremely well."

The newspaper quoted another observer who paid tribute to Southern's traditional strengths of management: "Southern has developed... perhaps the best management in the railroad industry.... They have at any given time about four potential chief executive officers in the wings. No other railroad has that. There's real depth there. Extreme depth."

The benefit of Southern's long-term emphasis upon development of executive talent had seldom been more obvious than it was after Hall moved up to the presidency of Southern in 1979. Earl L. Dearhart, executive vice-president, Marketing; and Karl A. Stoecker, senior vice-president, Finance, reached retirement age at the time. As usual, veteran managers were ready to step in and shoulder new responsibilities—Edward G. Kreyling, Jr., senior vice-president, Marketing Service, to take over from Dearhart; Arnold B. McKinnon, executive vice-president, Law, to add finance to his responsibilities.

Hall's entire career with Southern had been spent in an era of drastic change within the rail industry. Following World War II the industry had been jolted by major shocks in the wake of economic and technological change that fostered the growth of competitors—especially those whose growth had been subsidized by heavy government outlays. First, the railroads had lost the lucrative government mail contracts to the airlines, and then lost their passengers primarily to an expanding highway system.

Throughout his service as a senior officer, Hall realized that interstate freight service was and would remain the major function of American railroads. The era of passenger trains had ended, he felt, and would never return to importance. "Lots of people hated to see it go, but it was clear that those days were ended in early 1979, when we gave Amtrak $6.7 million to take the Southern Crescent off our hands. By then we were losing about $7 million per year on that train."

As the *Wall Street Journal* reported Southern's formula after an interview with Hall: "Keep track and equipment in good shape so trains will be on time and freight undamaged; set rates that will beat the competition and yet return a profit; and hire qualified and talented people, train them and motivate them with incentive

Harold Hall: "One of the Very Best"

pay and promotions." The paper concluded that Hall had such confidence in the formula that he was unlikely to "juggle it."

The new president expressed traditional Southern tenets of management when asked to analyze the railroad's strength. "We've always prided ourselves on keeping our operating costs low and lean," Hall said. "We've also prided ourselves on giving the best possible service to our customers. I think that's a hallmark of ours, and I think we've been successful in doing it over a rather long period of time. We're going to continue to do that in the future."

Though he expressed optimism to reporters, the new chief said frankly that the industry's unprecedented major problems made future developments uncertain. As for Southern itself, he pointed out, the picture was rosy. The year 1980 was the fifth straight in which the System had run up record profits—a net of $180.7 million, up 12.6 percent from the year before. And the road continued to enjoy the industry's second lowest operating ratio (the percentage of revenue required to run trains)—about 70 percent, as against 100 percent for Conrail and from the upper 70s to the low 80s for average railroads. In 1979 Southern had ranked number one among major railroads in rate of return on investment and in net railway operating income. (The year 1981 was to continue this success: it was the sixth straight year of record profits, with a net of $212.1 million—a jump of 17.2 percent from the preceding year. This was also the first time the System's profits had risen above $200 million—all this accomplished during a steady decline in the national economy.)

"Still," Hall said, "we are not as efficient or as profitable as we'd like to be. We'll have to strive for improvement every day." He felt that future improvements would be less impressive to the public than those of the Brosnan era, which he had seen in his youth. He stressed the importance of "a close watch on expenses," so that Southern could offer "good, reliable service at affordable cost." Competition from other modes of transportation would certainly continue, whatever deregulation brought to railroads, and the industry must continue to meet challenges in a positive manner. Piggybacking was one field in which Hall saw bright promise for all railroads.

Hall was also studying trucking companies, which had been deregulated in July 1980, in order to determine whether Southern should buy a major trucking firm. With the trucking industry in an uncertain state, Hall was determined to wait "until the dust set-

Harold Hall: "One of the Very Best"

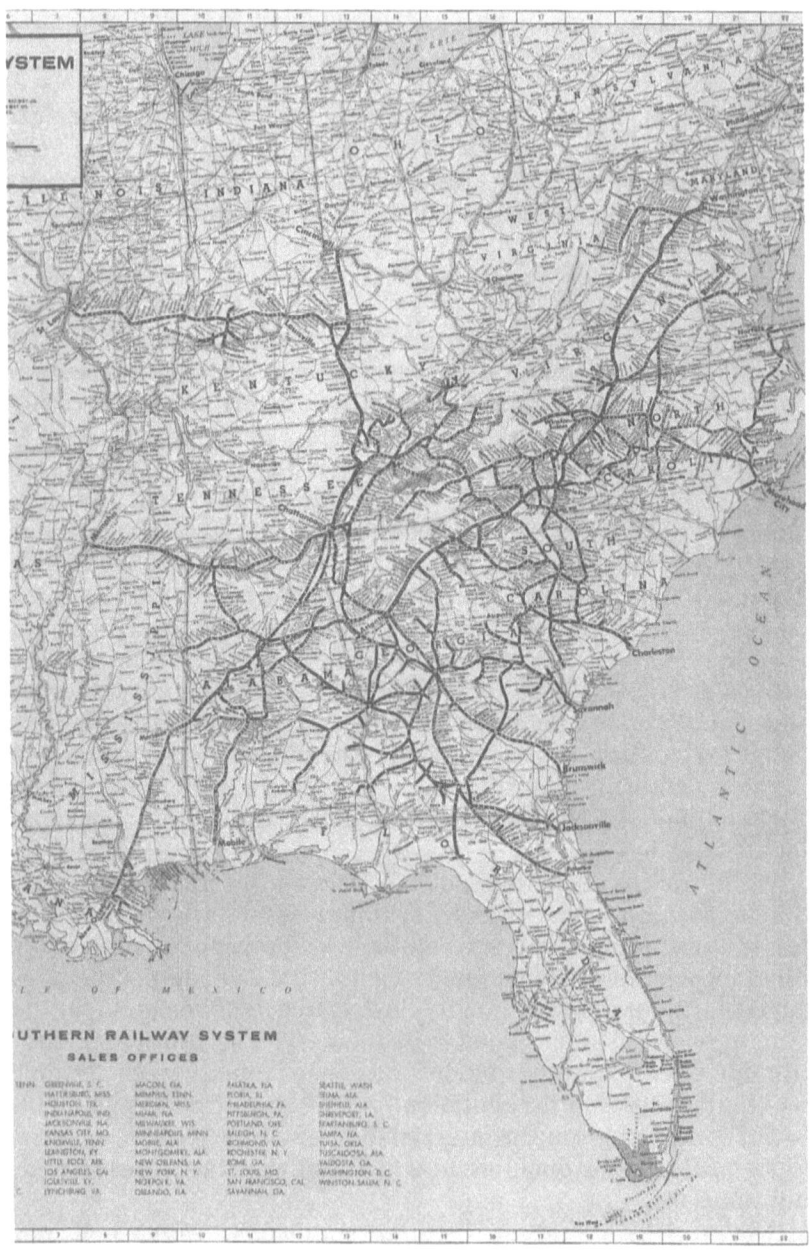

Map 3.

Harold Hall: "One of the Very Best"

tles" before moving into the new field. "We aren't testing the waters," he said, "but we're standing on the river bank and looking."

In development of new special cars and other equipment, Hall thought the pattern had been set for many years to come: "I expect no more major breakthroughs, but we can sure work on these operating problems daily, and get a little better each year. We can expect gradually improved efficiency in maintenance of way and marketing, for example. Our contract rates are studied daily, and this is where the profit is, in attention to detail. It's not so dramatic, but it has a lot to do with our profit picture."

He pointed out a basic change in Southern's traffic pattern—the rising importance of coal. In the second quarter of 1980 coal volume rose 46.7 percent, the largest increase in the quarter for any category. Hall said, "Coal now accounts for 16 percent of our revenue. It has become our volume leader in the past few years. We expect coal volume to increase." Much of this performance was due to use of unit coal trains, of which Southern now had a dozen. But the System was still far behind the industry's leaders in coal hauling.

Hall saw prospects of future improvement in communications, with encouraging results from the first tentative use of solar power on the system. But by now the microwave system was one of the wonders of the industry: 1.7 million circuit-miles were in use (the maximum use of this would be the equivalent of 1.7 million people speaking at once). The Atlanta center boasted more than two thousand channels; there was a data link analyzer to pinpoint the location of trouble on the system, and a lighted map to indicate problems more graphically. Fail-safe provisions included two transmitters and two receivers, sixteen-hour batteries to take over in case of commercial power loss, and standby generators in reserve; at strategic points on mountain tops were eight-hour standby batteries and propane generators.

Hall felt that the trend toward railroad mergers would continue. By 1990, he suggested, the United States might have only five or six railroads. The new chief saw no insurmountable barriers to this development. "After all, railroads are anything but a monopoly. Today there are few commodities that can't be moved by other forms of transportation. Efficiencies growing out of strong competition will be good for the public. So I believe that the long-term future for railroads is bright—for the strong ones, I mean."

Deregulation of the railroad industry, as Hall pointed out, was a

Harold Hall: "One of the Very Best"

mixed blessing. "It's really re-regulation," he said. "We do have more freedom in dealing with routes and rates, and it has already cut the delay between published dates and effective dates. There was a time lapse of up to a year, and that cost railroads dearly.

"Deregulation has established a cost-recovery index based on the Association of American Railroads indices of costs, which are on a quarterly basis. If costs are up 5 percent we can ask the Commission for a 5 percent increase ... but in practice we couldn't take more than 3 percent and still meet competition.

"Deregulation works against us in that it permits us to close gateways unless we are making 110 percent of the variable costs involved, as provided in the Staggers Act. Deregulation also removed our immunity to prosecution under antitrust legislation—in rate-making, that is. And, of course, we now learn of our competitors' pricing only when it is too late."

Inflation, too, was a continuing and perplexing problem whose future course could not be predicted. Hall was to operate in this climate of deregulation and inflation throughout his term. "We've coped with our problems because we have good people, and work hard," he said.

As to staff compensation, Hall continued support of the company's merit-pay-increase pool for non-agreement workers, as well as incentive bonuses for executives. In 1979, a total of 165 Southern officials had shared $1.9 million in bonuses because the company exceeded its pretax-profit goals.

Commenting on future expansion prospects, Hall said that he would like to have Southern experiment with an electrified line. He singled out the 336-mile route between Cincinnati and Chattanooga, which carried some of the nation's heaviest traffic. This segment of the network, he felt, would be ideal for the experiment, in case the federal government could be persuaded to share costs.

Personnel problems and labor relations were of vital importance to Southern's future. Negotiations with the brotherhoods continued to demand the attention of some of the most skilled people in top management, since Southern must negotiate with seventeen separate unions. As for training future executives, Hall took a pragmatic view: "You can run training programs until you're blue in the face, but they won't automatically produce leaders. All of us have a daily function here—to develop men who will be able to do a better job than we have done. All of us must be

Harold Hall: "One of the Very Best"

willing to do whatever it takes to broaden the horizons of men below us. And this effort should go far beyond our training courses."

Hall also directed all of his top executives to make a complete circuit of the System every two years, looking for potential trouble spots, and improving training in the bargain.

In its annual report for 1979 Southern announced that capital expenditures for the preceding six years had reached more than $1 billion, and that the pace was still increasing. By the end of 1981, Hall could report that the System had invested nearly $1 billion in its capital spending program in half that time—the three most recent years.

A substantial project of this type was the new forty-six-track automated Spencer classification yard at Linwood, ten miles north of Salisbury, North Carolina. This yard, the seventh major one on the System, was designed to handle three thousand cars daily. After its opening in 1979, it had begun speeding car movements on the busy eastern lines. This $48 million yard is operated by closed-circuit television, microwave communications, and computers, which monitor and expedite movement of cars through the yard, speeding newly assembled trains to destinations throughout the country.

New equipment continued to consume much of the capital budget. In two years, 1979 and 1980, Southern bought more than 6,000 freight cars of various designs and 157 new diesel locomotives; these purchases represented about 12 percent of the locomotives and 9 percent of the freight-car fleet Southern had owned at the end of 1978. Maintenance costs kept pace. Southern laid 860 miles of welded rail during these two years, resurfaced more than 5,000 miles of track, and laid 3.9 million new crossties. Other improvements were almost endless: a 5.3-mile pipeline to channel fuel to Macon, Georgia's, Brosnan Yard; relocation and expansion of piggyback facilities at Memphis; new office buildings at Somerset, Kentucky, and Macon; a 4,200-foot cutoff to bypass a narrow tunnel near Braswell, Georgia; automatic block signals between East St. Louis and Mt. Carmel, Illinois; solar panels on cabooses and solar-powered signals at isolated track sites; new rail-welding machines in Atlanta; yard track changes in half a dozen locations.

It was a picture of a huge system functioning at top speed and under remarkable control—with all eyes on the future. The territory served by Southern reflected healthy growth that promised a

Harold Hall: "One of the Very Best"

bright future for the region as well. During the first two years of Hall's regime, 233 new industrial projects had been completed in the territory, at an investment cost of $4.5 billion—plants, warehouses, and distribution centers built or expanded, enterprises that would create almost 17,000 new jobs, and add an estimated $72.3 million to Southern's annual revenues.

Some observers felt that the major contribution of Hall's career was in carrying through the merger with Norfolk & Western, for he was given much credit for making a sound, mutually beneficial marriage possible, after Southern had failed in previous attempts at large mergers. The key advantage, Hall felt, was that each partner would be able to penetrate promising new markets previously closed to it—including midwestern grain for Southern and increasing coal tonnage for Norfolk & Western's coal-hauling experts. Hall forecast a steady increase in coal volume for Norfolk & Western for several years, but could foresee few changes in Southern's service area, or its marketing approach. He was particularly optimistic regarding the basic financial strengths of the two roads and the resulting opportunities for the merged giants.

"We have ten common points to consolidate with NW [Norfolk & Western]" Hall said. Some will remain Southern and some NW—as in NW's Norfolk base."

In competition with the CSX (Chessie–Seaboard–Atlantic Coast Line) system, Hall noted, Southern was at a disadvantage because of lack of single-line service to the Midwest. But the merger with NW would lengthen single-line hauls in penetration of new markets.

He saw considerable promise in the merger, and added, "I have no real fear because of the talent we have—the people to cope with deregulation and other problems."

Though the merger would create a gigantic network of some 18,000 miles, employing about 41,000 people and grossing in excess of $3 billion, Hall emphasized that he would press vigorously for cost reductions. The new system would blanket the north-south region east of the Mississippi and command the strength to meet the challenge of competitors.

Outside observers praised the merger as one of the most successful in the modern era. *World*, the organ of Peat, Marwick & Mitchell, accountants, said: "It is a marriage that, if not made in heaven, must have been conceived on some high and favored

Harold Hall: "One of the Very Best"

cloud. Separately, the NW and the Southern are the nation's two most prosperous railroads; together they will stand as a colossus. The combination will result in the nation's fourth-largest system."

As *World* pointed out, the "ideal" merger could be understood with a few figures from balance sheets: In 1980, the NW had a record net of $232.4 million, and Southern a record $180.9 million. Both had returns of about 9 or 10 percent on investment, against an industry average of about 4.25 percent.

The NW had an operating ratio of 77.9 percent; Southern, 82.2 percent—the two best performances in the industry. The transportation ratio (percentage of revenues actually used in providing transportation service): NW, 36.6 percent; Southern, 37.6 percent. As Harold Hall commented, "If you look at the results of both companies, then you reach the conclusion pretty quickly that our objectives are the same. We both try to get more for our buck. On that and many other scores we're very compatible."

World predicted that the new Norfolk Southern Corporation would compete on very favorable terms with the giant CSX system: "The CSX operates 24,000 route miles, versus 17,642 for Norfolk Southern; has 70,000 employees, versus 44,443; had revenues of $4.5 billion, versus $3.2 billion for Norfolk Southern. The bottom line comes to this: In 1980 the CSX had a net income of $281.6 million; the NW and Southern, together, made $413.3 million. That's the kind of performance that makes security analysts sit up and take notice."

Consolidation of the two systems was expected to speed traffic and save fuel; yards were to be consolidated at common points, reducing manpower needs while improving switching operations. Such facilities as NW's car-building shops in Roanoke and Southern's rail-welding plant in Atlanta would, it was noted, "save millions of dollars." Computer centers in Atlanta and Roanoke could be linked, and, of major importance, the combined systems would have a coordinated marketing effort.

Perhaps the most important factor for the future was the shared conviction of the two railroads that the new company must think of itself as a transportation company, rather than a huge railroad. As Norfolk Southern Chairman Robert Claytor said, "We feel that intermodal transportation is the wave of the future," and he was seconded by Hall: "The present regulatory environment might not support such expansion," he said, "but all that is changing. Our customers don't care how their goods get to a destination as long as it's the most efficient, cost-effective method available. That means we ought to be in the transportation business."

The Southern Railway System, having grown with the South in a partnership of development for eighty-eight years, ended its independent life on 1 June 1982. From the time of Andrew Jackson to that of Ronald Reagan, this remarkable railroad, so uniquely southern in its outlook and operations, had grown from the first puny experiment on the continent into one of the nation's premier corporations. In the modern era, after the close of World War II, it was regarded by many as the number one American railroad, on the basis of superior management and creative operations. Its achievements would have made founder Samuel Spencer happy and proud. Its future, in the eyes of its managers and their staffs, was as bright at the time of merger as it had ever been in its long past.

Index

Abbeville, S.C., 102, 104, 178
Acheson, Dean, 233–34, 251
Adams, Brock, 283
Adel, Ga., 217
Aiken, William, 94–95, 97
Alabama & Chattanooga R.R., 184
Alabama & Miss. Rivers R.R., 125, 167, 172, 187–88
Alabama & Tenn. River R.R., 167, 172, 187–88
Alabama Central R.R., 190
Alabama Great Southern Ry., 29, 125, 182, 184, 185, 190
Alabama Power Co., 222
Albany, Ga., 228
Alderman, Edwin A., 55–56
Alexandria, Va., 17, 110, 111, 168, 169, 201, 213, 244
Alexandria, Loudon & Hampshire R.R., 168, 180, 194
Algiers, La., 126
Allen, Horatio, 95, 96
Allied Chemical Co., 242
Amelia C.H., Va., 177
American Car & Foundry Co., 87
American Farm Bureau Federation, 234
American Institute of Industrial Engineers, 271
American Society of Mechanical Engineers, 215, 271
American Telephone & Telegraph Co., 10, 248
Amtrak, 258, 274, 286
Anderson, Nathaniel, 118
Anderson, Oliver, 201
Anderson, S.C., 102, 104
Andrews, Alexander B., 28, 116, 197
Andrews, James J., raid of, 117
Andrews, N.C., 278
Appalachia, Va., 223

Appalachicola, Fla., 228
Appomattox C.H., Va., 178, 193
Appomattox River, 108
Arlington Heights, Ill., 71
Armellino, Michael R., 14
Army of Northern Va., C.S.A., 173, 174
Army of Tennessee, C.S.A., 176
Ashby, Turner, 113, 200
Ashby's Gap, Va., 169
Asheville, N.C., 10, 47, 57, 101, 113 ff., 196, 197, 279, 282
Association of American Railroads, 42, 77, 79, 269, 290
Atchison, Topeka & Santa Fe R.R., 12, 26
Athens, Ga., 29, 32, 102, 236
Athens, Tenn., 122, 123
Atlanta, Ga., 5, 14, 19, 29, 39, 43, 58, 66, 72, 105–6, 120, 124, 166, 171, 175, 190–91 ff., 202, 208, 221, 236, 237, 246 ff., 283, 289, 293
Atlanta & Charlotte Air Line R.R., 191
Atlanta & Florida R.R., 30
Atlantic & Danville R.R., 217
Atlantic & N.C. R.R. ("Old Mullet Line"), 115, 116, 167, 176, 181, 217
Atlantic & Yadkin R.R., 32
Atlantic Coast Line R.R., 30, 38, 76, 194, 218, 250
Atlantic, Tenn. & Ohio R.R., 167
Audubon, John J., 106
Augusta, Ga., 97, 99, 100 ff., 121, 124, 192, 236
Austell, Ga., 191

Baldwin, William H., Jr., 28, 29
Baldwin Locomotive Works, 35, 49, 57, 58
Baltimore, Md., 110, 121
Baltimore & Ohio R.R., 20–25, 38, 110, 116, 169, 194

Index

Baltimore, Chesapeake & Richmond Steamship Co., 194
Bangor, Me., 112
Barbour, John S., 111–12
Beaufort, N.C., 113, 115, 116
Beauregard, P.G.T., 126, 169–70, 176
Beaver Dam, Va., 40
Belton, S.C., 104
Bendix Corp., 244
Bennett (Bennitt), James, 178
Benter, Charles, 212
Bentonville, N.C., battle of, 176
Best, William J., 197
Bethania, N.C., 78
"Big John" cars, 14, 231–35
Birmingham, Ala., 13, 20, 49, 66, 81, 125, 185 ff., 221, 229, 236, 279, 281
Black, Alexander, 94
Blackville, S.C., 175–76
Black Warrior River, 10
Blairs Ferry, Tenn., 123
Blue Mountain, Ala., 172, 188
Blue Ridge R.R., 29, 104, 167
Boatwright, James S., 111, 250
Boulware, Aubin L., 28
Bowater Paper Co., 220
Bradley, Harvey, 283
Bragg, Braxton, 174
Braithwaite, La., 217
Branchville, S.C., 102, 175
Brandeis, Louis D., 250
Brashear, La., 126
Braswell, Ga., 291
Breckinridge, John C., 17, 183
Brinkley, Robert C., 119
Bristol, Tenn.-Va., 111, 124, 166
Broad River, 104
Broady, Joseph ("Steve"), 39–41
Brockmann, Max, 268
Brosnan, Dennis William, 6–9, 12, 13 and passim; acquisition of lines, 236–38; awards, 249; background, 227–28; and "Big John" case, 231–35; and black employees, 8–9; and carrier competition, 221, 231–35; and classification yards, 13, 207, 211, 239–40; and computers, 246–47; and cost reduction, 7, 89, 202–11, 216, 230, 238–39, 248–49; and Graham Claytor, 250–51, 254; and Stanley Crane, 222–24, 227, 231–35, 244–46, 269–70; and Harry DeButts, 80–81, 90–91, 199–200, 202, 208, 230–31; and diesel power, 6–9, 209, 230 and passim; and discipline, 7–9, 200, 202–11, 230–31; dislike of "staff work," 90; early career on Southern Railway, 76–77, 79–82, 229–30; and education, 249; elected to Board of Directors, 9; as Executive Vice President, 9, 202–11; and federal courts, 8–9, 231–35; and firemen, 6–9; and Golden Freight Car awards, 249; and Harold Hall, 227, 279–80; and Robert Hamilton, 209–10, 227, 231–35, 241–43, 249; and labor relations, 7–9, 13, 81–82, 203–8, 211, 223–24, 225, 229–30, 254; launches "Brosnan Revolution," 7–9, 12, 90, 202–11; and maintenance of right of way, 203–7, 238; as "Man of the Year," 249; and Ernest E. Norris, 76–77; and marketing, 14, 240–43 ff.; personality, 7–9, 90, 199–200, 202–6, 211, 225, 227 ff., 243–46; praise of, 13, 200, 205, 208, 225, 226, 249, 251, 254, 260, 270; as president, Southern Railway, 226–49; and repair shops, 210–11, 269–70; retirement, 249; and special cars, 14, 221 ff., 231 ff., 241–46, 269, 270; and training of executives, 227 and passim; as vice president, operations, 7, 279; and women employees, 81–82
Brosnan, Lou Geeslin, 229
Brotherhoods (railway unions), 6, 7–9, 60–61, 62, 65, 68, 207, 224, 225, 229–30, 282–83, 290
Brown, F. Hamlin, 80–81
Brown, W. S., 57
Brown, William, 104
Bruns, Henry, 262
Brunswick, Ga., 5, 11, 106, 190
Bryan, D. Tennant, 192
Bryan, John Stewart, 192
Bryan, Jonathan, 192
Bryan, Joseph, 192
Bryant, Charles, 268
Bryson City, N.C., 197, 279
Budd, E. G., 87
Buena, Va., 201

Index

Buford, Algernon S., 193–94, 197
Bureau of Railway Economics, 42
Burkeville, Va., 108, 166, 178
Burlington Northern R.R., 282
Burns, Miss., 120
Burnside, Ky., 84
Burrowes, R. S., 194
Burwell, Edward B., 276

Cabin John Bridge, 185
Cahawba, Marion & Greensboro R.R., 167, 188
Cain, "Doc," 204
Cairo, Ill., 168
Caldwell, Dr. Joseph, 113
Calhoun, James C., 125
Calhoun, John C., 17, 101, 102, 104, 125
Callaway, Thomas H., 123, 189–90
Camden, S.C., 178, 180
Camp Blanding, Fla., 80
Camp Lejeune R.R., 217
Canton, N.C., 219
Cargoes (Southern Railway), 11, 231 and passim; alumina, 231, 243; automobiles, 245; automobile parts, 246; cement, 231, 242, 243; chemicals, 14, 242; coal, 217, 222–23, 231, 242, 275, 289; electrical transformers, 243–44; fertilizer, 242; furniture, 14, 33, 242, 245; grain, 14, 231–35, 243; limestone, 33, 275; lumber, 14, 33, 242, 244–45; paper, 14, 219–20; petroleum, 82–83; steel, 33, 242; stone, 33; textiles, 14, 33; tobacco, 242, 245
Carrier competition: air lines, 75, 87–88, 286; barge lines, 221, 232–35, 261, 273–74; highway, 4, 36, 57, 75, 87–88, 221–22, 230–35, 242, 246, 261, 273, 286
Carroll, Charles 110
Carroll, Ga., 106
Case, Engineer C.F., 3, 4
Cash, Johnny, 41
Caswell Co., N.C., 114
Catawba River, 178
Catoosa, Ga., 174
Central of Georgia R.R., 20, 26, 175, 218, 236–38
Central Railroad & Banking Co. of Georgia, 103

Charleston, S.C., 4, 11, 31, 94–103, 119, 120, 124, 166, 179, 180
Charleston *Courier*, 101
Charlotte, N.C., 29, 31, 89, 114, 115, 178, 191, 203–4, 219 ff., 262
Charlotte & S.C. R.R., 106, 167, 174, 176, 178 ff.
Charlotte, Columbia & Augusta R.R., 29
Charlottesville, Va., 29, 111, 250
Chattanooga, Tenn., 3 ff., 10, 49, 58, 103, 111, 125, 166, 171 ff., 182 ff., 190, 223, 235 ff., 264 ff., 290
Chattanooga (Tenn.), battle of, 174
Chattanooga, University of, 249
Chattanooga *Times*, 123, 264
Cherrystone Creek, Danville, Va., 39
Chesapeake & Ohio Canal, 110
Chesapeake & Ohio R.R., 38, 224, 282
Chesapeake Bay 110
Chester, S.C., 31, 105
Chesterfield R.R., 107–8
Chicago, Ill., 37, 38, 42, 63, 72, 210
Chicago & Northwestern R.R., 72
Chicago, Indianapolis & Louisville R.R. *See* "Monon" R.R.
Chickamauga (Ga.), battle of, 174
Childersburg, Ala., 220
Cincinnati, Oh., 5, 10, 30, 58, 65, 90, 168, 182 ff., 190, 223, 238, 246, 248, 290
Cincinnati & Charleston R.R., 102
Cincinnati, New Orleans & Texas Pacific Ry. ("Rat Hole" Division of Sou. Ry.), 10, 30, 58, 183–84, 190, 212–13, 223–24
Cincinnati, Selma & Mobile R.R., 189
Cincinnati Southern Ry., 30, 182, 183
Civil War, 17, 19, 166–79, 237
Clark, Francis B., 185
Classification yards: Atlanta (Inman), 49, 207, 240; Birmingham (Norris), 13, 240; Chattanooga (Citico—later DeButts), 49, 240; Knoxville (Sevier), 13, 65, 240; Linwood, N.C., 13, 211, 240, 291; Macon (Brosnan), 240, 291; Memphis (Forrest), 58; New Orleans (Oliver), 240; Sheffield, Ala., 240, 257; yards as bottlenecks, 13, 239–40, 257
Claytor, Frances Hammond, 250
Claytor, Robert, 264, 293–94

Index

Claytor, W. Graham, Jr., 12, 223, 249, 250–66; and Amtrak, 258, 266; acquisition of lines, 262–63; background, 250–51; and "Big John" case, 251; and D. W. Brosnan, 250–51, 254; and budgeting, 252–54, 258–59; and carrier competition, 261; as Chairman of Board, 266; and computers, 256; and conglomerates, 261; and corporate communications, 258 ff.; and Stanley Crane, 251–52, 271–72; creates a "new" Southern Railway, 251 ff.; delegation of authority, 254, 257 ff.; and discipline, 255, 258; and divisional jealousies, 252; early career on Sou. Ry., 250–51; and financial simplification, 258; and Harold Hall, 255, 280; and Robert Hamilton, 256, 262; labor reduction, 260; labor relations, 254 ff.; and management committee, 258 ff.; praise of, 250–52, 266; as president, Southern Railway, 251–66; as railroad "buff," 250, 253; as Secretary of the Navy, 266; and steam excursions, 263–66; streamlines management, 252 ff.; and subsidiary lines, 262; as traveling president, 253; as vice president, law, 251; and Wall Street analysts, 261
Claytor Lake, Va., 264
Clemson University, 249
Cleveland, Grover, 184
Cleveland, Ohio, 63
Clinchfield R.R., 218
Clover Station, Va., 177
Clyde, Thomas, 194, 197
Coal Mine Bluff R.R., 126
Coal pipe lines, 16, 222
Coapman, Eugene P., 59
Cochran, A. E., 106
Coffeeville, Miss., 111
Cole, E. W., 190
Coleman, Thad, 196
Columbia, S.C., 4, 31, 101 ff., 176
Columbia & Greenville R.R., 29
Columbus, Ga., 19, 106, 121, 236, 237
Columbus, Ky., 38
Columbus, Miss., 4, 188, 191, 217
Columbus & Greenville R.R., 69
Comer, Braxton B., 46

Company Shops (Burlington), N.C., 115, 170
Concord, N.C., 115
Confederate States of America, 128 ff.
Conference on Data Systems Language, 247
Conrail, 277
Corinth, Miss., 120, 170, 172
Coster, Charles H., 26–27, 28
Cotton Belt R.R., 282
Covington & Burling, Attorneys at Law, 85, 250, 251
Cowen, John K., 23
Coxe, Frank, 197
Crane, L. Stanley, 12, 207–8, 222–24 and passim; awards, 271; background, 267; and D. W. Brosnan, 222–25, 227, 231–35, 244–46, 269–70; and car design, 222–23, 231 ff., 241–46, 269–70 ff.; and carrier competition, 273; as Chairman of Board, 276; and challenges to Southern Railway, 273–74; and Graham Claytor, 251–52, 271–72; and cushioned cars, 244–45, 269; and diesel lubricants, 268; early career on Southern Railway, 267; as executive vice president, operations, 255, 271; and Harold Hall, 276–77; and hot box detectors, 207–8, 269; joins Pennsylvania R.R., 270; and maintenance of right of way, 268–69, 275; as "Man of the Year," 271; and Management Information Service, 271–72; as metallurgist, 269; and national energy policy, 274; as oil chemist, 268; and passenger service, 274; as patent holder, 269 ff.; praise of, 222, 269, 272, 277; as President of Conrail, 277; as President, Southern Railway, 266–77; on reduced train crews, 274; on research, 267–69, 271; on steam excursions, 274–75; on technology lag, 276–77; and unit trains, 222–23; versatility, 269; and welded ribbon rail, 207
Crane, Leo V., 267
CSX (Chessie-Seaboard-Atlantic Coast Line), 292, 293
Culp, John W., 29
Culpeper, Va., 111, 201, 235

Index

Cumberland Gap, 102
Cumberland Mountains, 10
Cumberland River, 10, 84, 183
Cunningham, Dr. Samuel B., 124–25

Dalton, Ga., 123, 125, 166, 171, 188
Dalton & Gadsden R.R., 188
Dan River, 109
Danville, Ky., 5, 279
Danville, Va., 29, 39–41, 108, 109, 178, 217
Danville & Western R.R., 29
Darrell, Nicholas, 96
Davis, Jefferson, 17, 166, 175, 182; flight of, 176–78
Davison, Charles M., Jr., 85–87, 219, 223, 250–51
Dearhart, Earl L., 286
De Beauregard, Jacques T., 126
DeButts, Harry A., 4, 9, 12, 13, 53, 72–73, 75–76, 80–81, 86, 112, 212–21; acquisition of lines, 216–19, 237, 238; background, 200–201; and D. W. Brosnan, 80–81, 90–91, 199–200, 202, 208, 230–31; and computers, 247; early career on Southern Railway, 201; and end of steam era, 3, 212; expansion of Southern system, 224–25, 237; and labor relations, 198, 199; military service, 201; and E. E. Norris, 75–76, 80, 202; personality, 219, 225; praise of, 219, 226; as president, Southern Railway, 93, 198, 199–202, 208–9; retirement, 9, 226; as salesman, 199, 219, 221, 227; and Southern's goals, 198; and stockholders, 199, 216; as traveling president, 219; as vice president, operations, 201
DeButts, John, 200–201
DeButts, Richard E., 200
DeButts, Robert E., 112
Delano, Frederick H., 188
Delaplane, Va., 200
Delaware & Hudson R.R., 95
Denny, Charles F., 84
Deregulation of railroads, 277, 289–90
DeRamus, L. F., 229
De Saussure, C. A., 121
Detroit, Mich., 63
Diesel horns, 212–13

Diesel power, 212 and passim; benefits of, 4–9 and passim; Southern Railway's conversion to, 3–9, 10, 86–87. *See also* Locomotives, diesel
Dillard, William E., 238
Dix, Dorothea, 114
Doswell, Va., 111
Doughti, George F., 184
Douglas, Stephen A., 114
Dow Safety Award, 283
Drexel, Morgan & Co., 18, 22–29
Duke, Doris, 78
Dun's Review, 10–11, 259–61
DuPont, E. I., de Nemours & Co., 242
Durant, Miss., 111
Durham's Station (Durham), N.C., 178, 279

East St. Louis, Ill., 10, 126, 291
East Tenn. & Ga. R.R., 123–24, 166, 167, 181, 189
East Tenn. & Va. R.R., 124–25, 166, 167, 181, 189
East Tenn., Va. & Ga. R.R., 17, 26 ff., 184, 185, 188 ff., 193
Echols, George, 209
Eiford, "Dutch," 212–13
Elder, W. Cliff, 170
Elizabeth River, 30
Elyton Land Co., 185
Employee relations, 6–9, 12, 53–54, 65, 76, 81–82, 84–85, 199, 201, 202–3, 225, 246, 254–56, 263, 270, 283–85, 290
Energy efficiency of railroads, 16
Erlanger, Emile, 182–85, 186, 187
Erlanger, Baroness Emile (Matilda Slidell), 182 ff.
Erlanger, Ky., 182
Esch-Townsend Bill, 42
Etowah, Ga., 171
Evansville, Ind., 168
Ewen, W.A.C., 28

Fahnestock, Harris C., 28
Fairbanks, Charles W., 43
Fairfax C.H., Va., 113
"Family Lines" (Seaboard & Atlantic Coast Line), 218
Farmers' Union, 234

Index

Fauquier Co., Va., 112
Fayette Co., Tenn., 119
Felton, Samuel, 184
Ferguson, Edward A., 183, 184
Finley, William W., 12, 34, 37; and anti-railroad forces, 46–47; arrested, 47; background, 45; death, 51; expands Southern Railway agencies, 49; as financier, 51; and "good roads" movement, 50; and Fairfax Harrison, 48–49, 53; praise of, 50, 52; as president, Southern Railway, 45–52; and public relations, 45–46; and recession of 1907, 46–47; and Samuel Spencer, 34, 36, 41, 44, 45–46, 50; as traffic manager, 45, 49; as traveling president, 45–46
Finley Shops (Birmingham, Ala.), 65
First National Bank (N.Y.C.), 48
Fisher, Charles F., 115, 116–17, 170
Flagler, Henry M., 30
Fleming, Robert V., 213
Florence, S.C., 100
Florida East Coast R.R., 38
"Flying Dutchman," 96
Foley, Fla., 217
Fontana Dam, 278
Forbes magazine, 90, 92, 231, 232, 236, 239
Forrest, Nathan B., 17, 19, 188–89
Fort Sumter, S.C., 166, 179
Fortune magazine, 230–31
Foster, Reuben, 26
Fox, Herbert, 204, 209, 246
Fox, Robert, 203–5, 209, 246
Franklin, Richard E., 204, 206, 209–11, 227, 238, 246, 268, 270
Franklin, Tenn., 19
Fredericksburg, Va., 103
French, Daniel Chester, 43
French Broad River, 101, 102
Fruit Growers Express, 36

Gadsden, James, 101
Gadsden, Ala., 125
Gadsden Purchase, 101
Gainesville, Ga., 29, 232
Gainesville, Va., 113
Garrett, John W., 21–23
Garrett, Robert, 22–24

Gay, Walter, 3
General Electric Co., 242, 244
General Motors Corp., 259; Electro-Motive Division, 209
George, David, 40
George Washington University, 267
Georgia, University of, 19
Georgia Air Line R.R. Co., 105
Georgia & Alabama R.R., 188
Georgia & East Tenn. R.R., 172
Georgia & Florida R.R., 17, 238
Georgia & Western R.R., 106, 191
Georgia, Florida & Alabama R.R., 17
Georgia Institute of Technology, 228
Georgia Military Institute, 19
Georgia Pacific R.R., 29, 191–92
Georgia Power Co., 275
Georgia R.R., 100, 103, 105–6
Georgia Southern & Florida Ry., 17, 30, 80, 193
Gilbert, John, 201
Golden Freight Car Award, 275
Goldman, Sachs & Co., 14
Goldsboro, N.C., 29, 114, 115, 116, 176, 217
Gordon, John B., 17, 182, 191–92
Gordonsville, Va., 103, 111, 168
Graham, N.C., 115
Grand Junction, Tenn., 166, 172
Granger Movement, 46
Grant, Lemuel P., 105, 191
Grant, U. S., 170, 175, 178
Graves, Calvin, 114, 115
Graysville, Tenn., 171
Great Northern R.R., 5
Great Southern & Southwestern Mail Route, 111–12, 121
Great Western R.R., 106
Greeneville, Tenn., 124
"Green Light" of Southern Railway, 263 ff.
Greensboro, Ala., 189
Greensboro, N.C., 29, 32, 43, 72, 109, 114–15, 178, 262
Greenville, Miss., 217
Greenville, S.C., 29, 104
Greenville & Columbia R.R., 103–5, 167, 176
Greenville, Columbus & Birmingham R.R., 191

Index

Greenwood, S.C., 238
Guaranty Trust Co., 216
Gunnell, Bruce, 268
Guntersville, Ala., 125
Gurley, Thomas E., 276
Gwinett Co., Ga., 284
Gwynne, Walter, 115

Hagerstown, Md., 20
Hall, Harold H., 12, 227, 255; background, 278; and D. W. Brosnan, 227, 279-80; and Graham Claytor, 255, 280; and coal traffic, 289; and Stanley Crane, 276-77; and deregulation, 289-90; early career on Southern Railway, 278-81; and electrified lines, 290; as executive vice president, operations, 280; and labor relations, 282; and mergers, 289; and merit pay, 290; and N. & W. merger, 285, 292-94; personality, 278-79, 285; praise of, 255, 280, 285-86; as president, Southern Railway, 276 ff., 285-92; on profits and costs, 287; and run-through trains, 280-81; and safety programs, 282-85; as telegrapher, 278-79; and training programs, 290; and trucking lines, 287-88; as vice president, transportation, 255, 280
Hall, Mary Abernathy, 279
Hall, Odell C., 278
Hamburg (Bamberg), S.C., 97, 99-100
Hamilton, Robert W., 209, 210, 222, 227, 231-34, 241-43, 247, 252, 256, 260, 262, 270, 272
Hampton Roads, Va., 262
Hand, Judge Learned, 250
Hanover Bank (NYC), 48
Hardeeville, S.C., 218
Hardy, Capt. William H., 186
Harpers Ferry, Va. (later W. Va.), 110, 168, 169
Harriman, E. H., 237
Harriman, E. H., Memorial Gold Medal, 12-13, 283
Harriman, W. Averell, 13
Harrisburg, Pa., 21
Harrison, Burton, 48
Harrison, Constance Cary, 48

Harrison, Fairfax, 11, 12, 93, 238; appearance, 53; background, 48, 53; and Board of Directors, 55-56; and consolidation of lines, 66; death of, 70; eccentricities, 53, 66; and employee relations, 54, 66; and expansion of Southern Railway network, 58; and finance, 48, 61-62, 65-66, 67-69; and William W. Finley, 48-49, 53; and highway competition, 57; innovations, 52-54, 55-56, 63; and labor apprentice program, 54; and management training program, 53-54; and Ernest E. Norris, 69, 71; personality, 53, 66; praise of, 11, 53, 55, 65-66, 201-2, 228-29; as president, Southern Railway, 53-70; as president, "Monon" line, 49, 53; and private cars, 62; and public relations, 56, 64; and relations with black employees, 56; as traveling president, 62; and Railroad War Board, 59; and recession of 1914, 54, 57; and World War I, 56-60
Harrison, William Henry, 101
Harrisonburg, Va., 112, 113, 201
Harvard Business School, 280
Harvard Law Review, 250
Harvard Law School, 250
Harvie, Lewis E., 109, 176-77, 193
Hattiesburg, Miss., 186, 187
Haupt, Herman, 191
Havre de Grace, Md., 112
Hayne, Robert Y., 101, 102
Hazlehurst, George H., 192
Hendersonville, N.C., 217
High Bridge, Ky., 49
High Point, N.C., 220
Hillsboro, N.C., 114
Hiwassee R.R., 122-23
Hobbs, George S., 28
Hodges, S.C., 104
Hoffman, R. C., 30
Holly Springs, Miss., 188
Hood, John B., 19
Hooker, Joseph, 174
Hoopeston, Ill., 71
Hoover, Herbert, 69
Horry, Elias, 97, 100
Houston, Tex., 281

Index

Hubbard, David, 118
Huidekoper, F. W., 26
Hungerford, Clark, 81, 90
Huntington, Collis P., 31
Huntsville, Ala., 118, 171, 172

Ickes, Harold, 83
Illinois Central R.R., 45, 237
Ingham, George, 186
Ingram, John, 231–32
Inman, John H., 26
Inman, Samuel M., 28
Innovations (Southern Railway): all-diesel power, 3–9, 10, 13, 208; "Big John" cars, 231–35; computer usage, 247–56; run-through trains, 280–82; special cars, 14, 221 ff., 231 ff., 241, 243 ff., 269–70 ff; "true" marketing function, 240 ff.; unit trains, 222–23, 275, 289
Internal Revenue Service, 86–87
International Business Machines Co., 247, 256
Interstate Commerce Commission (ICC), 42, 85, 86, 215, 218, 231–36, 238, 241, 242, 245, 282
Interstate R.R., 217, 223
Iuka, Miss., battle of, 172

Jackson, Andrew, 38, 126, 294
Jackson, Thomas J. ("Stonewall"), 20, 169, 173
Jackson, Ala., 106
Jackson, Miss., 166
Jacksonville, Fla., 10, 11, 38, 193, 218, 282
Jacksonville Terminal Co., 38
Jacobs, Solomon D., 122–23
James River, 108, 172, 177
James River Canal, 122
Jasper, Ala., 222
Jeffries, L. E., 65
Jersey City, N.J., 39
Jesup, Morris, 192
Jetersville, Va., 108, 178
Johnson, Andrew, 120, 124, 181
Johnson, Lizzie, 200
Johnston, John W., 192
Johnston, Joseph E., 170, 173, 176, 178, 182, 188, 193
Jones, Alexander W., 188
Jones, Jack, 247–48
Jones, Jesse, 73–74
Jones, Jimmy, 119
Jonesboro, Tenn., 124
Journal of Commerce, 95

Kanawha River, 122
Kansas City, Mo., 235
Kaylor, Frank, 283
Keister, O. B., 80–81
Kemble, Fanny, 106
Kemble, Gouverneur, 95
Kennesaw Mountain, Ga., 171
Kentucky River, 49, 183
Kerr-McGee Corp., 10
Kilgo, John C., 55–56
Kilrain, Jake, 187
King, Mason, 219, 220, 272
King, Porter, 188
King, Thomas B., 106
King, William Rufus, 125
Kings Mountain R.R., 167
Kings Mountain (Ky.) Tunnel, 183
Kinston, N.C., 116
Kiplinger's Magazine, 90
Knoxville, Tenn., 13, 72, 90, 111, 122–24, 210
Knoxville *Register*, 122–23
Knoxville *Whig*, 124
Kokomo, Ind., 71
Kreyling, Edward G., Jr., 286
Kyan, John M., 97
Kyanizing, 97

Labor: blacks, 8–9, 56, 99, 185; Chinese, 184–85; conflicts with management, 6, 7–9, 62, 112–13, 185, 225; contributions to success, 6 and passim, 59–60, 65, 68, 81, 199, 239, 240, 260; costs, 13, 68, 85, 89, 207, 239, 244–45; 40-hour week, 89; hiring policies of S.R., 7–9, 56, 246; productivity, 12, 62, 65, 88, 239, 260, 262, 285; ratio of costs to revenues, 13, 62, 65, 88, 89, 206, 239, 248–49, 254, 260; reduction of force, 13, 202–11, 239, 246, 248–49; violence, 7, 12–13, 185

Index

LaGrange & Memphis R.R., 119
Lake Pontchartrain, 126
Lake Pontchartrain Bridge, 186
La Motte, L. H., 247
Lapley, John W., 125
Larson, Major, 80
Laurens, S.C., 104, 105, 178
Laurens Ry., 104, 105, 167
Lawyers Station, Va., 43
Lee, Robert E., 53, 173, 175, 200
Leesburg, Va., 110
Leslie's Weekly, 97
Lexington, Ky., 126, 183
Lexington & Danville R.R., 167, 182–83
Lincoln, Abraham, 17, 37, 172
Linden Station, Va., 112
Littlefield, Milton S., 196
Live Oak, Perry & Gulf R.R., 17, 217
Locomotives: classification of, 57n. *See also* Locomotives, diesel; Locomotives, steam
Locomotives, diesel: F-types, 5; F-7's, 6; switching, 4–5
—engines of note: #6100, 5, 84, 215
Locomotives, steam: Americans (4-4-0), 35, 68, 108; articulated, 58, 64; Atlantics (4-4-2), 35; Consolidations (2-8-0), 6, 35; engine write-offs, 86–87; Mallets, 58; Mikados (2-8-2), 3, 4, 5, 6, 49, 264–66; Moguls (2-6-0), 35, 68; Mountains (4-8-2), 57; Pacifics (4-6-2), 6, 35, 62–63, 64, 213–15; Santa Fes, 57–58; six-wheelers, 6; ten-wheelers, 6, 35, 39, 68
—engines of note: Best Friend of Charleston, 3, 94, 96, 97, 99; Big Liz, 58; The E.L. Miller, 99; The Orange, 111; The Phoenix, 99; The Roanoke, 108; The Stourbridge Lion, 95; The Texas, 171; #1102 (of "Old 97"), 39–40; #1401, 213–15; #4501, 264–66; #6330, 3, 4
Logan, Thomas M., 197
Lonergan, Kenerly, 122
Long, Stephen, 101
Long Island R.R., 22
Longstreet, James, 174, 182, 186
Lookout Mountain (Tenn.), battle of, 174

Louisa C.H., Va., 111
Louisa R.R., 110–11
Louisiana Southern R.R., 126, 187, 216–17
Louisville, Ky., 37, 38, 49, 102, 168, 190, 221
Louisville & Nashville R.R., 30, 37, 49, 82, 190, 218, 224
Louisville, Cincinnati & Charleston R.R., 100, 102
Louisville, Evansville & St. Louis R.R., 37
Louisville Southern R.R., 29, 190
Lula, Ga., 32
Lynchburg, Va., 29, 111, 122, 124, 166, 178
Lynchburg & Danville R.R., 194
Lynchburg & New River R.R., 122

McAdoo, William G., 59
McBee, Vardry E., 197
McBees Ferry, Tenn., 124
McCarthy, Charles J., 233
McClellan, George, 172
McDonough, Ga., 263
McKeller, R. L., 58
McKinnon, Arnold B., 286
McMinn Co., Tenn., 123
Macon, Ga., 20, 80, 103, 106, 193, 229, 236, 279, 291
Macon & Brunswick R.R., 106, 175, 190, 192–93
McPherson Square, Washington, D.C., 66
Madison, James, 103
Magrath, William J., 180
Manassas, Va., 66, 111, 112, 168, 169, 172, 173
Manassas/Bull Run (Va.), battle of, 117, 169–70, 173
Manassas Gap R.R., 110 ff. 168, 169, 173, 194, 200
Manchester, Va., 108
Marietta, Ga., 19
Marion Junction, Ala., 32, 186, 189
Marshall, Edward C., 112–13, 194
Marshall, John, 112, 194
Martinsburg, W. Va., 79
Maslin, George W., 29

Index

Mason, James M., 182
Mayer, Charles F., 25
Mayo, T. P., 56
Maysville, Ky., 102
Melious, Richard, 263
Memminger, Christopher G., 101
Memphis, Tenn., 10, 32, 57, 102, 118–22, 125, 172, 188, 291
Memphis & Charleston R.R., 119–22, 167, 170–71, 172, 181, 190
Memphis *Daily Appeal*, 120
Mercer University, 249
Merck & Co., 10
Meridian, Miss., 58, 125, 182, 184, 186, 190
Merriman, Paul, 264
Mexican Gulf R.R., 167, 187
Midlothian, Va., 107, 108
Midway, S.C., 175
Milbank, Jeremiah, 192
Military use of railroads, 80–85, 97, 166, 168–79
Miller, Ezra L., 95–96
Mills, Nicholas, 107, 110
Milneburg, La., 126
Milner, John T., 185
Mississippi Central R.R., 111–12
Mississippi River, 10, 17, 19–20, 37, 38, 187, 217, 232, 292
Missouri Pacific R.R., 282
Mitchel, Ormsby M., 171, 173
Mobile, Ala., 11, 32, 38, 49, 58, 121, 126, 185, 186, 201
Mobile & Alabama Grand Trunk R.R., 185
Mobile & Birmingham R.R., 32, 186, 190
Mobile & Ohio R.R., 38, 49, 69, 120, 190, 217
Modern Metals magazine, 249
Modern Railroads magazine, 249, 275, 276
"Monon" R.R., 37–38, 49
Monroe, Va., 39, 41
Monroe R.R., 103
Montevallo, Ala., 125, 172
Montgomery, Ala., 105, 110, 121, 126, 166, 236
Montgomery & West Point R.R., 126
Moore, Joe, 204, 209, 246

Moore, William, 270
Morehead, John M., 109, 113–15, 116
Morehead City, N.C., 11, 116, 176, 217
Morgan, David P., 12
Morgan, J. Pierpont, 22–28
Morgan, J. Pierpont, & Co., 48
Morgan, Junius S., 119
Morganton, N.C., 117
Moultrie, Ga., 238
Mount Carmel, Ill., 291
Mount Jackson, Va., 113
Murphey, Archibald, 113
Murphy, N.C., 29, 35, 196, 197
Murrell, George E., 50
Muscle Shoals, Ala., 102, 118, 121

Nancy Hanks, 237
Nantahala, N.C., 278
Nashville & Chattanooga R.R., 120
National Freight Traffic Officers' Association 221
National Grange, 234
National Museum of Transportation (St. Louis), 215
National Railway Historical Society, 250, 265
National Science Foundation, 16
New Albany Belt & Terminal R.R., 38
New Bern, N.C., 116, 173
Newberry, S.C., 104
New Jersey Southern R.R.., 20
New Orleans, La., 10, 11, 38, 39, 49, 58, 105, 111, 112, 119, 121, 126, 182, 186 ff., 191, 217, 238, 281, 282
New Orleans & Gulf R.R., 187
New Orleans & Northeastern R.R., 6, 17, 83, 182, 186–87, 279
New Orleans & Southern R.R., 187
New Orleans Belt & Terminal Co., 38
New Orleans, Jackson & Great Northern R.R., 45, 126
New Orleans, Opelousas & Great Western R.R., 126
New York, N.Y., 112, 121, 188, 192, 216
New York *American*, 50
New York Central R.R., 241
New York *Herald*, 24
New York Times, 271
Nicholasville, Ky., 126
Nolichucky R., 101

Index

Norcross, Jonathan, 105, 191
Norfolk, Va., 11, 17, 30, 72, 103, 111, 194, 217, 218, 262
Norfolk & Carolina R.R., 30
Norfolk & Western R.R., 16, 39, 79, 236, 250, 264
Norfolk Southern Corp., 16, 264
Norfolk Southern Ry., 262, 273
Norris, Ernest E., 4–6, 9, 12, 69, 70, 71–93, 216, 230; appearance, 71; background, 69, 71–73; and D. W. Brosnan, 76–77, 80; and competing lines, 76; and connecting lines, 76; and Harry DeButts, 75–76, 80, 202; defends land grants to railroads, 91; and diesel power, 4–5, 78, 86–87, 88; and employee relations, 76; and financial problems, 73, 86, 88–89; and Fairfax Harrison, 69, 71; and Mobile & Ohio, 69, 72; and The New Deal, 77; personality, 71, 72, 73–74, 76–77, 85, 86; praise of, 76, 77, 90–91, 93; and public relations, 78–79; and regional promotion, 92; retirement, 93; as salesman, 75–76; and "Sun Belt," 92; as traveling president, 75–76
North, John Ringling, 78
North Carolina, University of, 113
North Carolina R.R., 28, 31, 109, 114, 167, 170 ff., 181
Northeast & Southwest Alabama R.R., 167, 184
North Eastern R.R., 100
Northeastern R.R. of Georgia, 32
Northern Alabama R.R., 32
North Platte, Neb., 282
North Shore & Labrador R.R., 271
Nottoway, Va., 108

Oakdale, Tenn., 5, 77, 229
Ocmulgee R., 237
Ohio R., 10, 49, 65, 183, 194
Okie, F. W., 83–84
"Old 97," wreck of, 39–41
Oliver, Elmer R., 80, 219
O'Neall, John, 104
Oneida, Tenn., 263
Opelika, Ala., 20
Orange & Alexandria R.R., 110, 111–12, 168, 169, 172, 174, 180, 194

Paint Rock, Tenn., 196, 197
Palatka, Fla., 30, 193
Panama Canal, 38, 49
Parrish, Ala., 32
Pass Christian, Miss., 45
Passenger service, 4–5, 6, 63–64, 74–75, 84, 87–88, 274, 286; operating deficits, 215, 274, 286; streamliners, 75, 87–88; terminated, 15, 215
—trains: The Cracker, 5; Crescent Ltd. (later Southern Crescent), 15, 63, 64, 74, 88, 274, 286; Florida Express, 15, 37; Goldenrod, 4; Joe Wheeler, 5; Kansas City-Florida Special, 74; Memphis Special, 74; New York & Florida Ltd., 15, 36–37; Ponce de Leon, 74; Queen & Crescent, 74–75; Royal Palm, 37, 74; Southerner, 75; Sunnyland, 74; Suwannee River Special, 63; Tennessean, 75; United States Fast Mail, 37; Washington & Southwestern Vestibuled Ltd., 15, 36
Patterson, Cissie, 77
Paul, George S., 252, 263
Peabody, George, 119
Pearl Harbor, 75, 82
Peat, Marwick & Mitchell, 292–93
Pelley, John J., 83
Pennsylvania Central R.R., 224
Pennsylvania R.R., 12, 23, 38, 270, 277, 282
Pere Marquette R.R., 28
Petersburg, Va., 103, 108, 111, 121
Philadelphia, Pa., 121
Philadelphia, Tenn., 122
Piedmont Air Line R.R., 52, 191
Piedmont R.R., 167, 178
Piedmont Station, Va., 169
Pierce, Franklin, 111
Pigeon R., 197
Pinehurst, N.C., 37
Pinner's Point, Norfolk, Va., 30, 218
The Pioneer (S.C.R.R.), 96
The Pioneer (Cumberland Valley R.R.), 214
Pittsburg Rail & Coal Co., 126
Plant, Henry B., 30, 192
Pocahontas, Tenn., 120
Poinsett, Joel R., 17, 101, 103
Polk, James K., 110, 119

Index

Pontotoc, Miss., 188
Port Chalmette, New Orleans, La., 38
Portsmouth, Va., 117
Portsmouth & Roanoke R.R., 115
Potomac R., 111, 112, 185
Potomac Yard, Alexandria, Va., 212, 214
Potter, Stewart, 234
Powell, A. M., 117
Pride, Ala., 275
Progressive Railroading magazine, 271
Pullman Standard Co., 63, 66–67, 87, 244

Queen & Crescent Ltd., 186
Queen & Crescent Route, 30, 182 ff., 238

Rabun Gap, Ga., 102
The Railroad Advocate, 122
Railroad Credit Corp., 69
Railroad Gazette, 28
Railroad Literary Bureau, 42
Railroad Management, 252
Railway Age, 13, 55
Raleigh, N.C., 29, 47, 115, 176, 178, 262
Rapidan R., 174
Ravenel, John, 100
Rawlings, Isaac, 118
Reagan, Ronald, 294
Reconstruction Finance Corp., 69, 73, 75, 216
Resaca, Ga., 171
Reynolds Aluminum Co., 231
Reynolds Industries, 10
Richards, M. V., 33–34, 49
Richmond, Va., 29, 103, 121, 166 ff., 172 ff., 265
Richmond & Danville R.R., 25 ff., 63–64, 105, 108–9, 166, 168, 176–77, 180, 185, 191 ff.
Richmond & West Point Terminal Ry. & Warehouse Co., 26, 197
Richmond & York River R.R., 110, 168, 172–73, 180, 194
Richmond, Fredericksburg & Potomac R.R., 38, 110
Richmond Terminal System, 25 ff., 184, 186, 190, 194
Richmond Times, 192
Riley, James Whitcomb, 37

Ringgold, Ga., 171, 174
Rives, Alfred L., 185
Roanoke, Va., 250, 293
Roanoke Valley R.R., 167
Robinson, John M., 30
Rogersville & Jefferson R.R., 168, 181
Rome, Ga., 125, 172
Roosevelt, Franklin D., 77, 91, 213
Rosman, N.C., 217
Rucker, Edward W., 188
Rudder, Paul R., 276
Rust, John A., 231
Ryan, Thomas F., 28

Safety program, 54, 282–85; awards for, 283; crossing fatalities, 284; Operation Lifesaver, 284–85
St. Augustine, Fla., 37
St. John's Episcopal Church (Washington, D.C.), 43
St. Johns R., 17, 193
St. Louis, Mo., 37, 232
St. Louis & San Francisco R.R. (The Frisco), 218, 237
St. Michaels, Md., 19
St. Petersburg, Fla., 63
St. Simons Island, Ga., 106
Sales & Marketing Executives International, 249
Salisbury, N.C., 29, 115, 117, 196, 197
San Diego, Cal., 117
San Francisco, Cal., 106
Santa Fe R.R., 5
Savannah, Ga., 11, 38, 94, 96, 120, 124, 175, 236, 237
Savannah & Memphis R.R., 20
Savannah & Western R.R., 20, 22
Savannah, Florida & Western R.R., 250
Savannah R., 96, 97, 100
Sawyersville, Ala., 189
Schiff, Charles, 184
Seaboard Airline Ry., 30, 38, 76, 80, 100, 194, 218
Seaboard Allied Milling Corp., 235
Sears Roebuck & Co., 259
Seay, Thomas H. 87
Selma, Ala., 125, 172, 188, 201, 229
Selma, N.C., 30, 218
Selma & Tennessee R.R., 125
Selma, Marion & Memphis R.R., 188–89

Index

Selma, Rome & Dalton R.R., 188, 190
Selma (Ala.) *Times and Messenger*, 188
727th Railway Operating Batt'n., U.S.A., 84
Seward, Clarence A., 184
Sharp, Thomas R., 20, 22, 169
Sheffield, Ala., 132
Shelbyville Tenn., 171
Shenandoah Valley (Va.), 112, 173
Shephard's Point Land Co., 116
Sherman, George, 27
Sherman, William T., 19, 168–69, 175–76, 178, 237
Sherrod, Benjamin, 118
Shiloh (Tenn.), battle of, 170–71
Sibley, Hiram W., 191
Silverside coal cars, 222–23
6th N.C. Infantry, C.S.A., reenactment brigade, 170
Slidell, John, 182
Slidell, La., 182
Slogans: "The Southern Serves the South," 65; "Look Ahead—Look South," 79, 84, 219, 263; "Southern—The Railroad that Gives a Green Light to Innovation," 263–64
Smith, John, 204
Smithfield, N.C., 176
Smith Machine Shop, Alexandria, Va., 111
Smithsonian Institution, 103, 213–14
Smoot, George, 111
Somerset, Ky., 228, 291
Sorrell, G. Moxley, 174
South Carolina & Georgia R.R., 31, 100, 103
South Carolina Canal & R.R. Co., 17, 94–100
South Carolina R.R. ("Charleston & Hamburg"), 100, 166, 167, 174 ff.
Southeastern region, U.S.: history, 15, 16 and passim; industrial growth, 14–15, 16, 33, 49 ff., 215, 220, 224–25, 273, 291–92; migration of European colonists into, 34
Southern Field, 34
Southern Governors' Conference, 234
Southern Pacific R.R., 31, 281
Southern Railway System: abandonment of lines, 68, 217, 218, 260; agricultural promotion, 14, 33–34, 49–50, 231–36; bells donated to churches, schools, 78; Board of Directors, 4, 28–29, 55–56 and passim; budgeting, 15, 68, 251–54, 258–59;computer usage, 14, 246–48, 256; discipline, 7–9, 11–12, 199, 202–11, 226, 229–31, 253, 255, 258; dividends, 48, 51, 61, 67–68, 216, 277; double tracking of lines, 39, 47, 49, 58, 65, 205; employees enlist in WW II, 83–84, 278–79; executive bonuses, 290; financial crises, 47–48, 54, 67–69, 89, 202 ff., 259; founding of, 16–17, 26–29, 184; headquarters buildings, 66, 67; industrial parks, 14, 219; industrial promotion, 14–15, 33, 221 and passim; investment in plant and equipment, 4, 5, 11, 29, 30, 47, 49, 51, 57–58, 64, 65, 87, 92, 221 ff., 231–35, 237–39, 245–48, 257, 273, 291; Land and Industrial Dept., 33; logo, 65; management awards, 10, 11, 259–61; management strengths, 10–15 and passim, 285–86; marketing, 14–15, 222–23, 231–35; materials testing, 267–68; merger with Norfolk & Western, 16, 264, 280, 285, 292–94; military traffic in World War I, 56–57; military traffic in World War II, 82–83, 86–87; morale, 6, 11–12, 51, 54, 56, 84–85, 246, 251 ff., 271–72; as "mountain line," 10, 39, 49, 57–58, 223–24; *News Bulletin*, 52, 79; nicknames of component lines, 17; predecessor lines, 94–98; presidential succession, 12; profitability, 11, 14, 29, 43, 47 ff., 60, 62, 215–16, 236, 240–41, 242 ff., 254, 259, 260, 261–62, 272–73, 277, 287; rate reduction, 14, 220 ff., 231–35, 239, 242 ff., 257; steam excursion program, 263–66, 274–75; steam power phased out, 3–9; stockholders, 51, 55, 61, 67–68, 216, 273; stock issues, 27, 29, 48, 61, 67–68, 216, 217, 273; taxes, 85–86; *Ties*, 71, 79, 84, 85; trains terminated, 15, 215; voting trustees, 55. *See also* Innovations; Passenger service; Technological advances
Southern Railway System Employees

Index

Pension Assn., 65
South Georgia Ry., 217
Southside R.R., 108, 111, 166
Southwest R.R. of Georgia, 237
Spanish-American War, 31, 34
Spartanburg, S.C., 29
Spartanburg & Union R.R., 167
Special trains, freight: The Clipper, 92; The Jack Pot, 92; The Southern Flash, 92; The Spark Plug, 92, 246
Spence, Richard, 281
Spencer, Henry, 21, 36
Spencer, Lambert, 19–20
Spencer, Louisa Benning, 20
Spencer, Samuel, 12, 18, 19–44 ff., 184, 294; acquires Southern Railway network, 27 ff., 30–32, 37–38, 43–44; background, 19–20; and birth of Southern Railway, 25–29; death of, 42–43; and diversified traffic, 33–34; early railroad career, 20–25; and William Finley, 34, 36, 41, 44, 45–46, 50; and "good roads" movement, 35–36; and passenger service, 36–37; praise of, 23, 25, 43–44; and public relations, 42; regional promotion, 33
Spencer, N.C., 41, 57, 208, 211
Staggers Act (railroad deregulation), 290
Stanly, W. R., 116
Stanton, David N., 184
Stanton, John C., 184, 185
Statesville, N.C., 117
Staunton, Va., 111, 168
Stetson, Francis L., 28
Stevenson, Ala., 120
Stillhouse Trestle, Danville, Va., 39
Stockton, Ala., 121
Stoecker, Karl A., 286
Strasburg, Va., 20, 29, 111, 112, 113, 168, 169, 201
Stubbs, J. C., 50
Stump House Mountain (S.C.), 104
Sullivan, John L., 187
Summerville, S.C., 97
Swannanoa Tunnel (N.C.), 196–97
Swanson, Robert E., 212
Swepson, George W., 196

Talladega, Ala., 125
Tate, Sam, 120, 185
Technological advances (Southern Railway), 49, 51, 221 ff., 239–40; ballast tampers, 205; bolt-cutters, 206; bolt-tighteners, 206; bush hog, 206; Centralized Traffic Control, 87; closed circuit television, 13, 240, 291; computer usage, 14, 246–48; cushioned cars, 243–44; data link analyzer, 289; headlights, 96; hot box detector, 14, 207–8; microwave system, 13–14, 247–48, 289, 291; piggyback freight, 245–46, 273, 291; radar speed meter, 13, 240; solar power, 291; spiker-nipper, 206; test cars, 14; tie-changing machine, 204–5; tie-notcher, 206; treated cross-ties, 97; trestles, 96; valve gear improvements, 49, 57, 63; welded ribbon rail, 13, 206–7, 291; wheel-mounting, 210
Tennessee, University of, 278
Tennessee R., 10, 58, 101, 123, 124, 125, 170, 183
Tennessee R.R., 262–63
Tennessee Valley, 119, 173
Tennessee Valley Authority, 232–33, 278
Tennessee Valley R.R. Museum, 264–65
Terminal Railroad Assn. of St. Louis, 38
Texarkana, Tex., 191
Texas & Pacific R.R., 45
Textile industry migration, 33
Thackeray, William M., 106
Thomas, Anthony J., 27, 28
Thomas, Charles B., 181
Thomas, Samuel, 28
Thomas, William Holland, 116
Thompson, Jacob,' 188
Thrall, Walter H., 213
Tilton, Ga., 171
Tombigbee R., 10
Track gauge, 96, 167, 183–84, 191
Training programs (Southern Railway): laborer's apprentice, 54; management, 11, 53–54, 201–2, 228–29, 263, 290–91; technical training center, 263
Trains, 12, 264–65

Index

Transylvania R.R., 217
Trautwine, John C., 122
Traveler (war horse of Gen. Robert E. Lee), 53
Tredegar Iron Works, 108
Trent, 182
Troost, Lewis, 125
Truman, Harry 7
Tudor Hall, Va., 111, 112
Tunstall, Whitmell P., 107–8
Tupper, Tristram, 100
Turner, James C., 116, 117
Tuscaloosa, Ala., 106
Tuscumbia, Ala., 5, 118, 120, 172
Tuscumbia, Courtland & Decatur R.R., 118–20, 126

Union Pacific R.R., 50, 282
Unit train system, 14, 222–23
United States Department of Agriculture, 234
United States Department of Commerce, 215
United States Department of Transportation, 261
United States Railroad Administration, 59, 60

Valdosta, Ga., 30, 38, 193, 238
Vance, Zebulon B., 196–97
Van Dyke, T. Nixon, 123
Victor Co., 40–41
Virginia, University of, 20, 55, 250
Virginia & Tenn. R.R., 111, 124, 166
Virginia Central R.R., 110–11, 168
Virginia Midland R.R., 21–22, 194
Virginia Military Institute, 200

Walhalla, S.C., 104
Walters, H. G., 30
Washington, D.C., 10, 31, 38, 39, 43, 58, 66, 72, 77, 112, 121, 168, 170, 213–14, 220, 244, 248, 264
Washington, Ga., 178
Washington Co., Tenn., 124

Washington *Times-Herald*, 77
Waynesville, N.C., 197
Weldon, N.C., 103
Wesser Creek, N.C., 278
Western & Atlantic R.R., 103, 123, 166, 171
Western N.C. R.R., 10, 28, 115, 116–17, 167, 196–97
Western Union Telegraph Co., 191
Westinghouse Corp., 244
West Point, 110
West Point, Va., 110, 172, 219
West Point Foundry Assn., 95
West Point Route, 166
West Virginia, 92
Weyerhaeuser Co., 219
White Hall (later Atlanta), Ga., 103
White Oak Mountain (Va.), 39
Whitter, Henry, 40–41
Whittier, Cal., 213
Williamsburg, Va., 271–72
Wills Valley R.R., 126, 168, 175, 184
Wilmer, Skipwith, 28
Wilmington, N.C., 103, 121
Wilmington & Weldon R.R., 30, 176
Wilson, James H., 172
Wilson, James W., 196, 197
Wilson, Richard T., 190
Wilson, Woodrow, 59
Wilsonville, Ala., 222
Winchester, Marcus B., 118
Winchester, Va., 169
Wise, John, 177
Wise Co., Va., 217
Witcher, Vincent, 108
World War I, 11, 56–60, 91, 201
World War II, 74, 79–87, 91, 250, 286, 294; Southern employees enlist, 83–84, 278–79
Wycoff, Daryl, 15, 240–41, 252, 266

York River (Va.), 110, 172
York River R.R., 173
Yorktown, Va., 172
Young, Bernard E., 78–79

www.ingramcontent.com/pod-product-compliance
Lightning Source LLC
Chambersburg PA
CBHW021355290426
44108CB00010B/247